Collection Editor: Jennifer Grünwald • Assistant Editor: Sarah Brunstad • Associate Managing Editor: Alex Starbuck • Editor, Special Projects: Mark D. Beazley
Senior Editor, Special Projects: Jeff Youngquist • SVP Print, Sales & Marketing: David Gabriel • Book Design: Jeff Powell

Editor in Chief: Axel Alonso • Chief Creative Officer: Joe Quesada • Publisher: Dan Buckley • Executive Producer: Alan Fine

BLACK WIDOW VOL. 1: THE FINELY WOVEN THREAD. Contains material originally published in magazine form as BLACK WIDOW #1-6 and ALL-NEW MARVEL NOW! POINT ONE #1. First printing
ISBN# 978-0-7851-8819-3. Published by MARVEL WORLDWIDE, INC., a subsidiary of MARVEL ENTERTAINMENT, LLC. OFFICE OF PUBLICATION: 135 West 50th Street, New York, NY 10020. Copyr
2014 Marvel Characters, Inc. All rights reserved. All characters featured in this issue and the distinctive names and likenesses thereof, and all related indicia are trademarks of Marvel Characters,
similarity between any of the names, characters, persons, and/or institutions in this magazine with those of any living or dead person or institution is intended, and any such similarity which may exist is
coincidental. **Printed in Canada.** ALAN FINE, EVP - Office of the President, Marvel Worldwide, Inc. and EVP & CMO Marvel Characters B.V.; DAN BUCKLEY, Publisher & President - Print, Animation &
Divisions; JOE QUESADA, Chief Creative Officer; TOM BREVOORT, SVP of Publishing; DAVID BOGART, SVP of Operations & Procurement, Publishing; C.B. CEBULSKI, SVP of Creator & Content Develo
DAVID GABRIEL, SVP Print, Sales & Marketing; JIM O'KEEFE, VP of Operations & Logistics; DAN CARR, Executive Director of Publishing Technology; SUSAN CRESPI, Editorial Operations Manage
MORALES, Publishing Operations Manager; STAN LEE, Chairman Emeritus. For information regarding advertising in Marvel Comics or on Marvel.com, please contact Niza Disla, Director of
Partnerships, at ndisla@marvel.com. For Marvel subscription inquiries, please call 800-217-9158. **Manufactured between 5/23/2014 and 6/30/2014 by SOLISCO PRINTERS, SCOTT, QC, C**

10 9 8 7 6 5 4 3 2 1

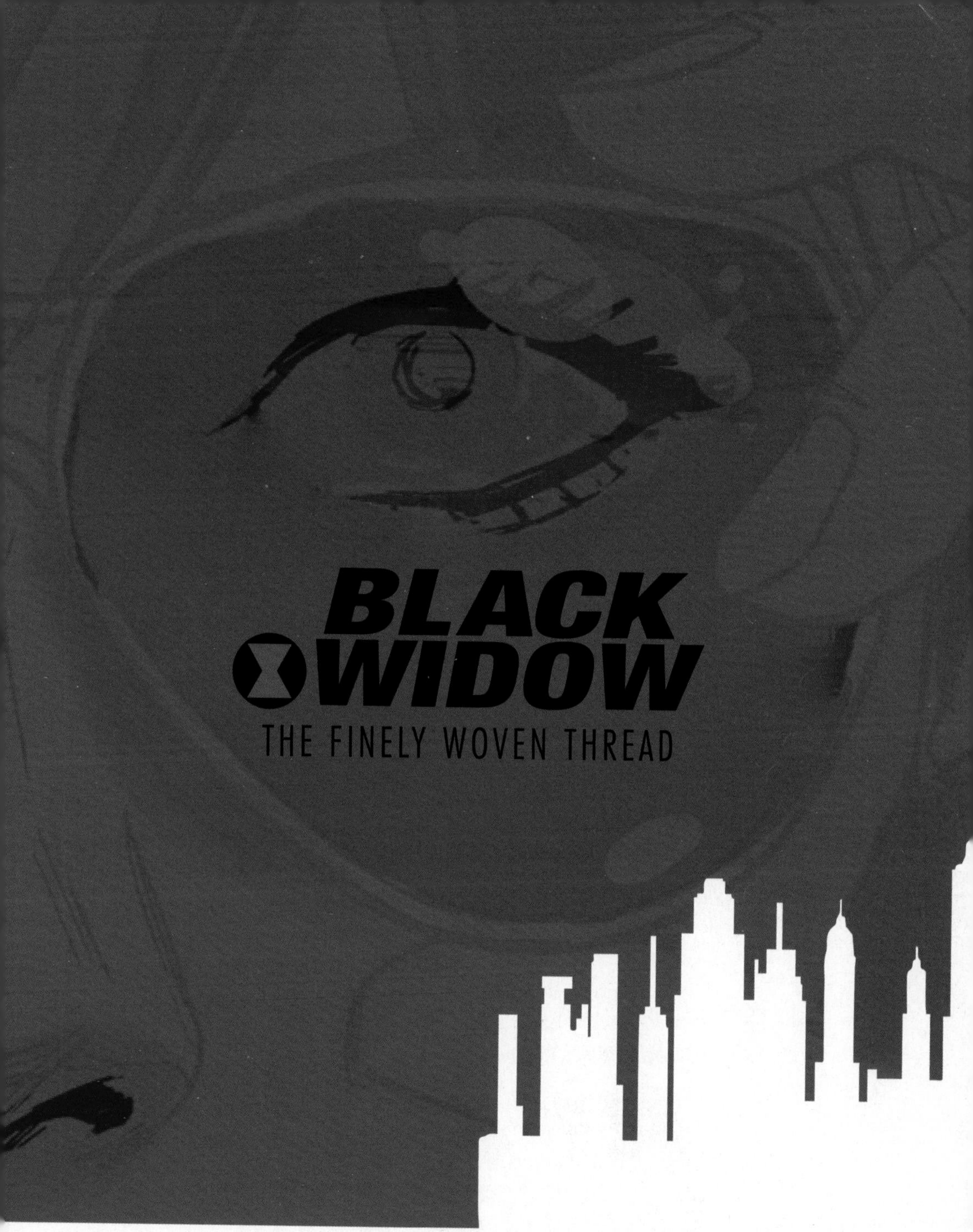

BLACK WIDOW

THE FINELY WOVEN THREAD

WRITER
NATHAN EDMONDSON

ARTIST/COVER ART
PHIL NOTO

LETTERER
VC'S CLAYTON COWLES

EDITOR
ELLIE PYLE

Natasha Romanov is an Avenger, an agent of S.H.I.E.L.D. and an ex-KGB assassin, but on her own time, she uses her unique skill set to atone for her past. She is:

BLACK WIDOW

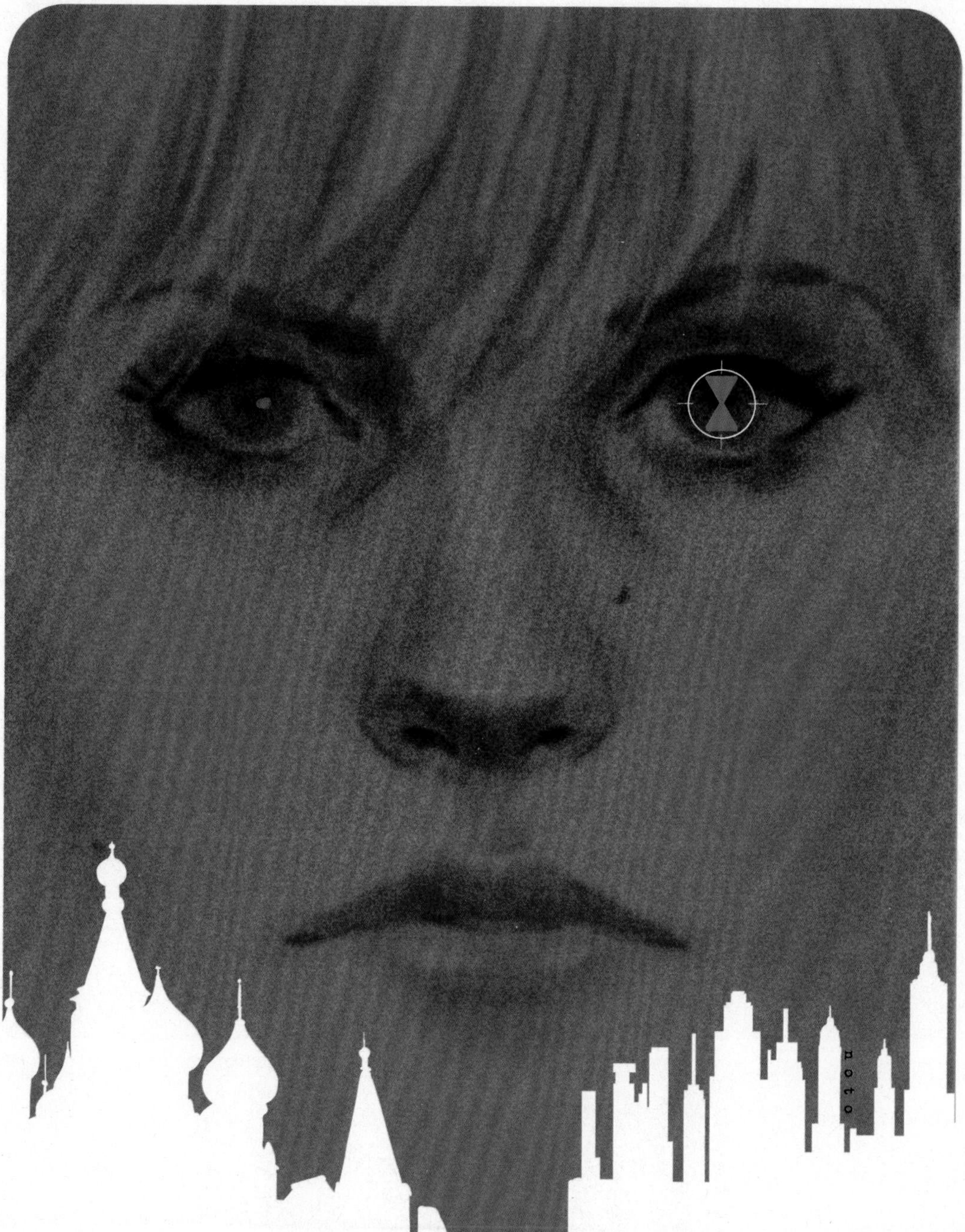
noto

1

RAISON D'ETRE

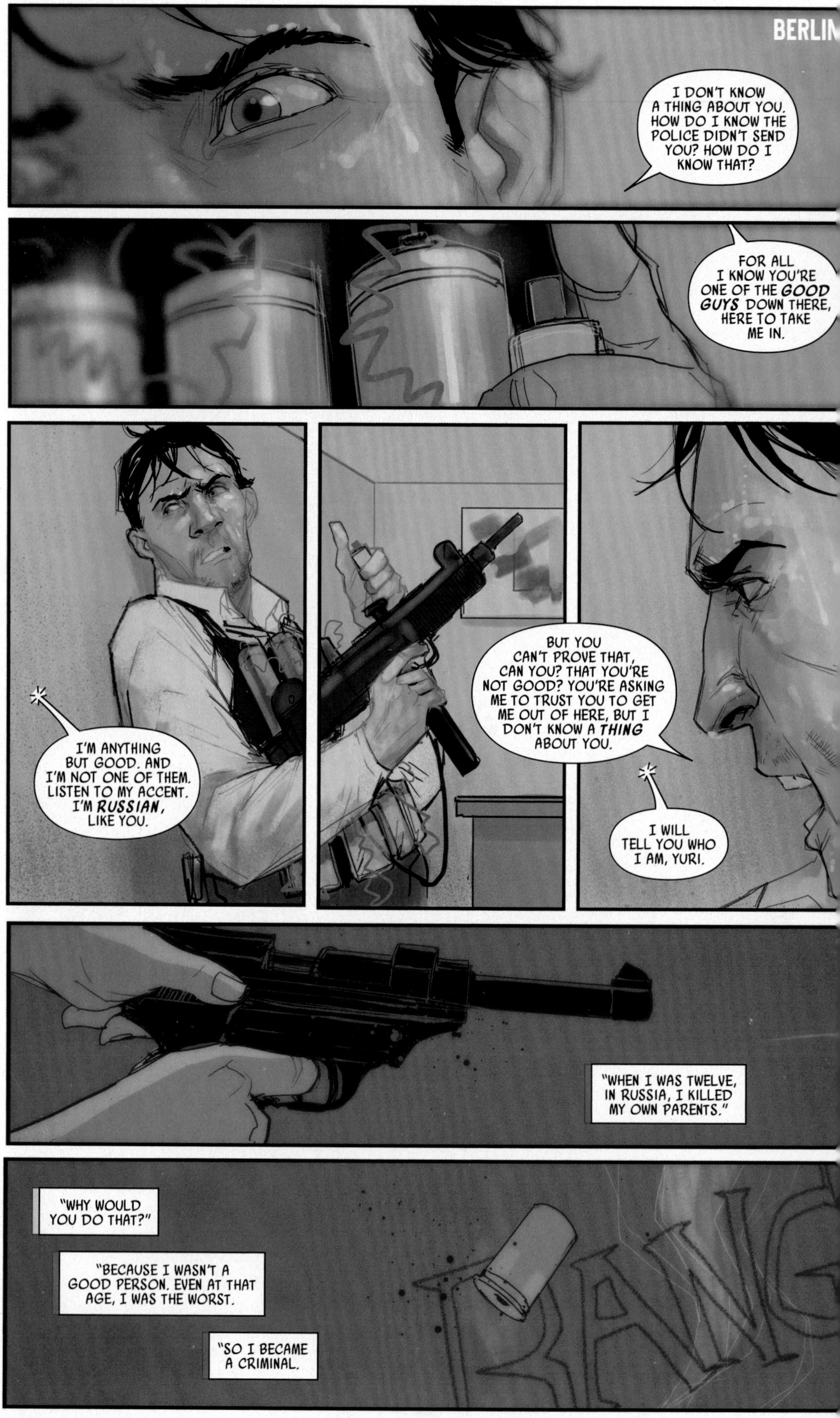
BERLIN
I DON'T KNOW A THING ABOUT YOU. HOW DO I KNOW THE POLICE DIDN'T SEND YOU? HOW DO I KNOW THAT?
FOR ALL I KNOW YOU'RE ONE OF THE GOOD GUYS DOWN THERE, HERE TO TAKE ME IN.
I'M ANYTHING BUT GOOD. AND I'M NOT ONE OF THEM. LISTEN TO MY ACCENT. I'M RUSSIAN, LIKE YOU.
BUT YOU CAN'T PROVE THAT, CAN YOU? THAT YOU'RE NOT GOOD? YOU'RE ASKING ME TO TRUST YOU TO GET ME OUT OF HERE, BUT I DON'T KNOW A THING ABOUT YOU.
I WILL TELL YOU WHO I AM, YURI.
"WHEN I WAS TWELVE, IN RUSSIA, I KILLED MY OWN PARENTS."
"WHY WOULD YOU DO THAT?"
"BECAUSE I WASN'T A GOOD PERSON. EVEN AT THAT AGE, I WAS THE WORST.
"SO I BECAME A CRIMINAL.
BANG

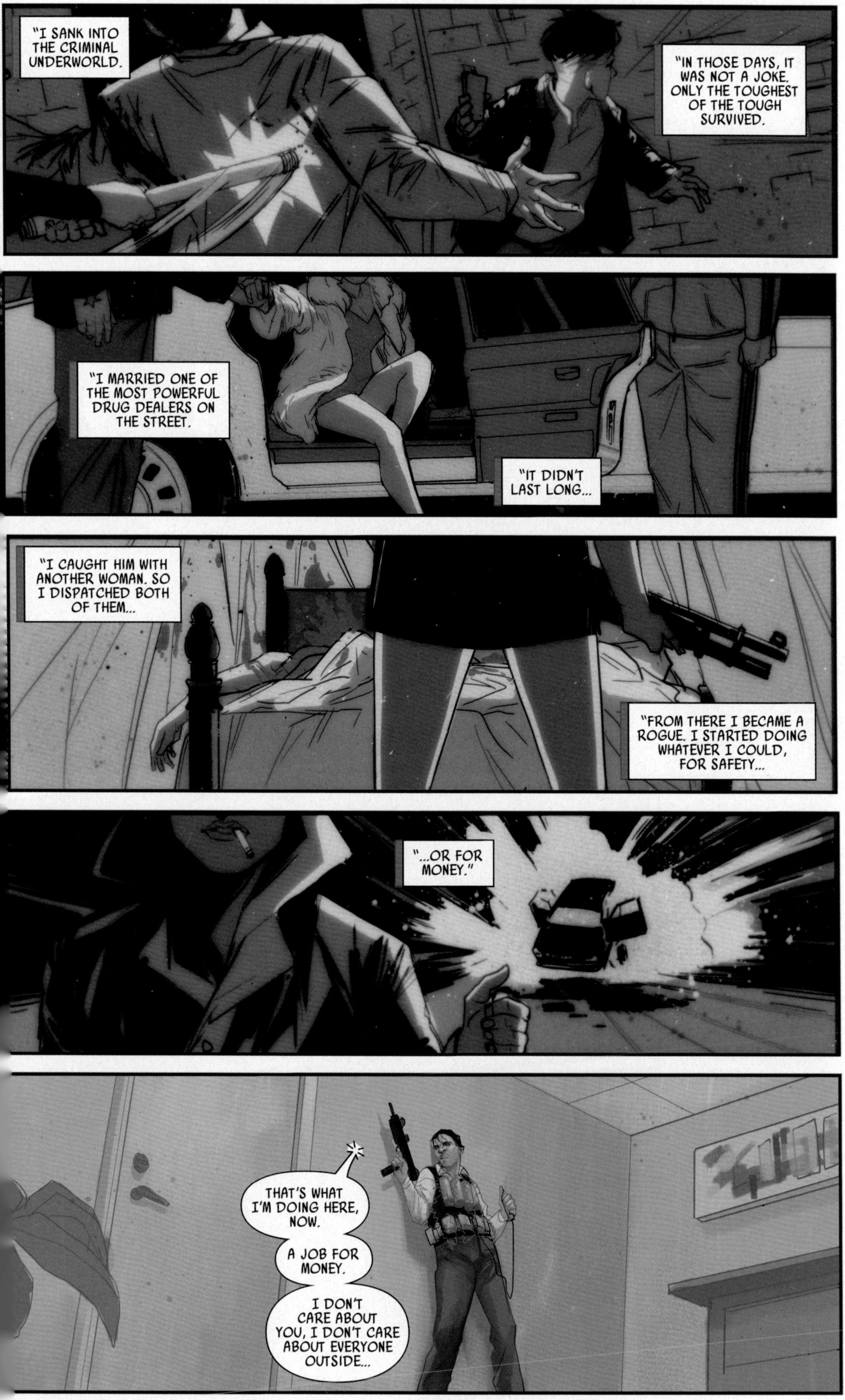
"I SANK INTO THE CRIMINAL UNDERWORLD.
"IN THOSE DAYS, IT WAS NOT A JOKE. ONLY THE TOUGHEST OF THE TOUGH SURVIVED.
"I MARRIED ONE OF THE MOST POWERFUL DRUG DEALERS ON THE STREET.
"IT DIDN'T LAST LONG...
"I CAUGHT HIM WITH ANOTHER WOMAN. SO I DISPATCHED BOTH OF THEM...
"FROM THERE I BECAME A ROGUE. I STARTED DOING WHATEVER I COULD, FOR SAFETY...
"...OR FOR MONEY."
THAT'S WHAT I'M DOING HERE, NOW.
A JOB FOR MONEY.
I DON'T CARE ABOUT YOU, I DON'T CARE ABOUT EVERYONE OUTSIDE...

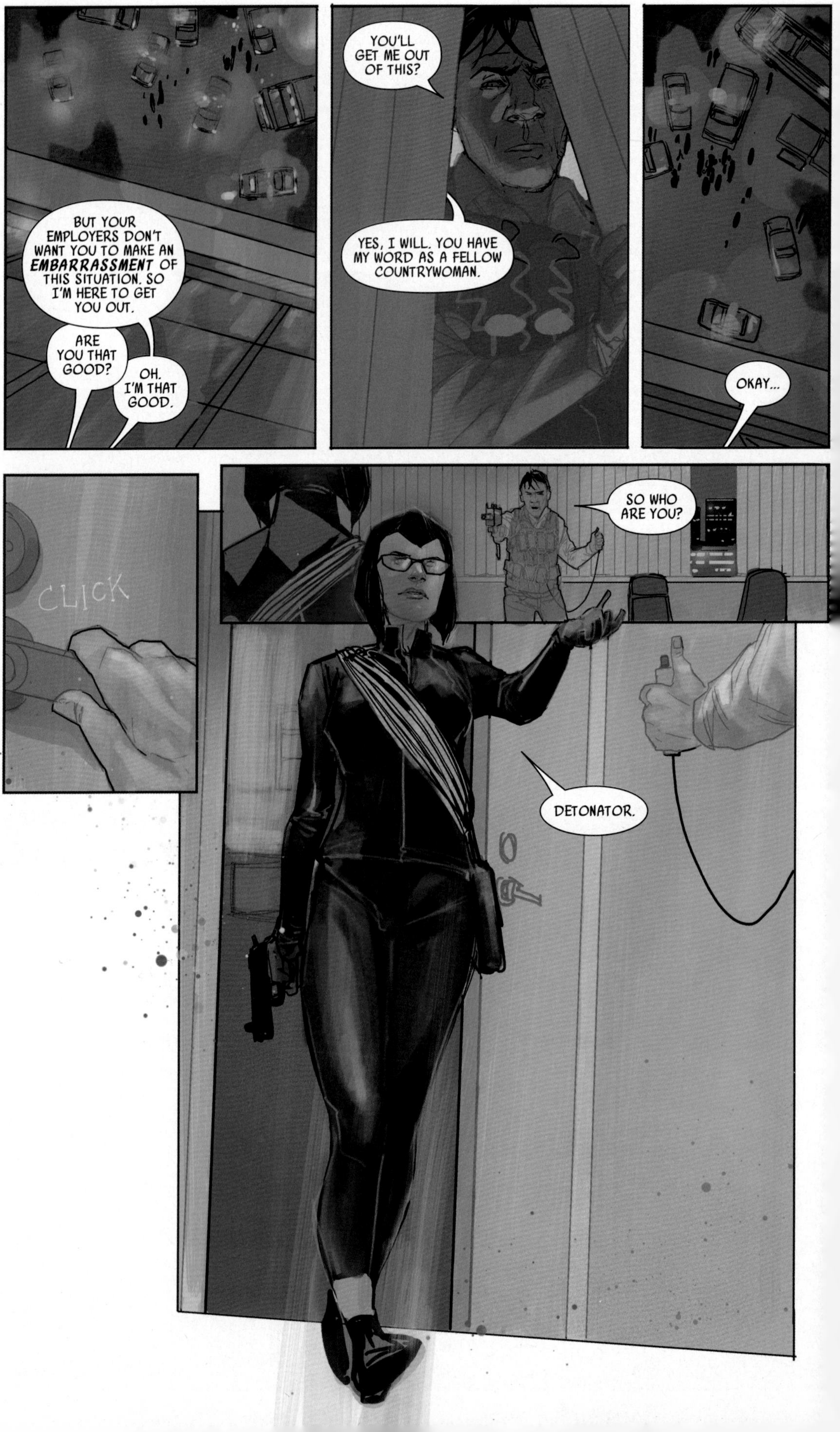
BUT YOUR EMPLOYERS DON'T WANT YOU TO MAKE AN EMBARRASSMENT OF THIS SITUATION. SO I'M HERE TO GET YOU OUT.
ARE YOU THAT GOOD?
OH. I'M THAT GOOD.
YOU'LL GET ME OUT OF THIS?
YES, I WILL. YOU HAVE MY WORD AS A FELLOW COUNTRYWOMAN.
OKAY...
CLICK
SO WHO ARE YOU?
DETONATOR.

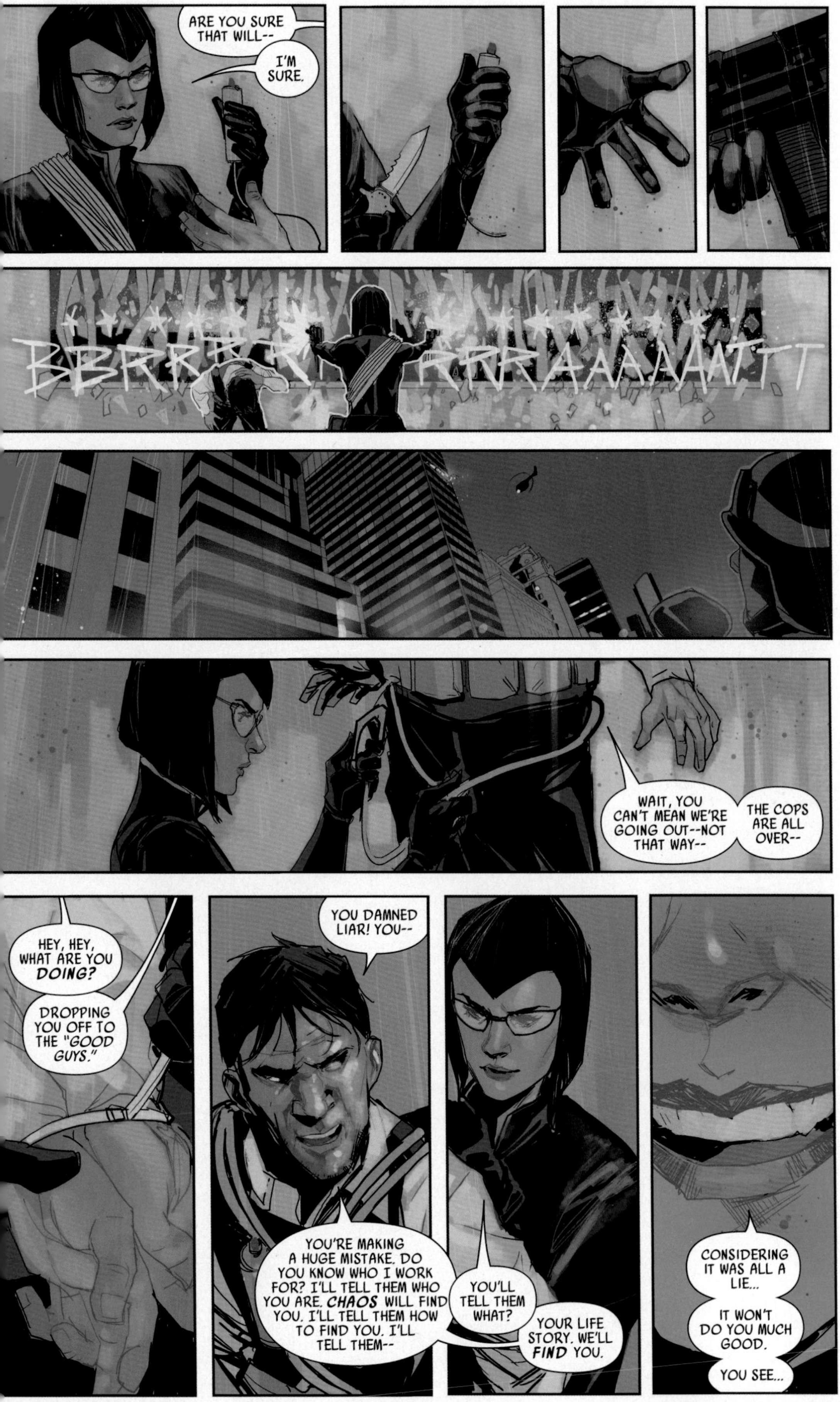
ARE YOU SURE THAT WILL--
I'M SURE.
BBRRRRRRRRRRRAAAAAATTTT
WAIT, YOU CAN'T MEAN WE'RE GOING OUT--NOT THAT WAY--
THE COPS ARE ALL OVER--
HEY, HEY, WHAT ARE YOU *DOING?*
DROPPING YOU OFF TO THE "GOOD GUYS."
YOU DAMNED LIAR! YOU--
YOU'RE MAKING A HUGE MISTAKE. DO YOU KNOW WHO I WORK FOR? I'LL TELL THEM WHO YOU ARE. *CHAOS* WILL FIND YOU. I'LL TELL THEM HOW TO FIND YOU. I'LL TELL THEM--
YOU'LL TELL THEM WHAT?
YOUR LIFE STORY. WE'LL *FIND* YOU.
CONSIDERING IT WAS ALL A LIE...
IT WON'T DO YOU MUCH GOOD.
YOU SEE...

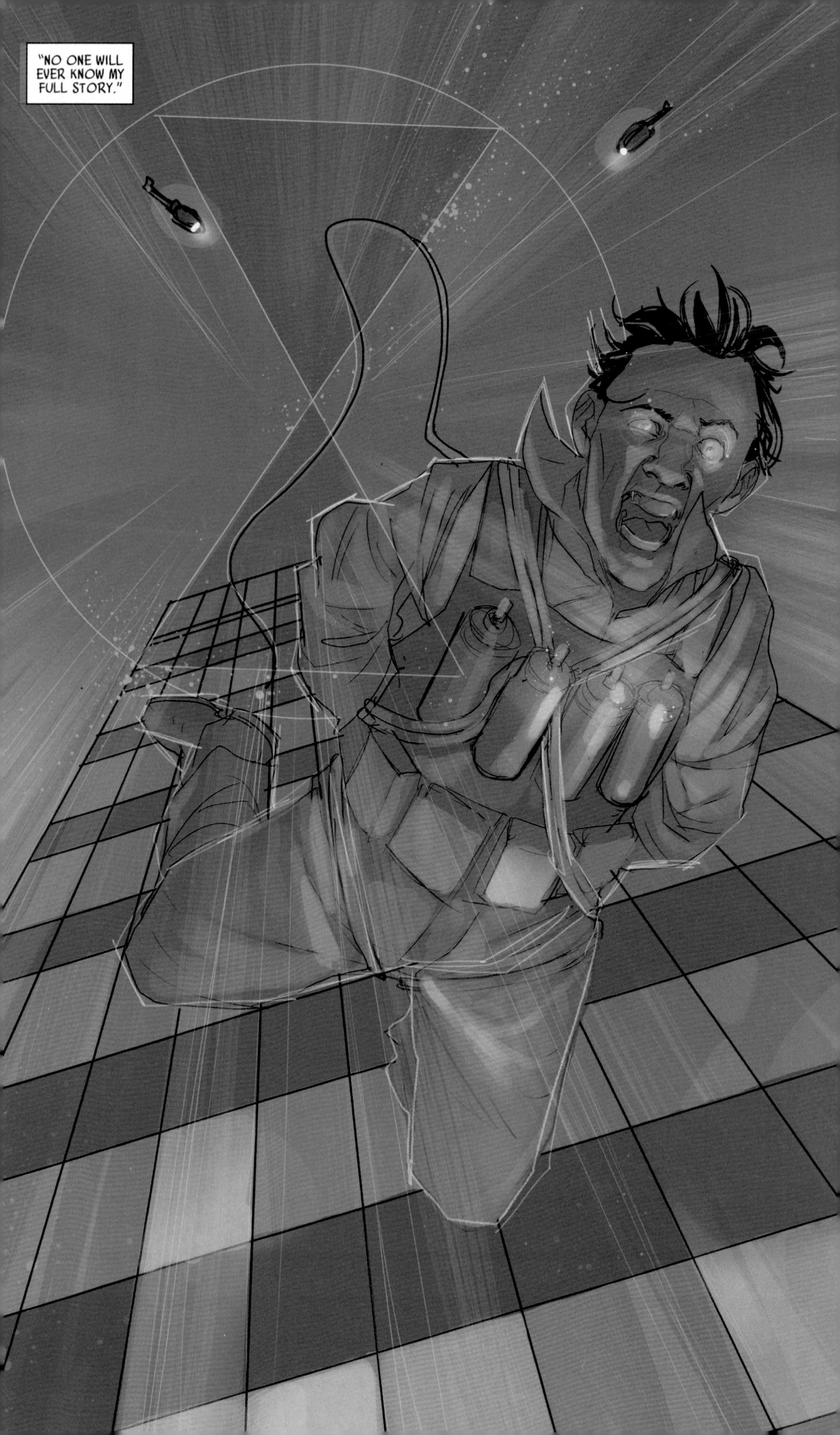
"NO ONE WILL EVER KNOW MY FULL STORY."

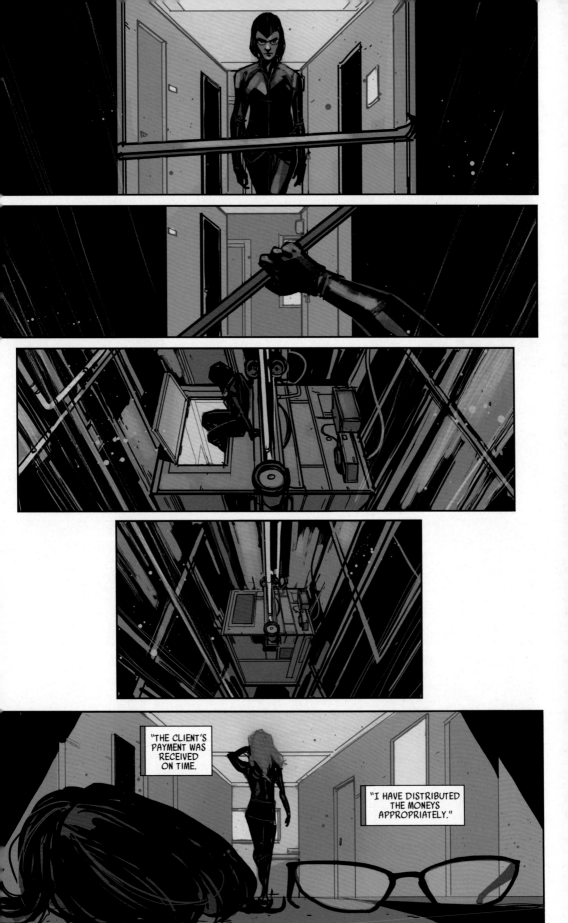

"THE CLIENT'S PAYMENT WAS RECEIVED ON TIME.

"I HAVE DISTRIBUTED THE MONEYS APPROPRIATELY."

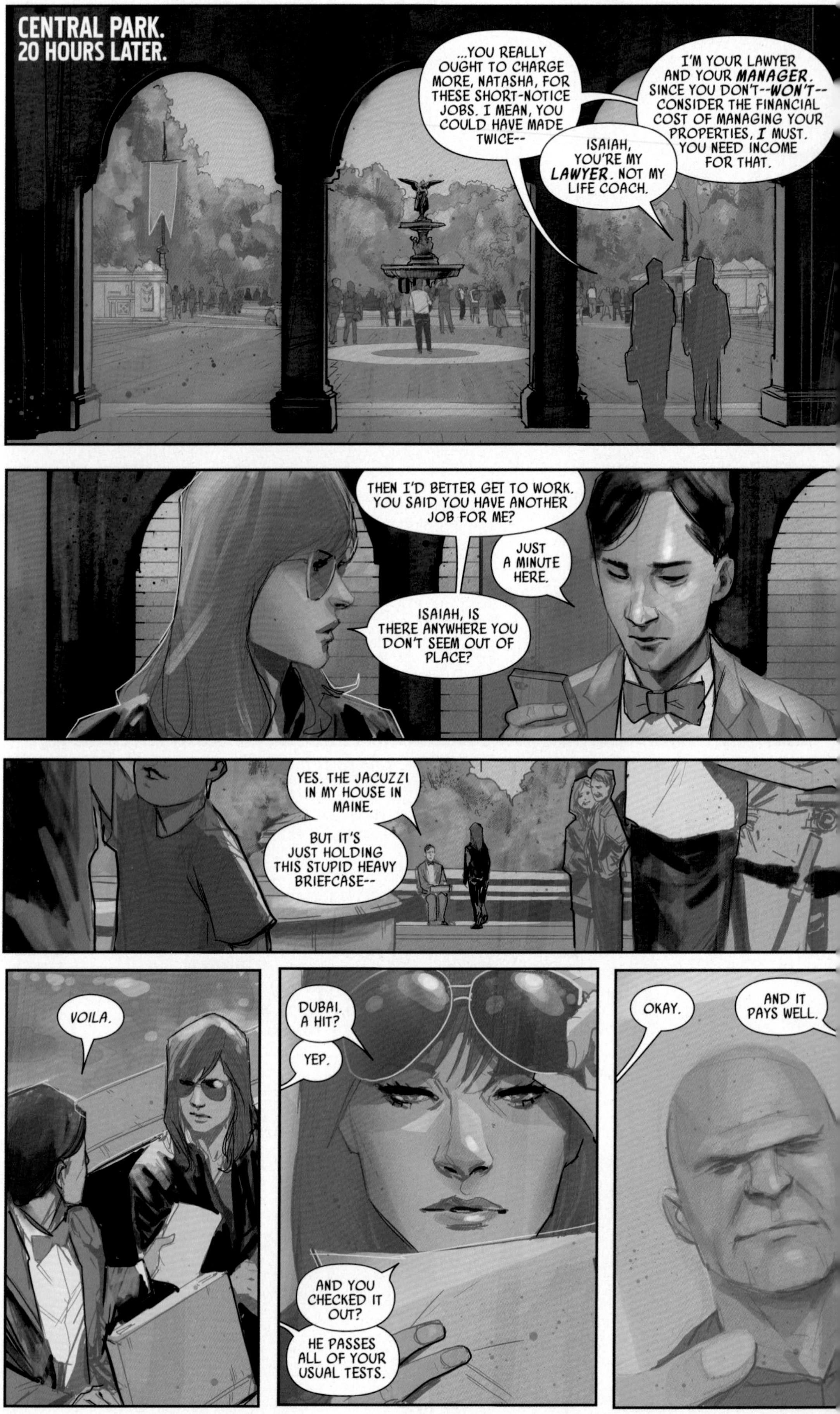
CENTRAL PARK. 20 HOURS LATER.
...YOU REALLY OUGHT TO CHARGE MORE, NATASHA, FOR THESE SHORT-NOTICE JOBS. I MEAN, YOU COULD HAVE MADE TWICE--
ISAIAH, YOU'RE MY LAWYER. NOT MY LIFE COACH.
I'M YOUR LAWYER AND YOUR MANAGER. SINCE YOU DON'T--WON'T--CONSIDER THE FINANCIAL COST OF MANAGING YOUR PROPERTIES, I MUST. YOU NEED INCOME FOR THAT.
THEN I'D BETTER GET TO WORK. YOU SAID YOU HAVE ANOTHER JOB FOR ME?
JUST A MINUTE HERE.
ISAIAH, IS THERE ANYWHERE YOU DON'T SEEM OUT OF PLACE?
YES. THE JACUZZI IN MY HOUSE IN MAINE.
BUT IT'S JUST HOLDING THIS STUPID HEAVY BRIEFCASE--
VOILA.
DUBAI. A HIT?
YEP.
AND YOU CHECKED IT OUT?
HE PASSES ALL OF YOUR USUAL TESTS.
OKAY.
AND IT PAYS WELL.

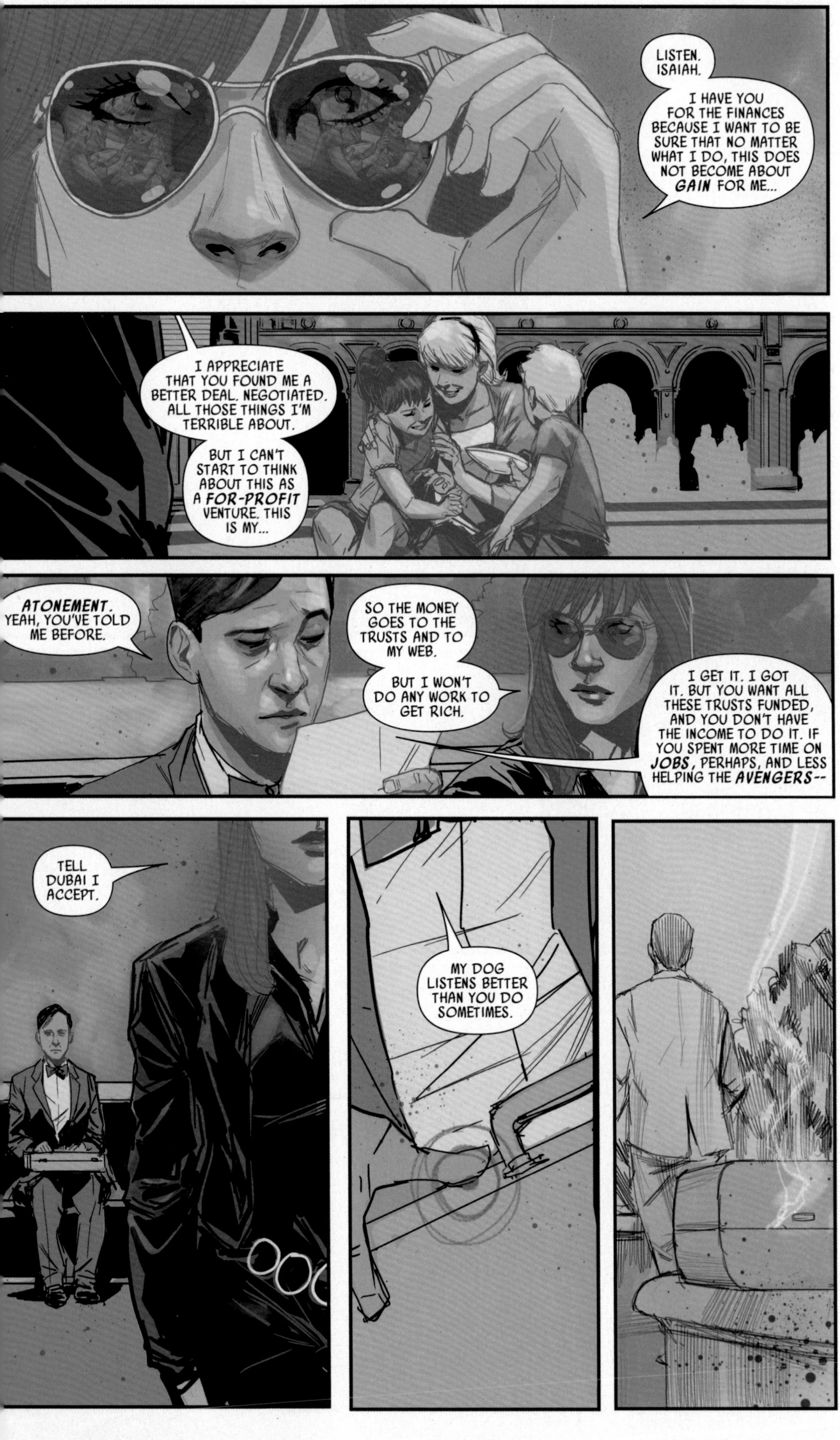
LISTEN. ISAIAH.
I HAVE YOU FOR THE FINANCES BECAUSE I WANT TO BE SURE THAT NO MATTER WHAT I DO, THIS DOES NOT BECOME ABOUT GAIN FOR ME...
I APPRECIATE THAT YOU FOUND ME A BETTER DEAL. NEGOTIATED. ALL THOSE THINGS I'M TERRIBLE ABOUT.
BUT I CAN'T START TO THINK ABOUT THIS AS A FOR-PROFIT VENTURE. THIS IS MY...
ATONEMENT. YEAH, YOU'VE TOLD ME BEFORE.
SO THE MONEY GOES TO THE TRUSTS AND TO MY WEB.
BUT I WON'T DO ANY WORK TO GET RICH.
I GET IT. I GOT IT. BUT YOU WANT ALL THESE TRUSTS FUNDED, AND YOU DON'T HAVE THE INCOME TO DO IT. IF YOU SPENT MORE TIME ON JOBS, PERHAPS, AND LESS HELPING THE AVENGERS--
TELL DUBAI I ACCEPT.
MY DOG LISTENS BETTER THAN YOU DO SOMETIMES.

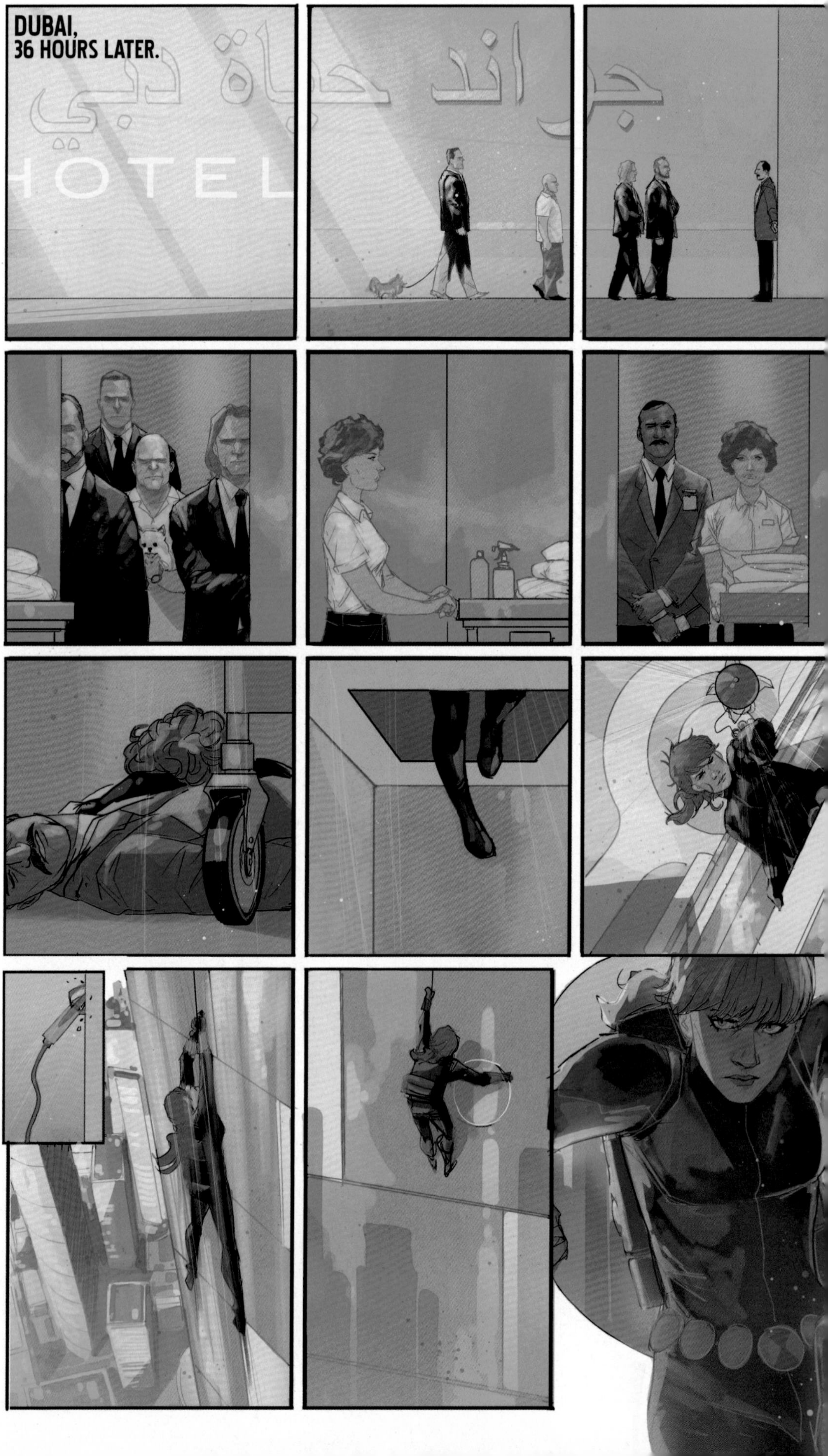
DUBAI,
36 HOURS LATER.
HOTEL

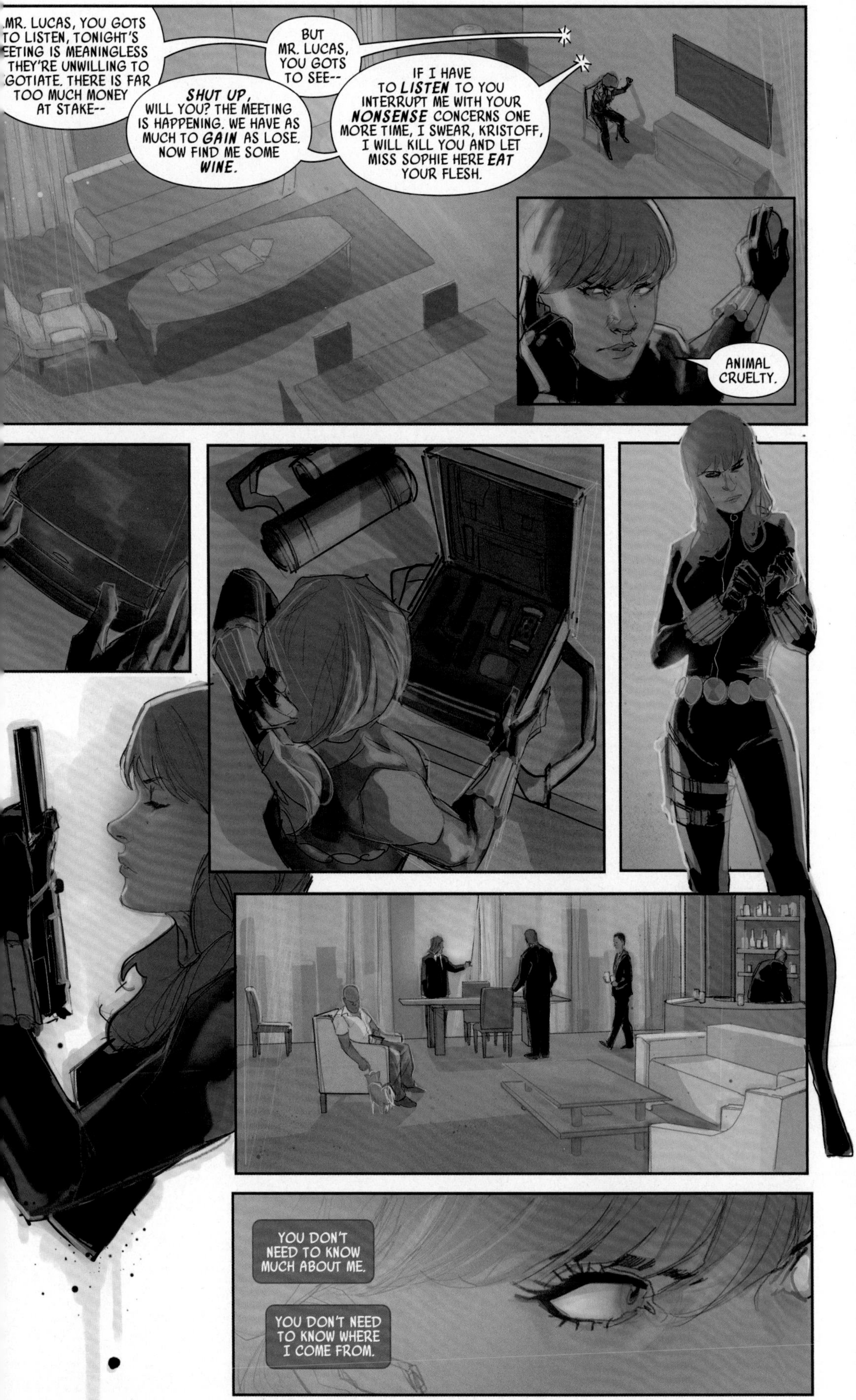
.MR. LUCAS, YOU GOTS TO LISTEN, TONIGHT'S EETING IS MEANINGLESS THEY'RE UNWILLING TO GOTIATE. THERE IS FAR TOO MUCH MONEY AT STAKE--
SHUT UP, WILL YOU? THE MEETING IS HAPPENING. WE HAVE AS MUCH TO GAIN AS LOSE. NOW FIND ME SOME WINE.
BUT MR. LUCAS, YOU GOTS TO SEE--
IF I HAVE TO LISTEN TO YOU INTERRUPT ME WITH YOUR NONSENSE CONCERNS ONE MORE TIME, I SWEAR, KRISTOFF, I WILL KILL YOU AND LET MISS SOPHIE HERE EAT YOUR FLESH.
ANIMAL CRUELTY.
YOU DON'T NEED TO KNOW MUCH ABOUT ME.
YOU DON'T NEED TO KNOW WHERE I COME FROM.

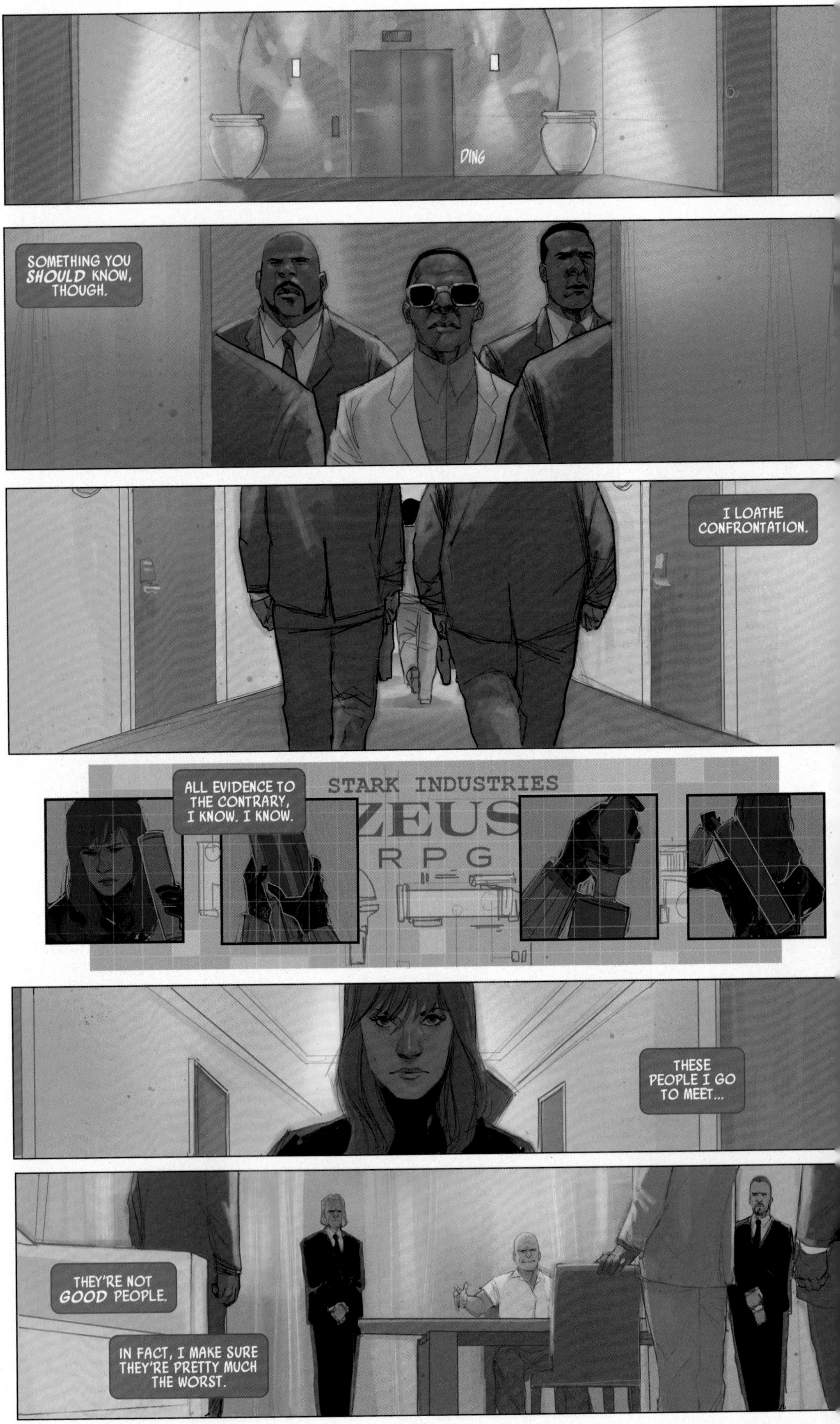
DING
SOMETHING YOU SHOULD KNOW, THOUGH.
I LOATHE CONFRONTATION.
ALL EVIDENCE TO THE CONTRARY, I KNOW. I KNOW.
STARK INDUSTRIES
ZEUS
RPG
THESE PEOPLE I GO TO MEET...
THEY'RE NOT GOOD PEOPLE.
IN FACT, I MAKE SURE THEY'RE PRETTY MUCH THE WORST.

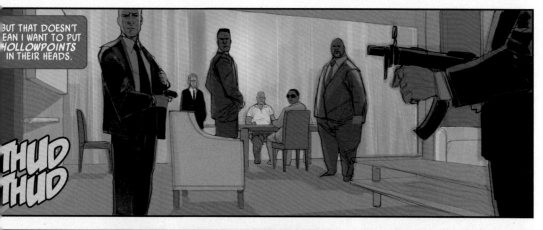

BUT THAT DOESN'T MEAN I WANT TO PUT HOLLOWPOINTS IN THEIR HEADS.

THUD THUD

YOU KNOW, NOT NECESSARILY.

WELL? WHAT *IS* IT?

NOT SURE, MR. LUCAS. NO ONE HERE...

CHECK IT OUT TO BE *SURE!*

YOU GO OUT THERE TOO! WE'RE FINE IN HERE!

DON'T-A-WORRY, MR. LUCAS, WE GOTS THIS--

ZZZAATT

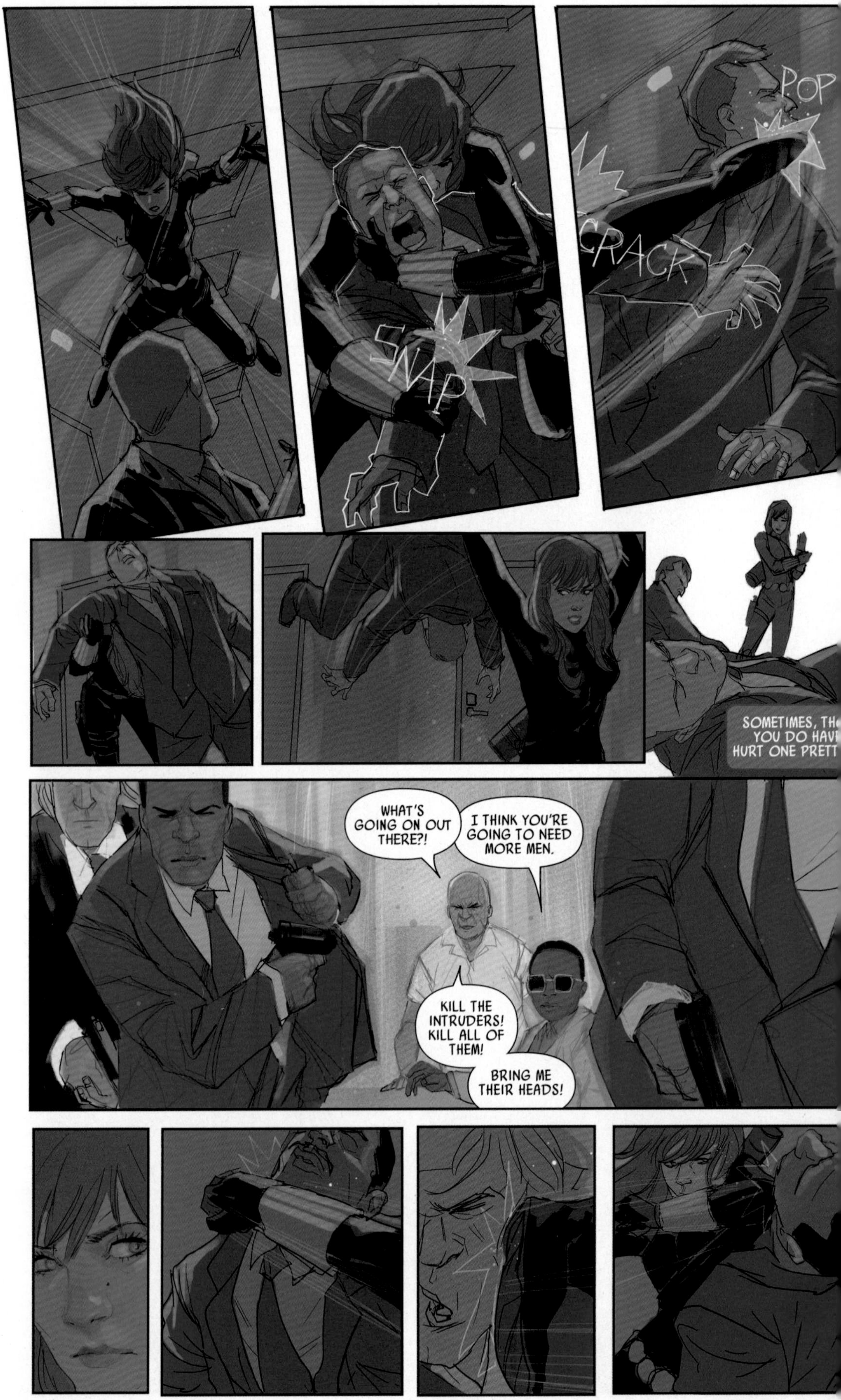
POP
CRACK
SNAP
SOMETIMES, TH
YOU DO HAV
HURT ONE PRETT
WHAT'S GOING ON OUT THERE?!
I THINK YOU'RE GOING TO NEED MORE MEN.
KILL THE INTRUDERS! KILL ALL OF THEM!
BRING ME THEIR HEADS!

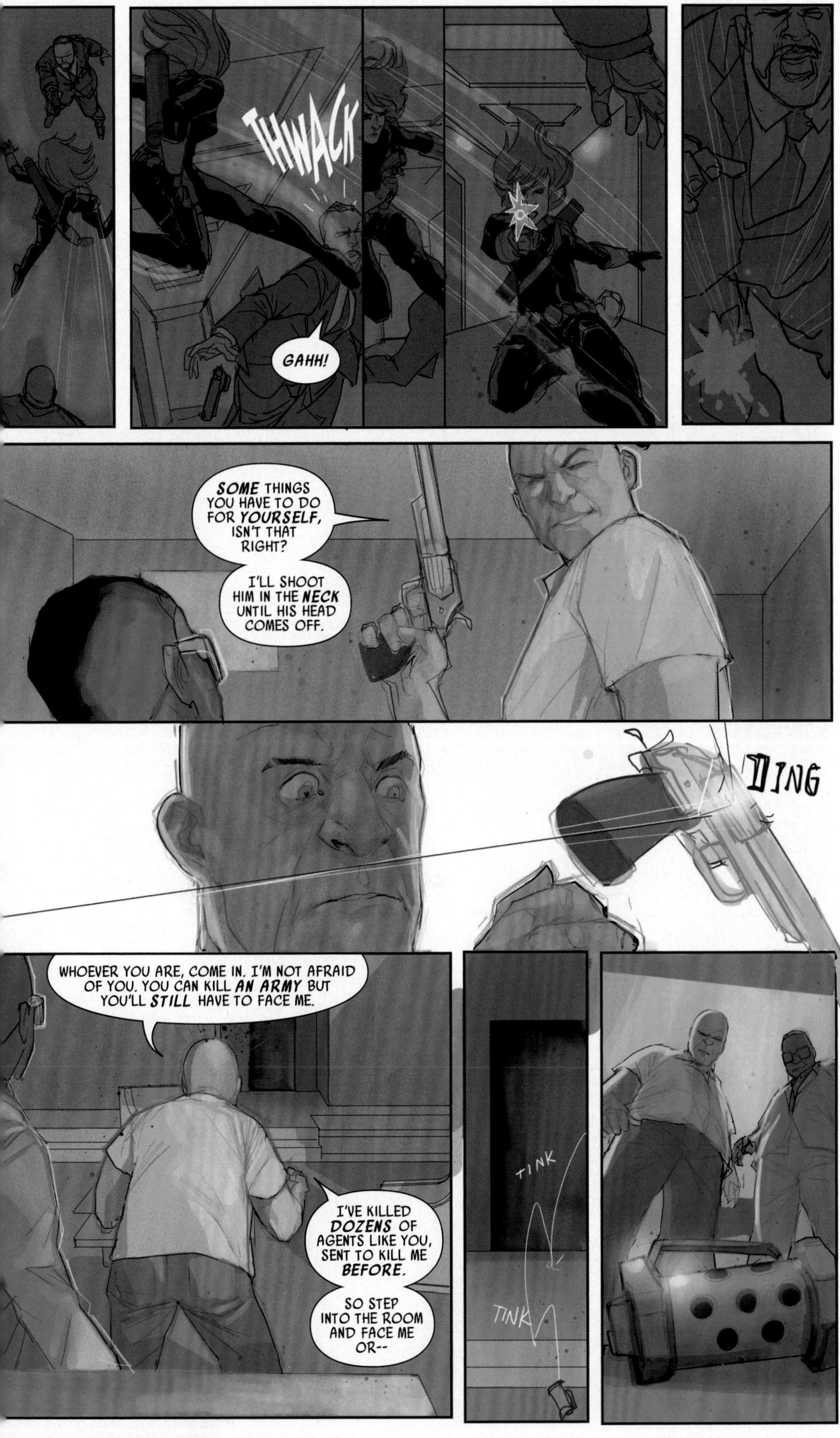
THWACK
GAHH!
SOME THINGS YOU HAVE TO DO FOR YOURSELF, ISN'T THAT RIGHT?
I'LL SHOOT HIM IN THE NECK UNTIL HIS HEAD COMES OFF.
DING
WHOEVER YOU ARE, COME IN. I'M NOT AFRAID OF YOU. YOU CAN KILL AN ARMY BUT YOU'LL STILL HAVE TO FACE ME.
I'VE KILLED DOZENS OF AGENTS LIKE YOU, SENT TO KILL ME BEFORE.
SO STEP INTO THE ROOM AND FACE ME OR--
TINK
TINK

IF YOU'RE GOING TO **KILL** ME DO IT TO MY **FACE**, DON'T THROW YOUR **TOYS** AROUND LIKE A COWARD!

PUT ON THIS KEVLAR VEST.

I WASN'T HIRED TO KILL YOU, MR. LUCAS.

I WAS HIRED TO KILL YOUR ASSASSIN.

STAND BY THE WINDOW.

WHAT? **WHY?** WHY WOULD I--

BECAUSE IF YOU DON'T, I **WILL** KILL YOU.

AND BECAUSE YOUR **REAL** KILLER HAS A SNIPER RIFLE SOMEWHERE IN THE BUILDING ACROSS THE WAY.

WAIT, YOU CAN'T BE--YOU DON'T MEAN-- NO!

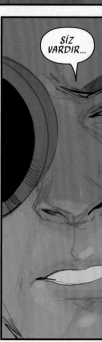

SÍZ VARDIR...

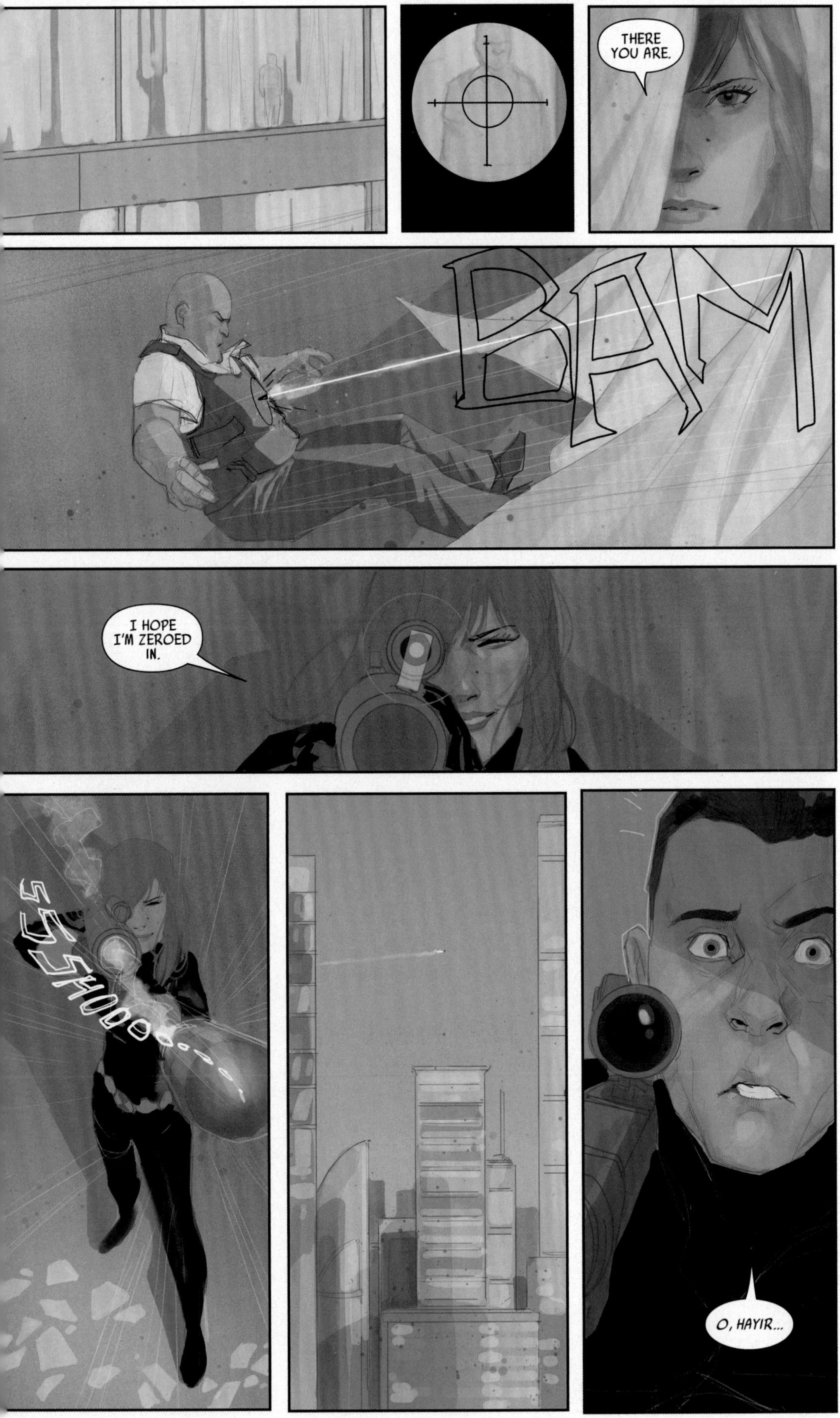
THERE YOU ARE.
BAM
I HOPE I'M ZEROED IN.
SSSHOOOooooo
O, HAYIR...

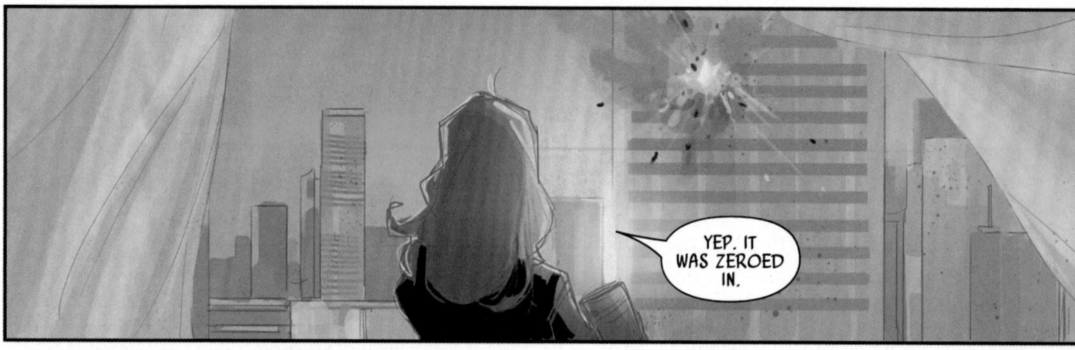
YEP. IT WAS ZEROED IN.

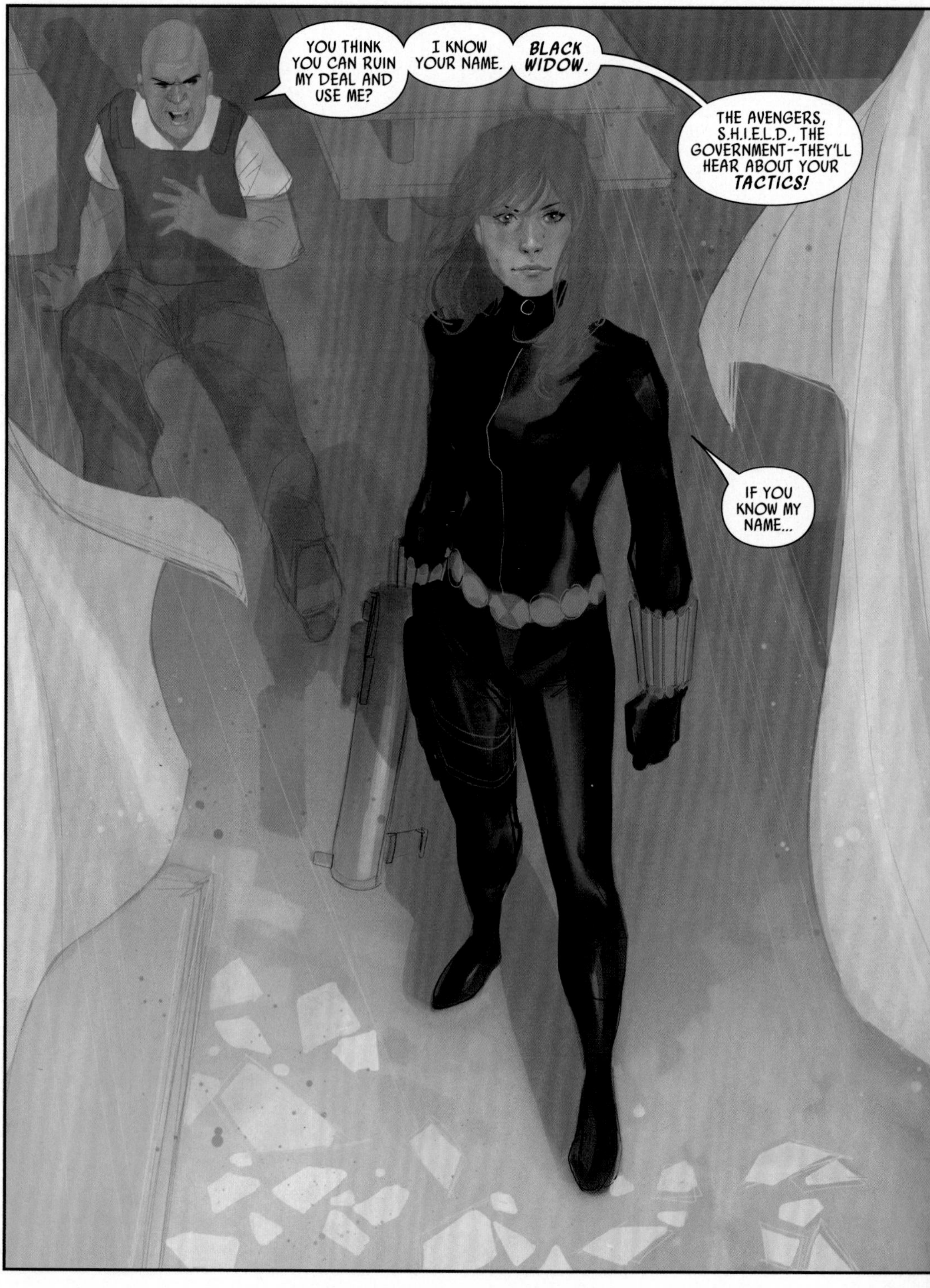
YOU THINK YOU CAN RUIN MY DEAL AND USE ME?
I KNOW YOUR NAME.
BLACK WIDOW.
THE AVENGERS, S.H.I.E.L.D., THE GOVERNMENT--THEY'LL HEAR ABOUT YOUR TACTICS!
IF YOU KNOW MY NAME...

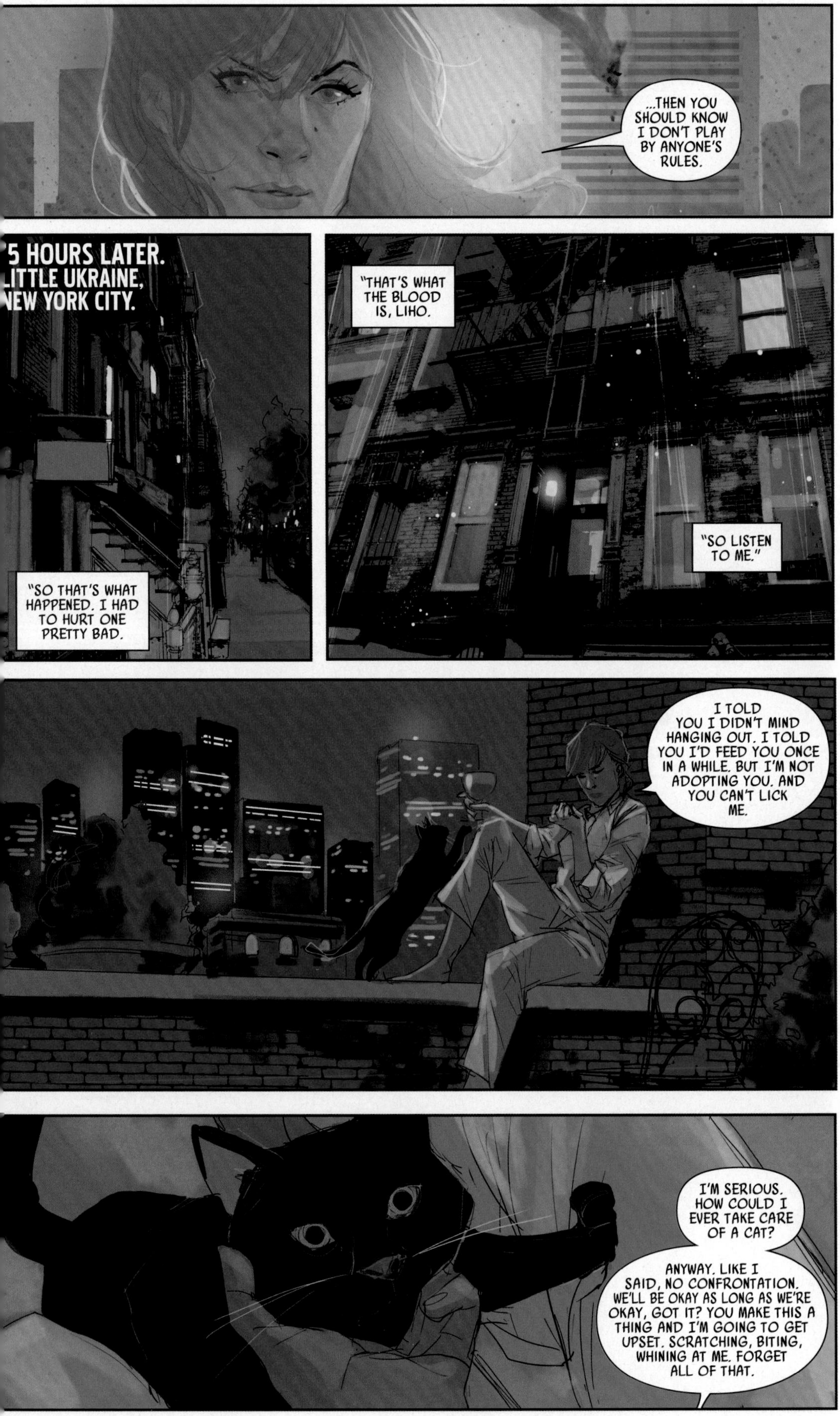
...THEN YOU SHOULD KNOW I DON'T PLAY BY ANYONE'S RULES.
5 HOURS LATER. LITTLE UKRAINE, NEW YORK CITY.
"SO THAT'S WHAT HAPPENED. I HAD TO HURT ONE PRETTY BAD.
"THAT'S WHAT THE BLOOD IS, LIHO.
"SO LISTEN TO ME."
I TOLD YOU I DIDN'T MIND HANGING OUT. I TOLD YOU I'D FEED YOU ONCE IN A WHILE. BUT I'M NOT ADOPTING YOU. AND YOU CAN'T LICK ME.
I'M SERIOUS. HOW COULD I EVER TAKE CARE OF A CAT?
ANYWAY. LIKE I SAID, NO CONFRONTATION. WE'LL BE OKAY AS LONG AS WE'RE OKAY, GOT IT? YOU MAKE THIS A THING AND I'M GOING TO GET UPSET. SCRATCHING, BITING, WHINING AT ME. FORGET ALL OF THAT.

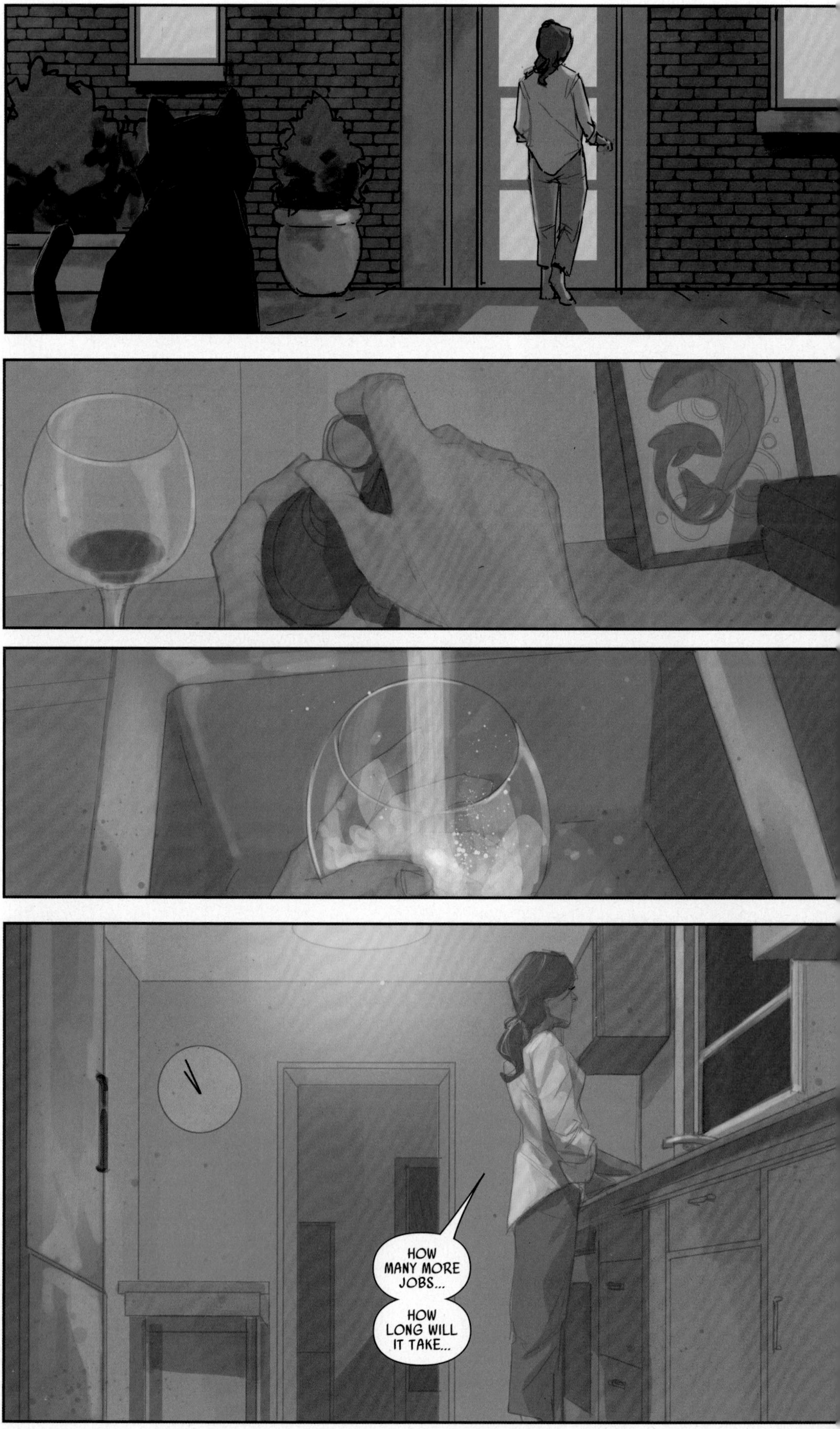
HOW MANY MORE JOBS...
HOW LONG WILL IT TAKE...

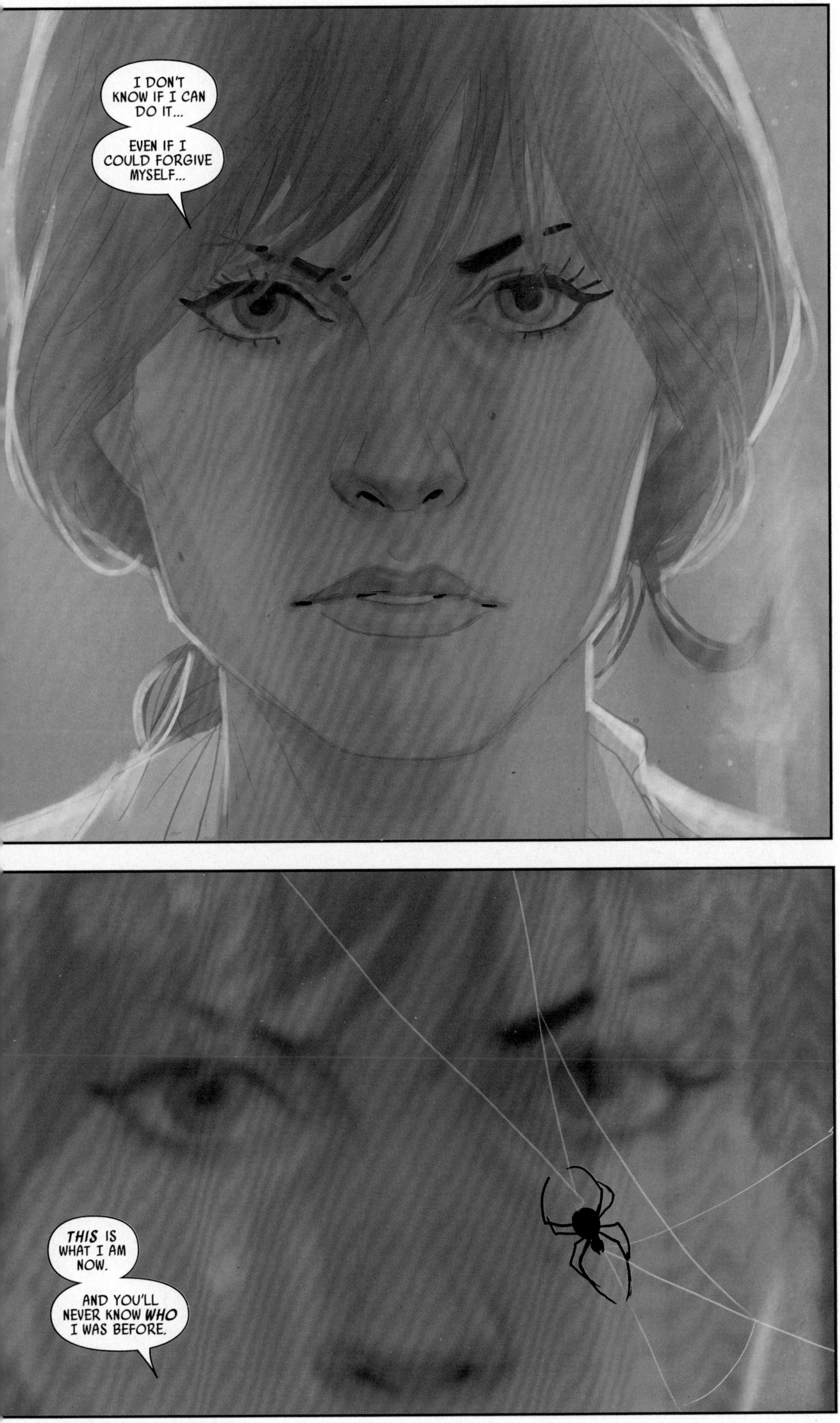
I DON'T KNOW IF I CAN DO IT...
EVEN IF I COULD FORGIVE MYSELF...
THIS IS WHAT I AM NOW.
AND YOU'LL NEVER KNOW WHO I WAS BEFORE.

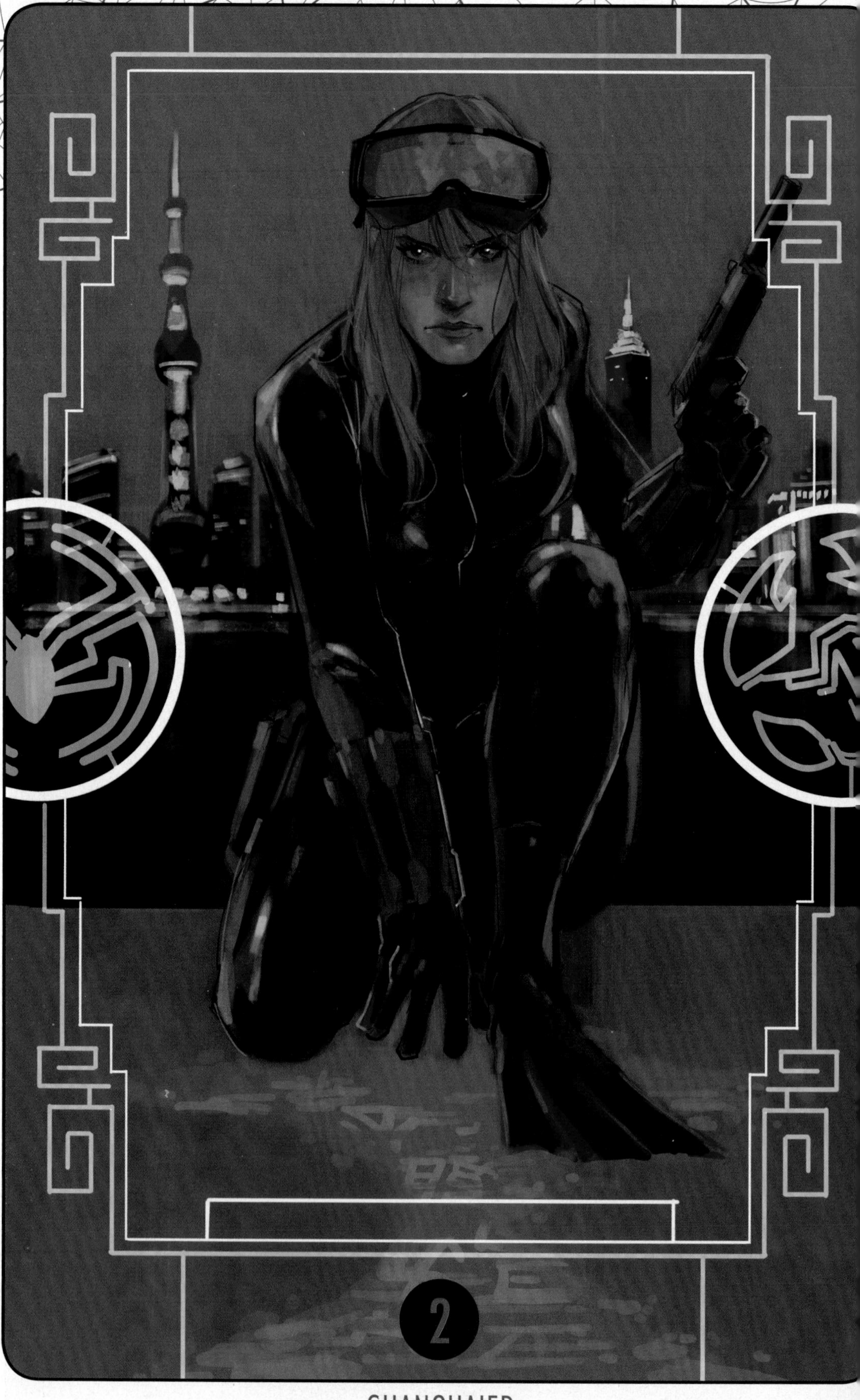
2

SHANGHAIED

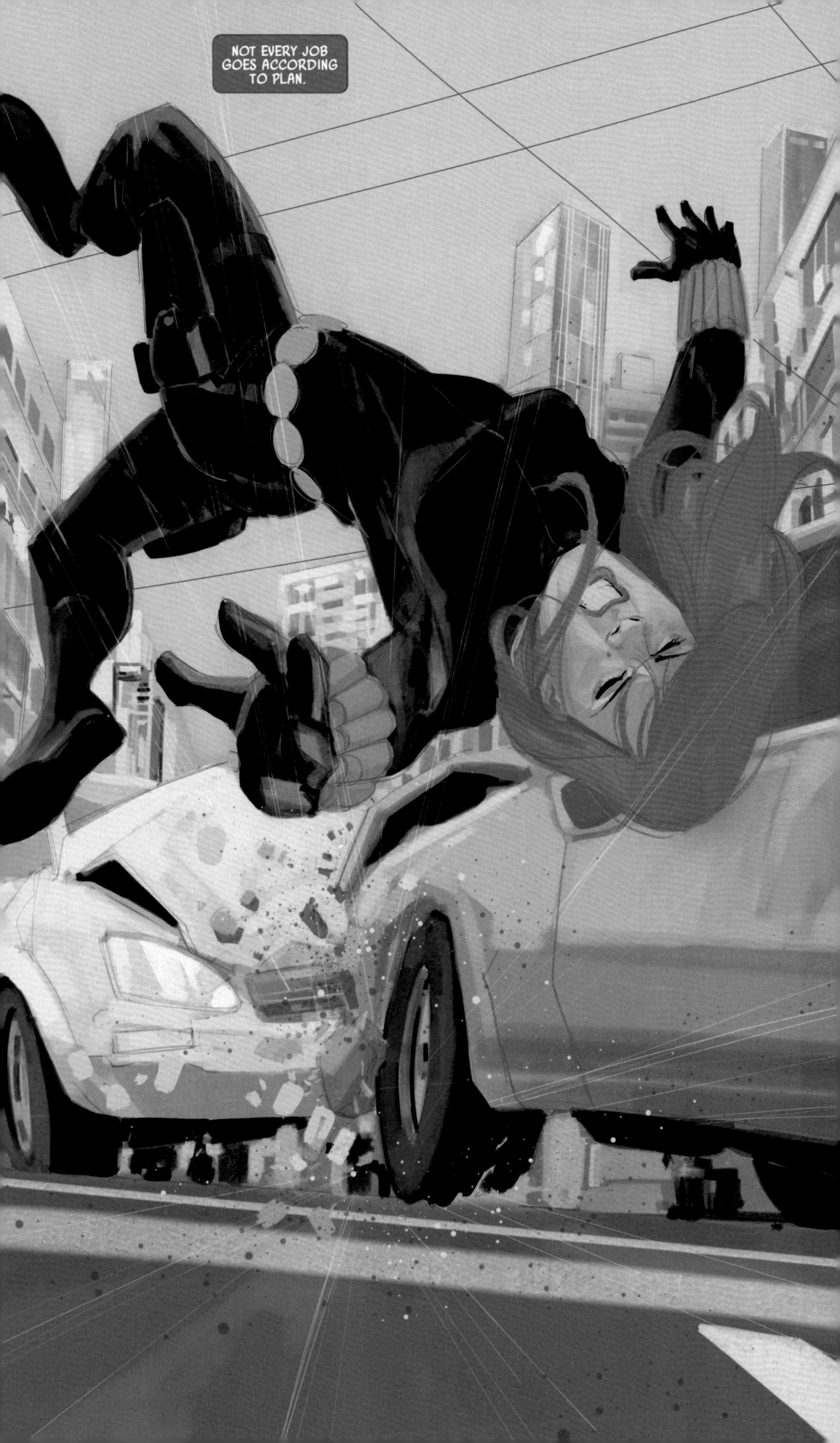
NOT EVERY JOB GOES ACCORDING TO PLAN.

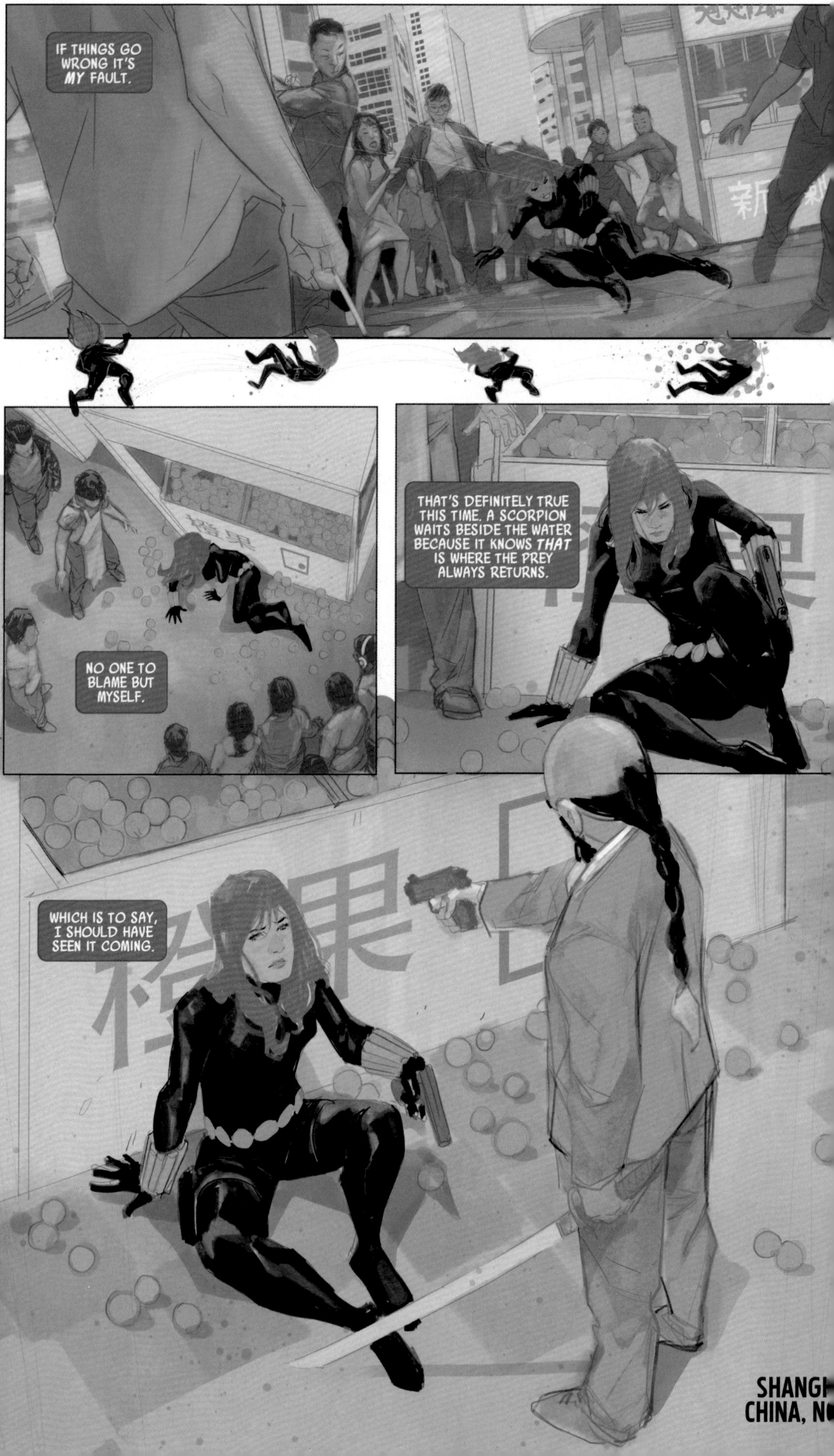
IF THINGS GO WRONG IT'S *MY* FAULT.
NO ONE TO BLAME BUT MYSELF.
THAT'S DEFINITELY TRUE THIS TIME. A SCORPION WAITS BESIDE THE WATER BECAUSE IT KNOWS *THAT* IS WHERE THE PREY ALWAYS RETURNS.
WHICH IS TO SAY, I SHOULD HAVE SEEN IT COMING.
SHANGI
CHINA, N

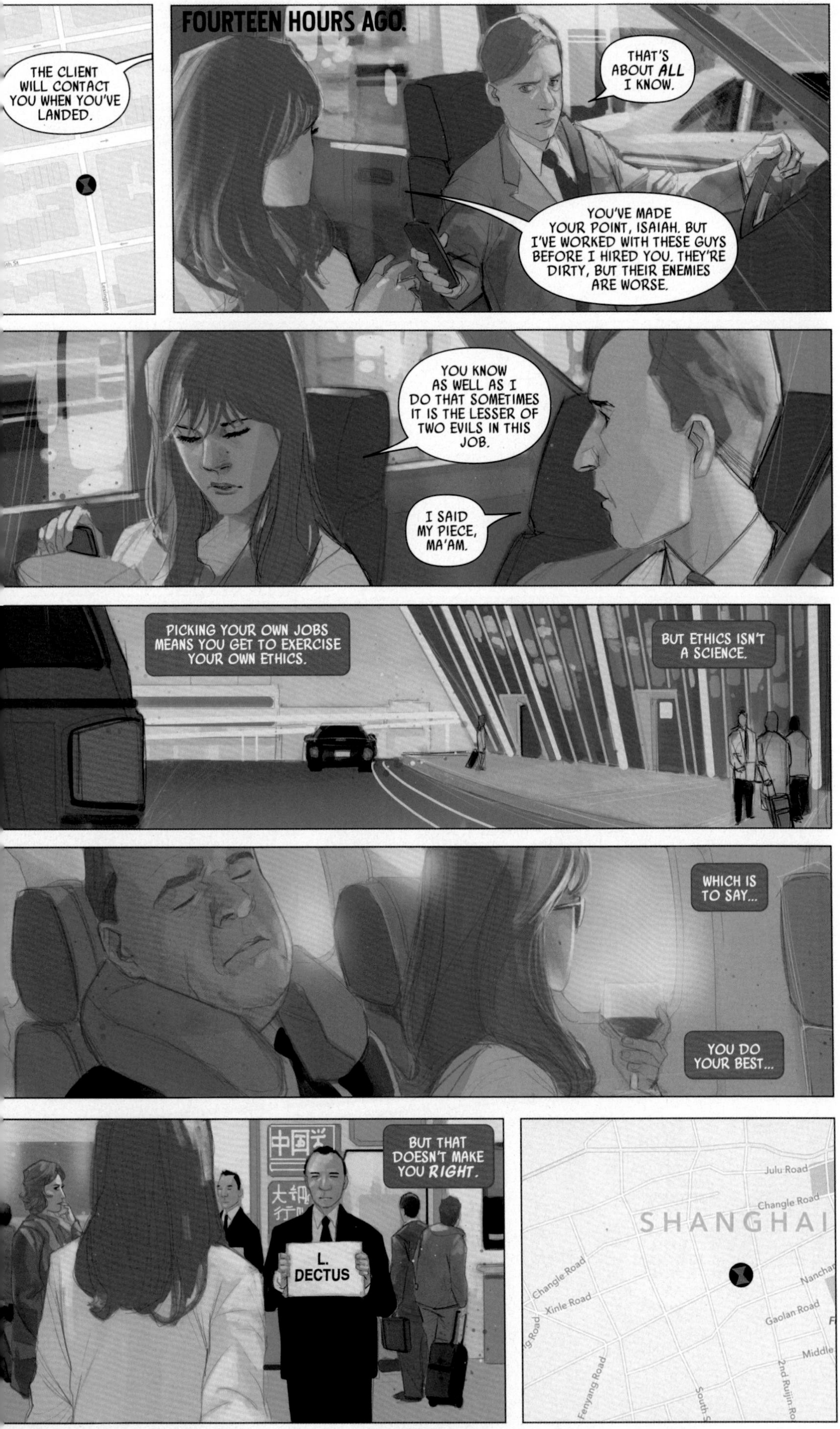
THE CLIENT WILL CONTACT YOU WHEN YOU'VE LANDED.
Lexington
FOURTEEN HOURS AGO.
THAT'S ABOUT ALL I KNOW.
YOU'VE MADE YOUR POINT, ISAIAH. BUT I'VE WORKED WITH THESE GUYS BEFORE I HIRED YOU. THEY'RE DIRTY, BUT THEIR ENEMIES ARE WORSE.
YOU KNOW AS WELL AS I DO THAT SOMETIMES IT IS THE LESSER OF TWO EVILS IN THIS JOB.
I SAID MY PIECE, MA'AM.
PICKING YOUR OWN JOBS MEANS YOU GET TO EXERCISE YOUR OWN ETHICS.
BUT ETHICS ISN'T A SCIENCE.
WHICH IS TO SAY...
YOU DO YOUR BEST...
BUT THAT DOESN'T MAKE YOU RIGHT.
L. DECTUS
Julu Road
Changle Road
SHANGHAI
Changle Road
Xinle Road
Gaolan Road
Fenyang Road
Middle
2nd Ruijin Ro

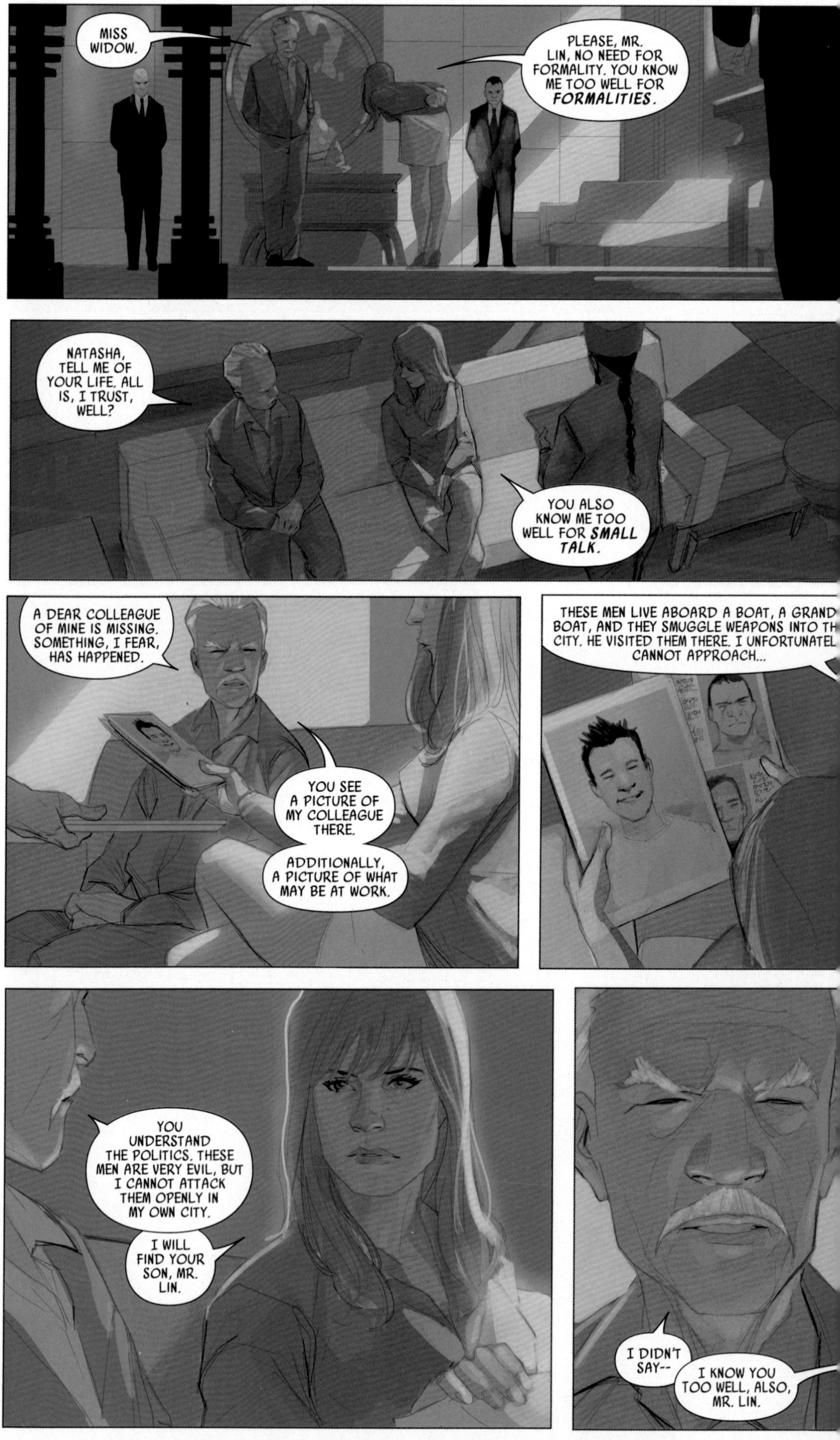
MISS WIDOW.
PLEASE, MR. LIN, NO NEED FOR FORMALITY. YOU KNOW ME TOO WELL FOR FORMALITIES.
NATASHA, TELL ME OF YOUR LIFE. ALL IS, I TRUST, WELL?
YOU ALSO KNOW ME TOO WELL FOR SMALL TALK.
A DEAR COLLEAGUE OF MINE IS MISSING. SOMETHING, I FEAR, HAS HAPPENED.
YOU SEE A PICTURE OF MY COLLEAGUE THERE.
ADDITIONALLY, A PICTURE OF WHAT MAY BE AT WORK.
THESE MEN LIVE ABOARD A BOAT, A GRAND BOAT, AND THEY SMUGGLE WEAPONS INTO TH CITY. HE VISITED THEM THERE. I UNFORTUNATEL CANNOT APPROACH...
YOU UNDERSTAND THE POLITICS. THESE MEN ARE VERY EVIL, BUT I CANNOT ATTACK THEM OPENLY IN MY OWN CITY.
I WILL FIND YOUR SON, MR. LIN.
I DIDN'T SAY--
I KNOW YOU TOO WELL, ALSO, MR. LIN.

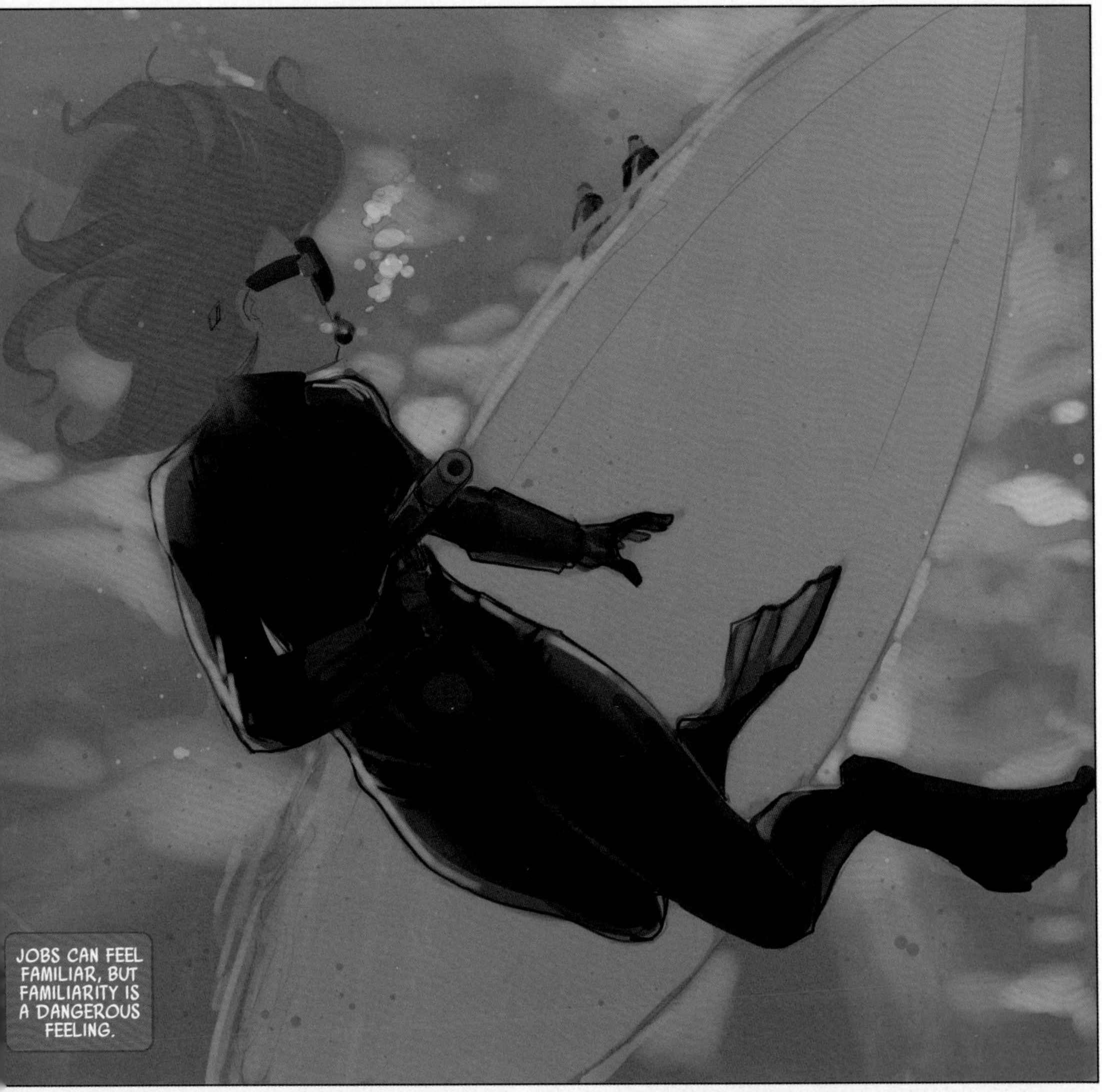
JOBS CAN FEEL FAMILIAR, BUT FAMILIARITY IS A DANGEROUS FEELING.

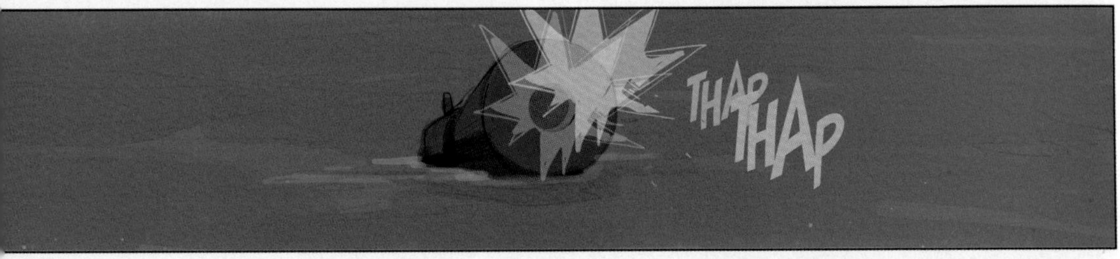
THAP
THAP

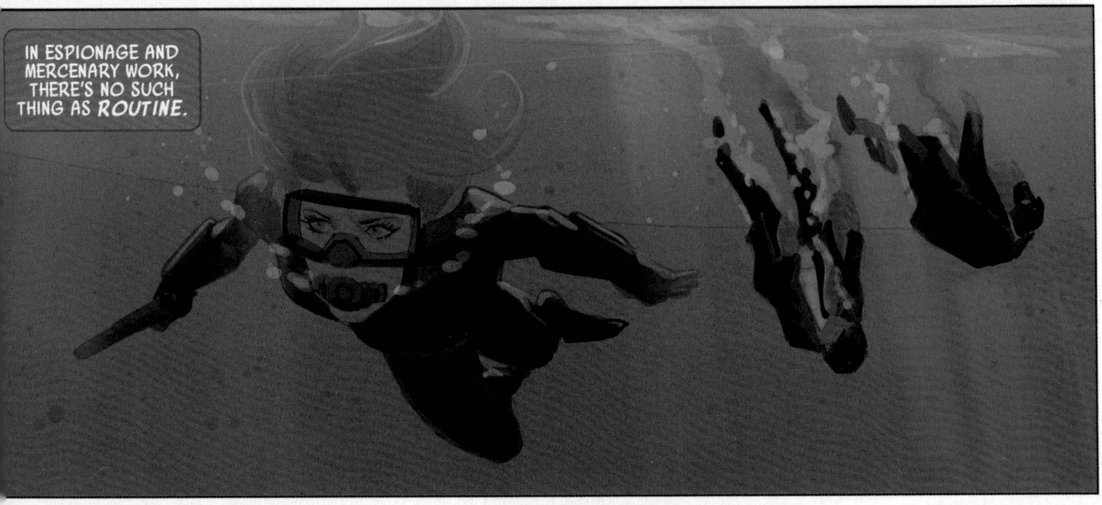
IN ESPIONAGE AND MERCENARY WORK, THERE'S NO SUCH THING AS ROUTINE.

AND SO HERE, I'M MAKING MY SECOND MISTAKE.

THIS FEELS FAMILIAR, BUT NOT FAMILIAR ENOUGH...

I SHOULD HAVE REMEMBERED THE BLACK SEA JOB.

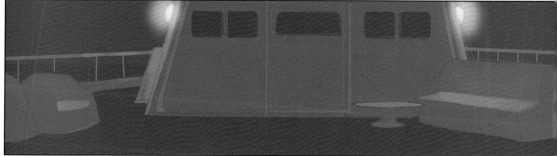

WHERE IS EVERYONE?

I WOULD HAVE GOTTEN A BAD FEELING LONG BEFORE NOW.

СКОРПИОНА...?

CRAP.

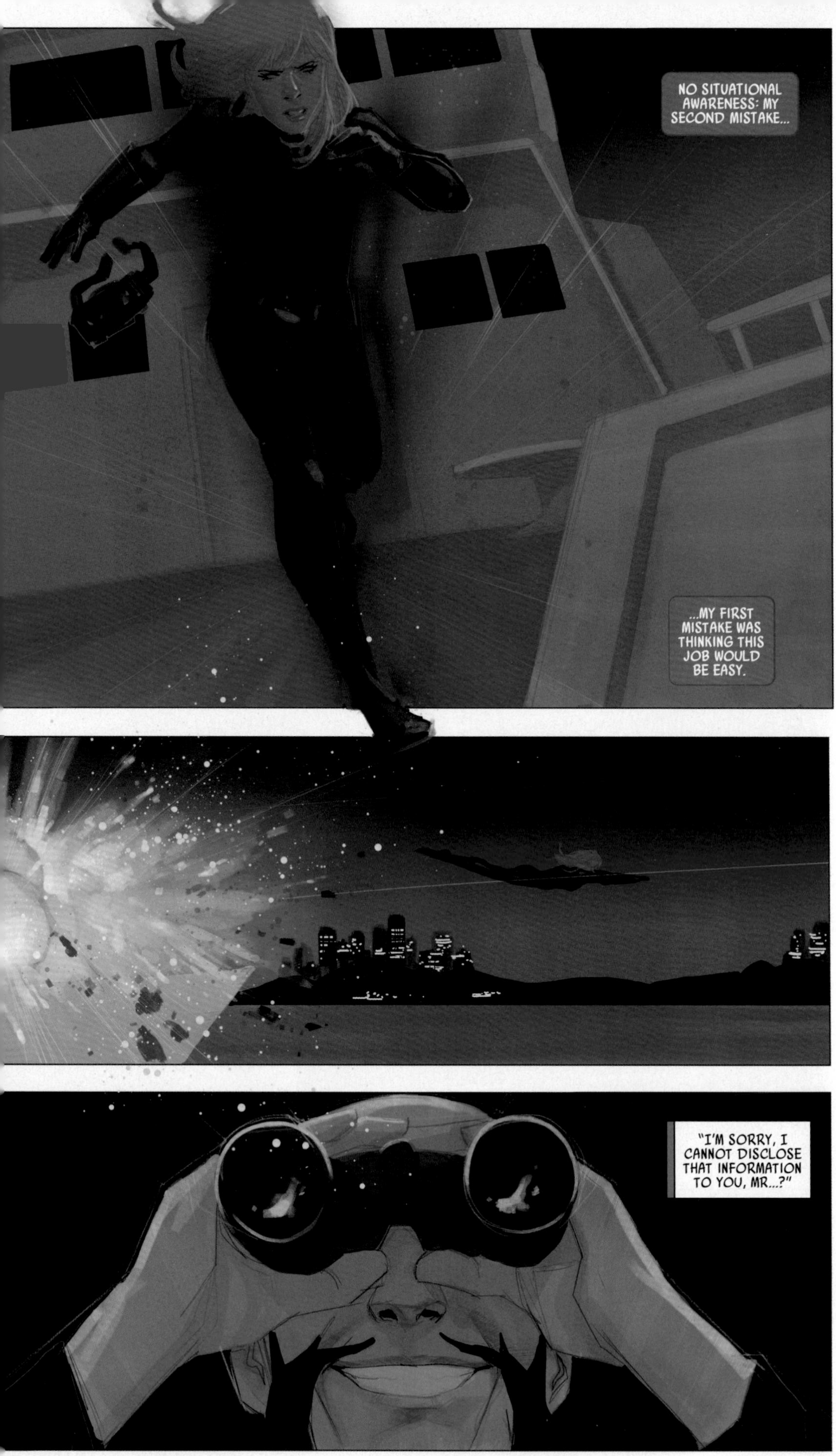
NO SITUATIONAL AWARENESS: MY SECOND MISTAKE...
...MY FIRST MISTAKE WAS THINKING THIS JOB WOULD BE EASY.
"I'M SORRY, I CANNOT DISCLOSE THAT INFORMATION TO YOU, MR...?"

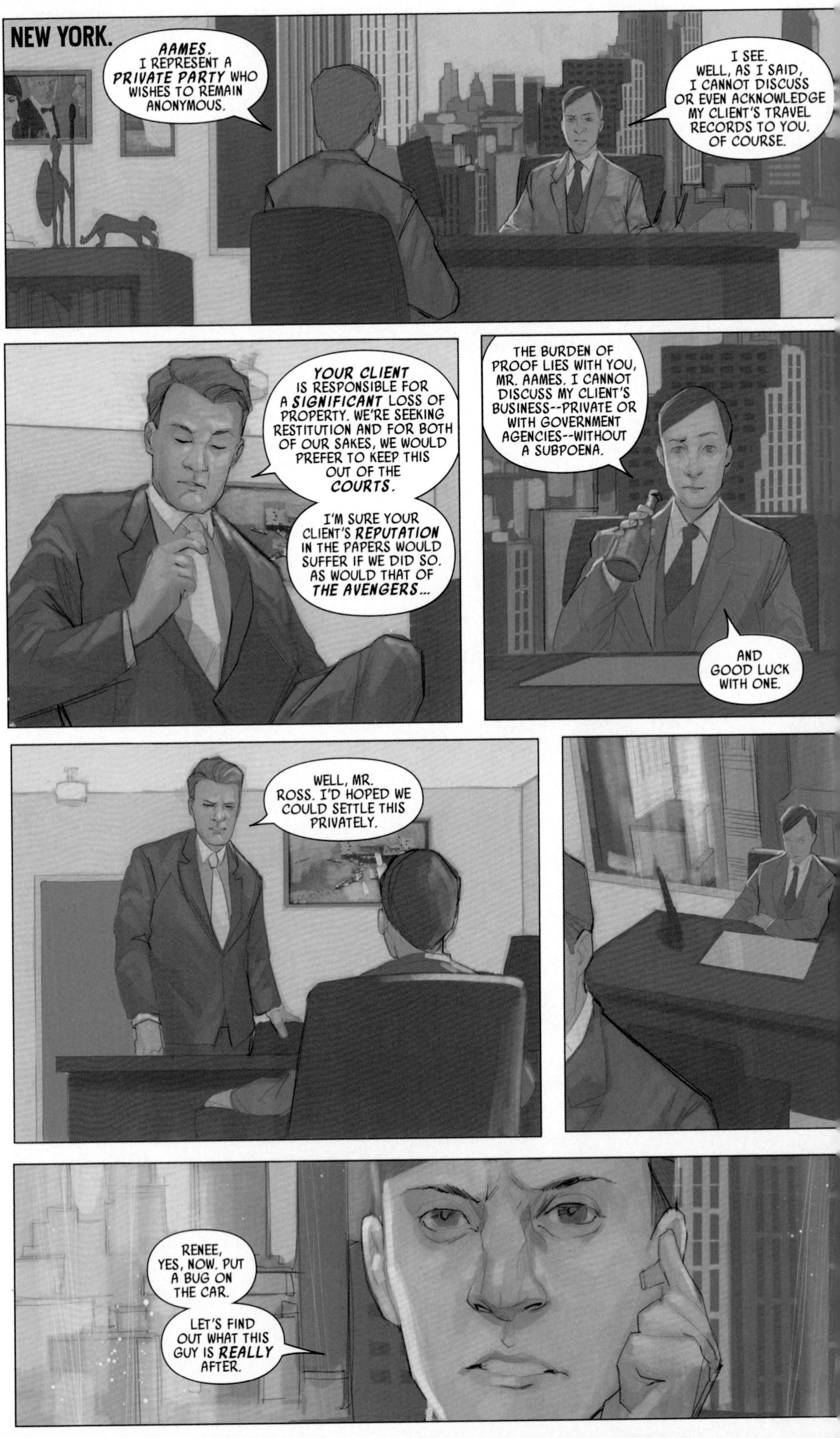
NEW YORK.
AAMES. I REPRESENT A PRIVATE PARTY WHO WISHES TO REMAIN ANONYMOUS.
I SEE. WELL, AS I SAID, I CANNOT DISCUSS OR EVEN ACKNOWLEDGE MY CLIENT'S TRAVEL RECORDS TO YOU. OF COURSE.
YOUR CLIENT IS RESPONSIBLE FOR A SIGNIFICANT LOSS OF PROPERTY. WE'RE SEEKING RESTITUTION AND FOR BOTH OF OUR SAKES, WE WOULD PREFER TO KEEP THIS OUT OF THE COURTS.
I'M SURE YOUR CLIENT'S REPUTATION IN THE PAPERS WOULD SUFFER IF WE DID SO. AS WOULD THAT OF THE AVENGERS...
THE BURDEN OF PROOF LIES WITH YOU, MR. AAMES. I CANNOT DISCUSS MY CLIENT'S BUSINESS--PRIVATE OR WITH GOVERNMENT AGENCIES--WITHOUT A SUBPOENA.
AND GOOD LUCK WITH ONE.
WELL, MR. ROSS. I'D HOPED WE COULD SETTLE THIS PRIVATELY.
RENEE, YES, NOW. PUT A BUG ON THE CAR.
LET'S FIND OUT WHAT THIS GUY IS REALLY AFTER.

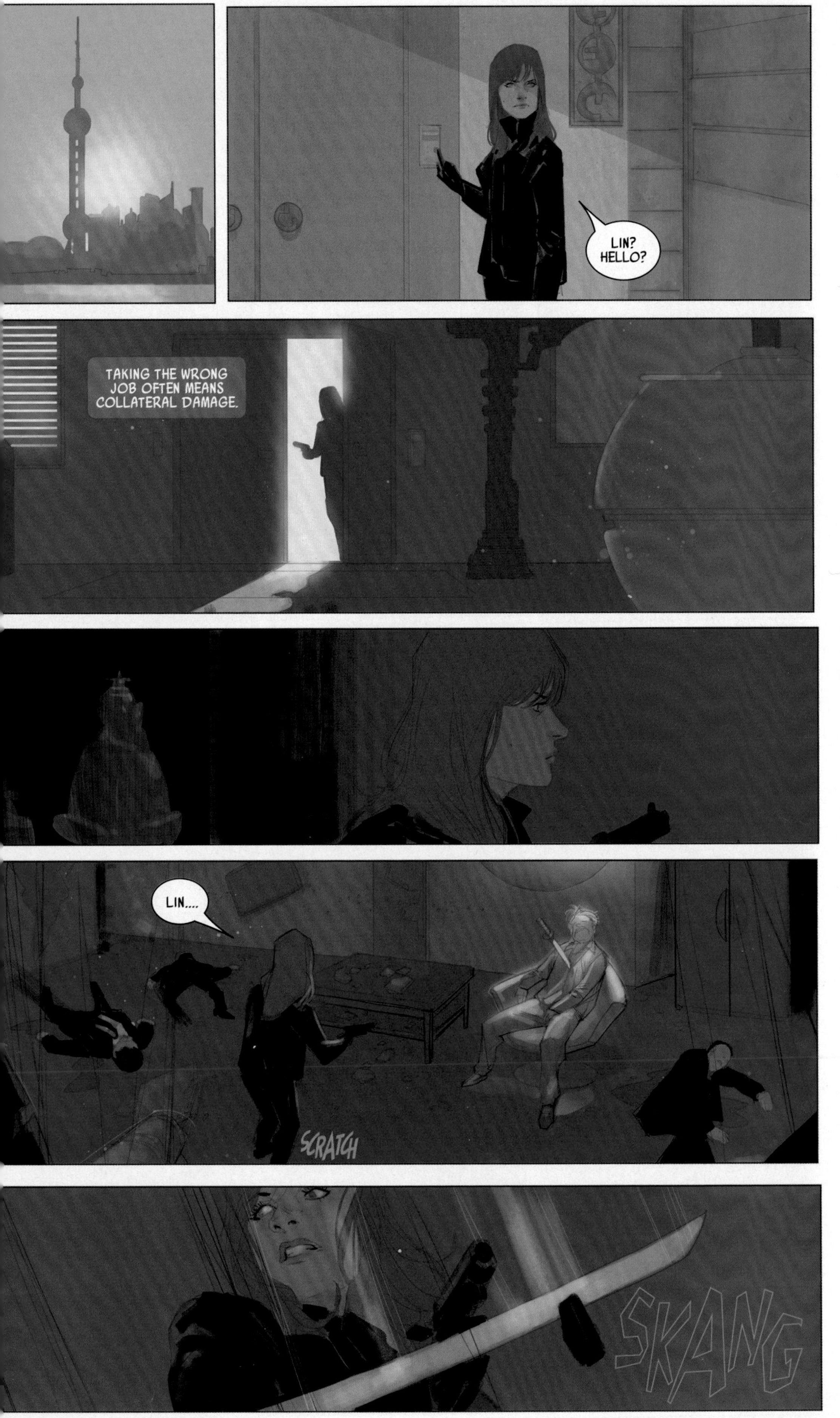
LIN? HELLO?
TAKING THE WRONG JOB OFTEN MEANS COLLATERAL DAMAGE.
LIN....
SCRATCH
SKANG

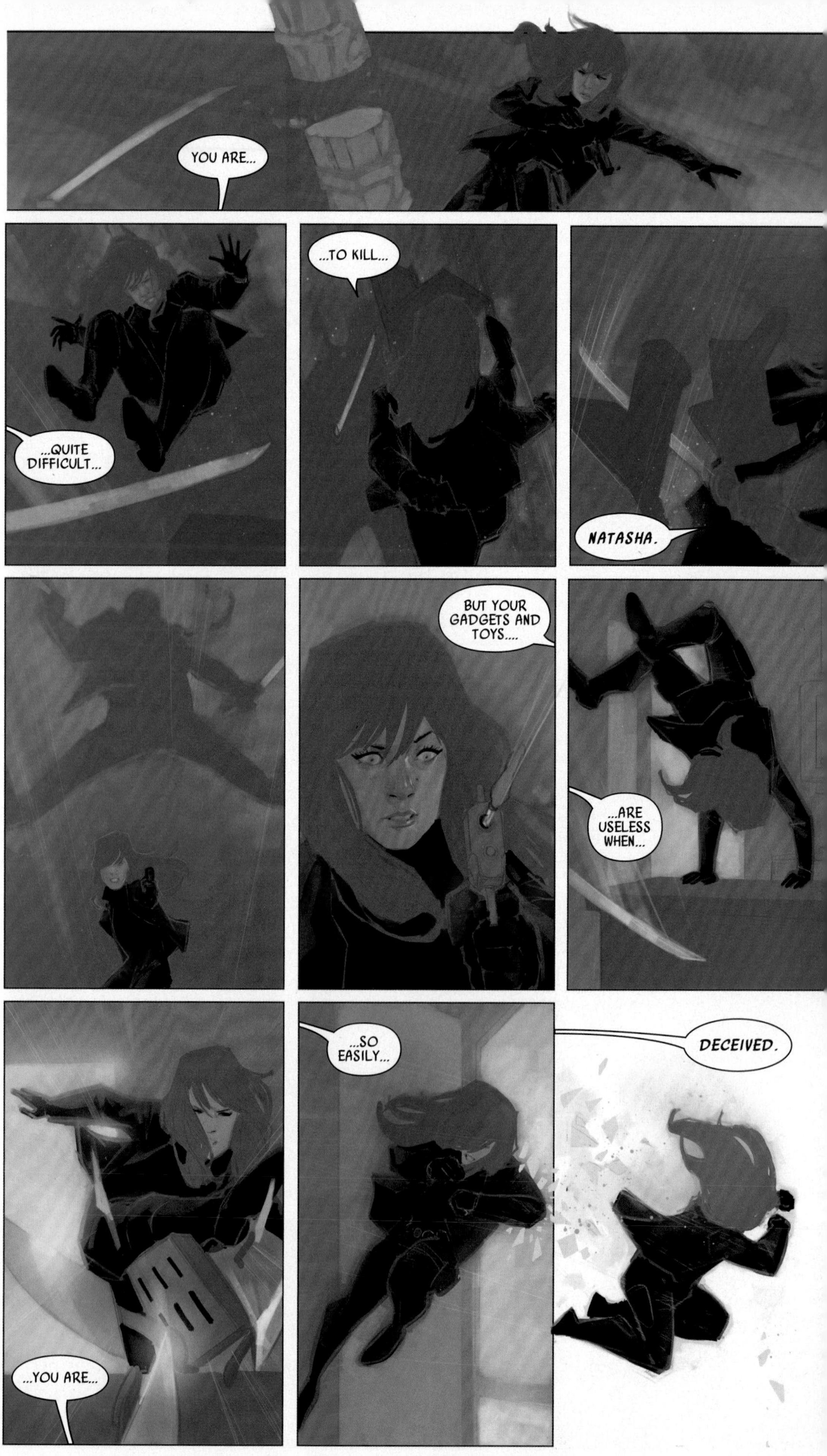
YOU ARE...
...QUITE DIFFICULT...
...TO KILL...
NATASHA.
BUT YOUR GADGETS AND TOYS....
...ARE USELESS WHEN...
...YOU ARE...
...SO EASILY...
DECEIVED.

HE'S NOT WRONG.

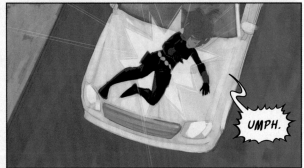

UMPH.

OW.

THIS WAS MY THIRD MISTAKE...

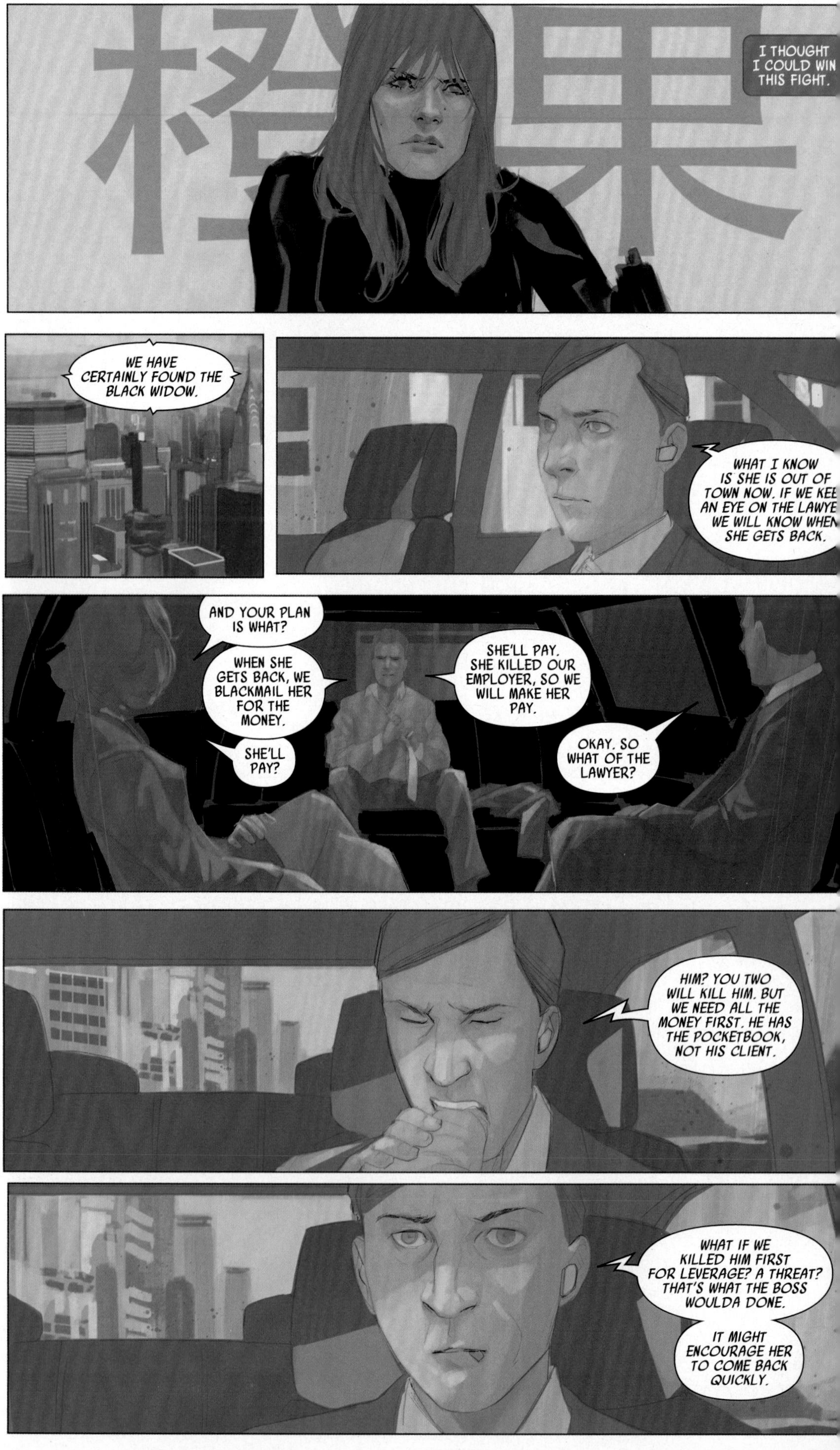
I THOUGHT I COULD WIN THIS FIGHT.
WE HAVE CERTAINLY FOUND THE BLACK WIDOW.
WHAT I KNOW IS SHE IS OUT OF TOWN NOW. IF WE KEE
AN EYE ON THE LAWYE
WE WILL KNOW WHEN
SHE GETS BACK.
AND YOUR PLAN IS WHAT?
WHEN SHE GETS BACK, WE BLACKMAIL HER FOR THE MONEY.
SHE'LL PAY?
SHE'LL PAY. SHE KILLED OUR EMPLOYER, SO WE WILL MAKE HER PAY.
OKAY. SO WHAT OF THE LAWYER?
HIM? YOU TWO WILL KILL HIM. BUT WE NEED ALL THE MONEY FIRST. HE HAS THE POCKETBOOK, NOT HIS CLIENT.
WHAT IF WE KILLED HIM FIRST FOR LEVERAGE? A THREAT? THAT'S WHAT THE BOSS WOULDA DONE.
IT MIGHT ENCOURAGE HER TO COME BACK QUICKLY.

THE WIDOW. THE RUSSIAN AVENGER. THE SLAVIC SHADOW. THE RED DEATH.

THEY HAVE SO MANY NAMES FOR YOU.

YOU ARE HIS SERVANT...

"A DISGUISE, WIDOW."

YOU CAN CALL ME IRON SCORPION.

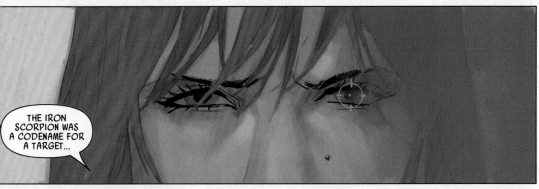

THE IRON SCORPION WAS A CODENAME FOR A TARGET...

"SIX YEARS AGO, ON THE BLACK SEA..."

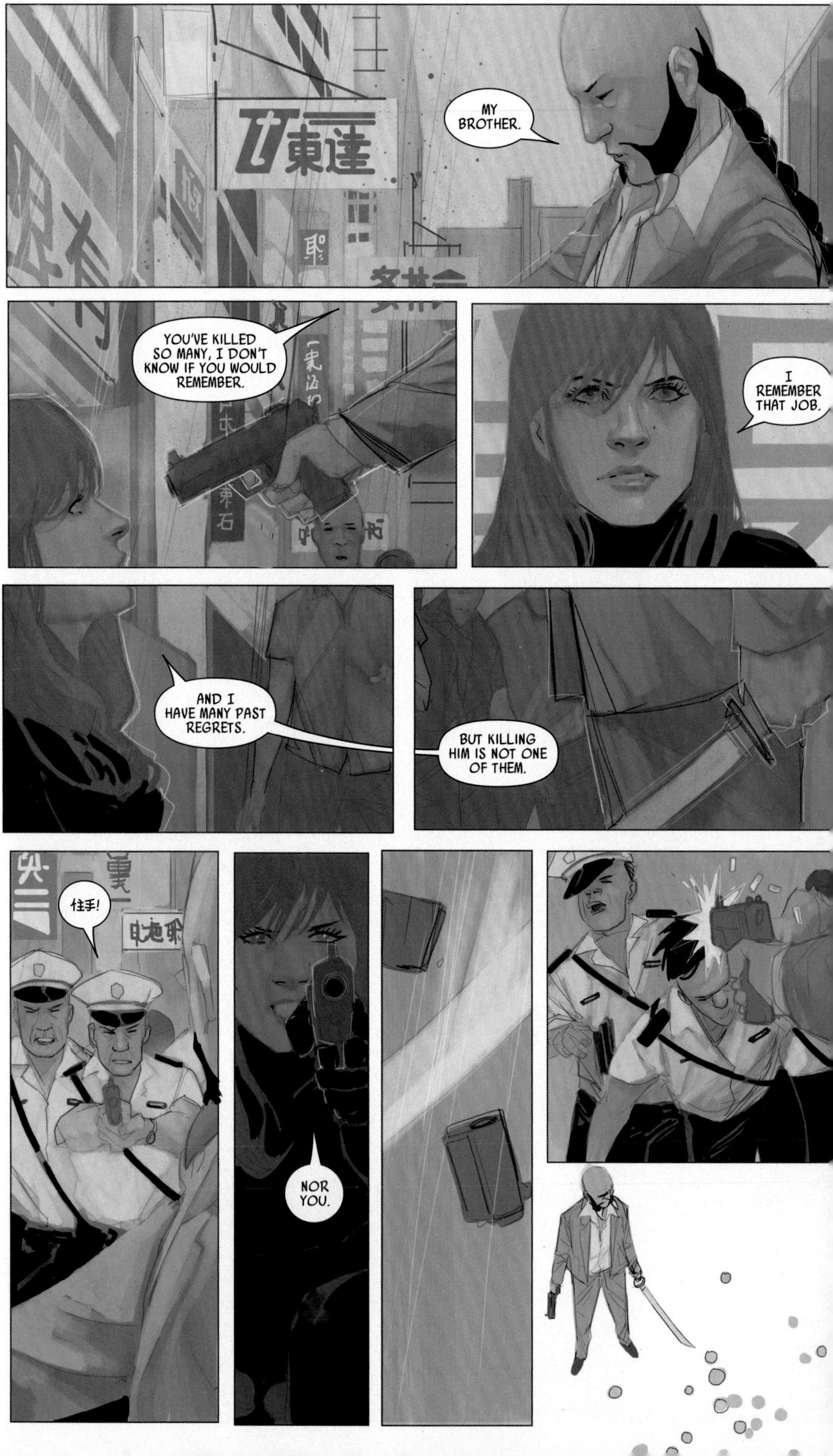
MY BROTHER.
YOU'VE KILLED SO MANY, I DON'T KNOW IF YOU WOULD REMEMBER.
I REMEMBER THAT JOB.
AND I HAVE MANY PAST REGRETS.
BUT KILLING HIM IS NOT ONE OF THEM.
住手!
NOR YOU.

WHERE HAVE YOU GONE, LITTLE SPIDER...

...YOU HAVE NO WEAPON, NO FRIENDS...

HERE.

I DO HAVE...

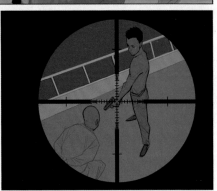

ONE REGRET:

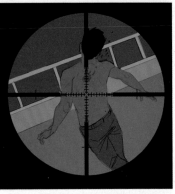

I HESITATED.

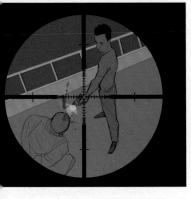

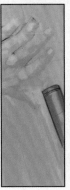

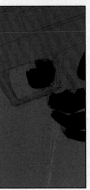

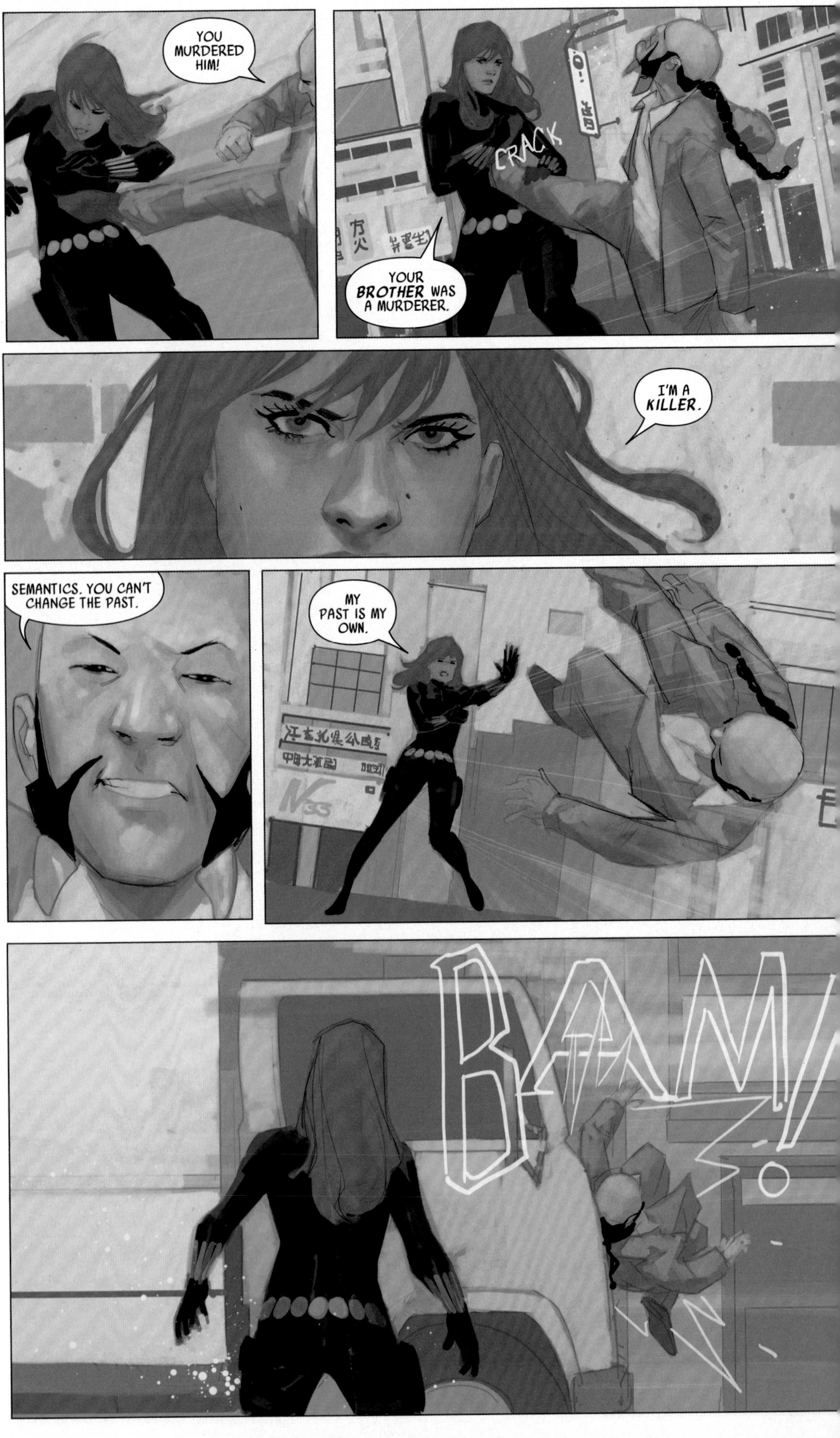
YOU MURDERED HIM!
CRACK
YOUR BROTHER WAS A MURDERER.
I'M A KILLER.
SEMANTICS. YOU CAN'T CHANGE THE PAST.
MY PAST IS MY OWN.
BAM!

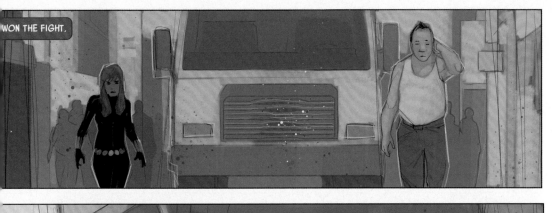

WON THE FIGHT.

BUT THE IRON SCORPION IS STILL OUT THERE.

HE'LL FIND ME AGAIN. I CAN COUNT ON THAT.

THAT'S MY FOURTH MISTAKE...

...BUT I'M DONE COUNTING FOR TODAY.

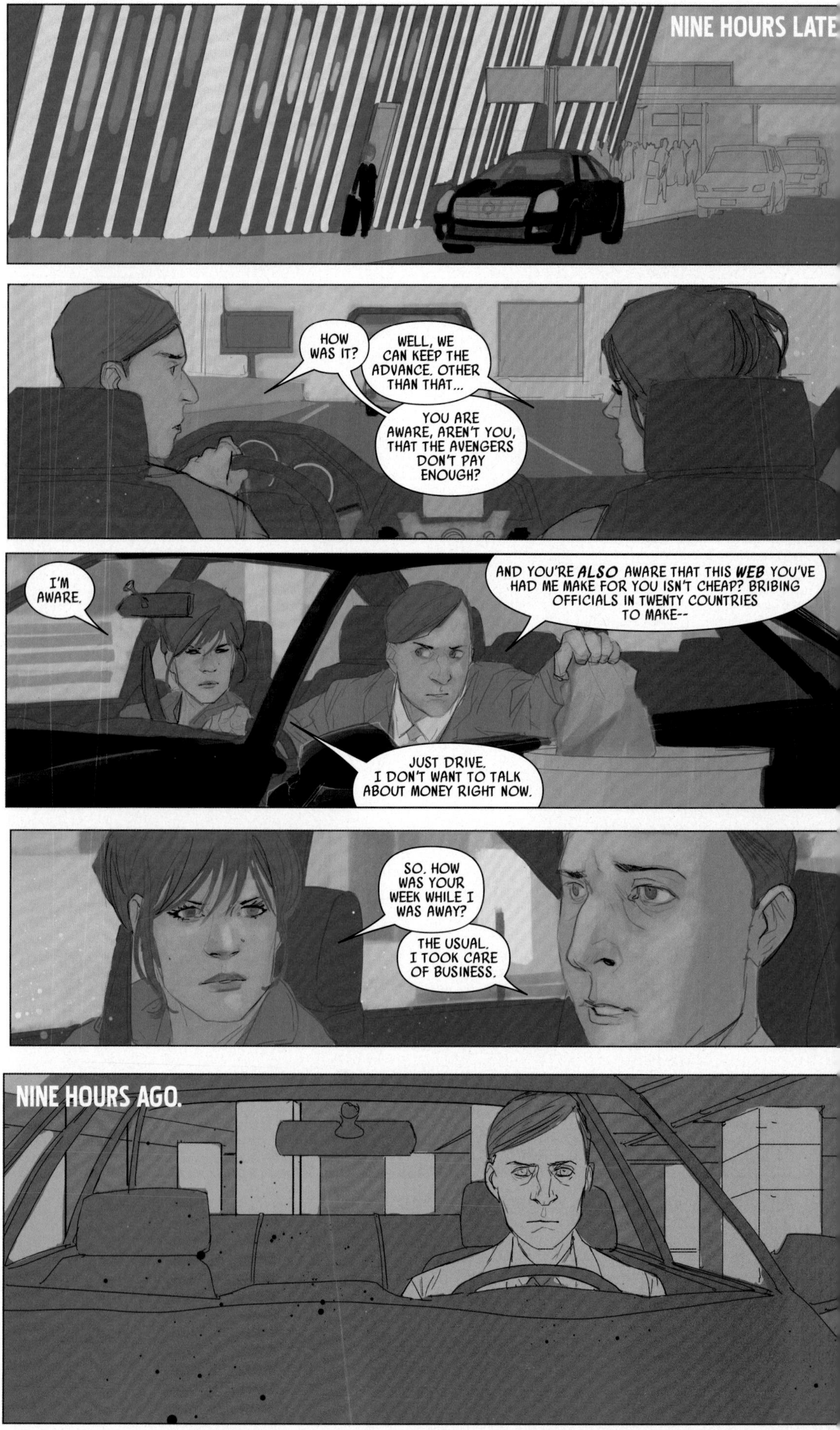
NINE HOURS LATE
HOW WAS IT?
WELL, WE CAN KEEP THE ADVANCE. OTHER THAN THAT...
YOU ARE AWARE, AREN'T YOU, THAT THE AVENGERS DON'T PAY ENOUGH?
I'M AWARE.
AND YOU'RE ALSO AWARE THAT THIS WEB YOU'VE HAD ME MAKE FOR YOU ISN'T CHEAP? BRIBING OFFICIALS IN TWENTY COUNTRIES TO MAKE--
JUST DRIVE. I DON'T WANT TO TALK ABOUT MONEY RIGHT NOW.
SO. HOW WAS YOUR WEEK WHILE I WAS AWAY?
THE USUAL. I TOOK CARE OF BUSINESS.
NINE HOURS AGO.

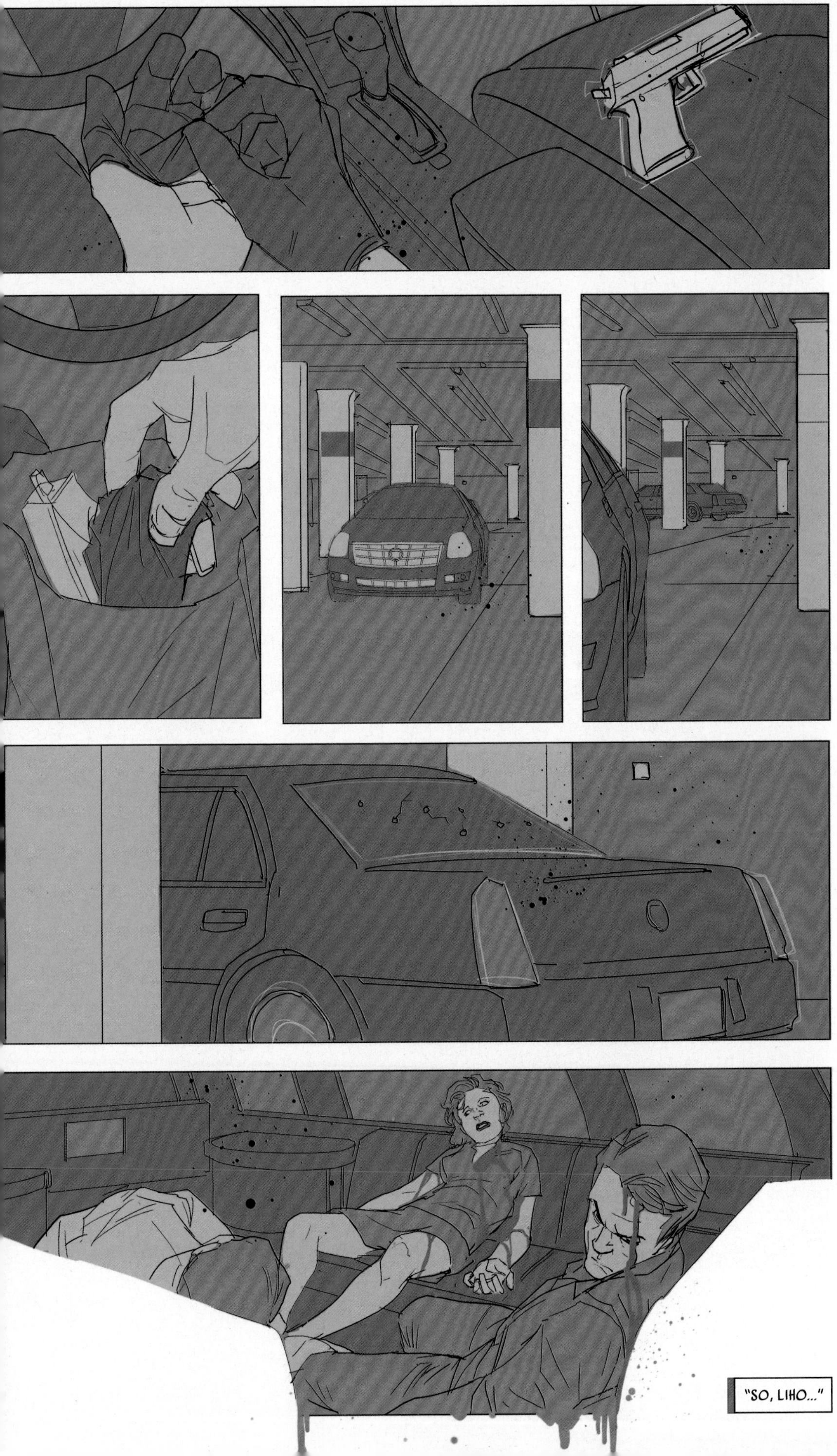
"SO, LIHO..."

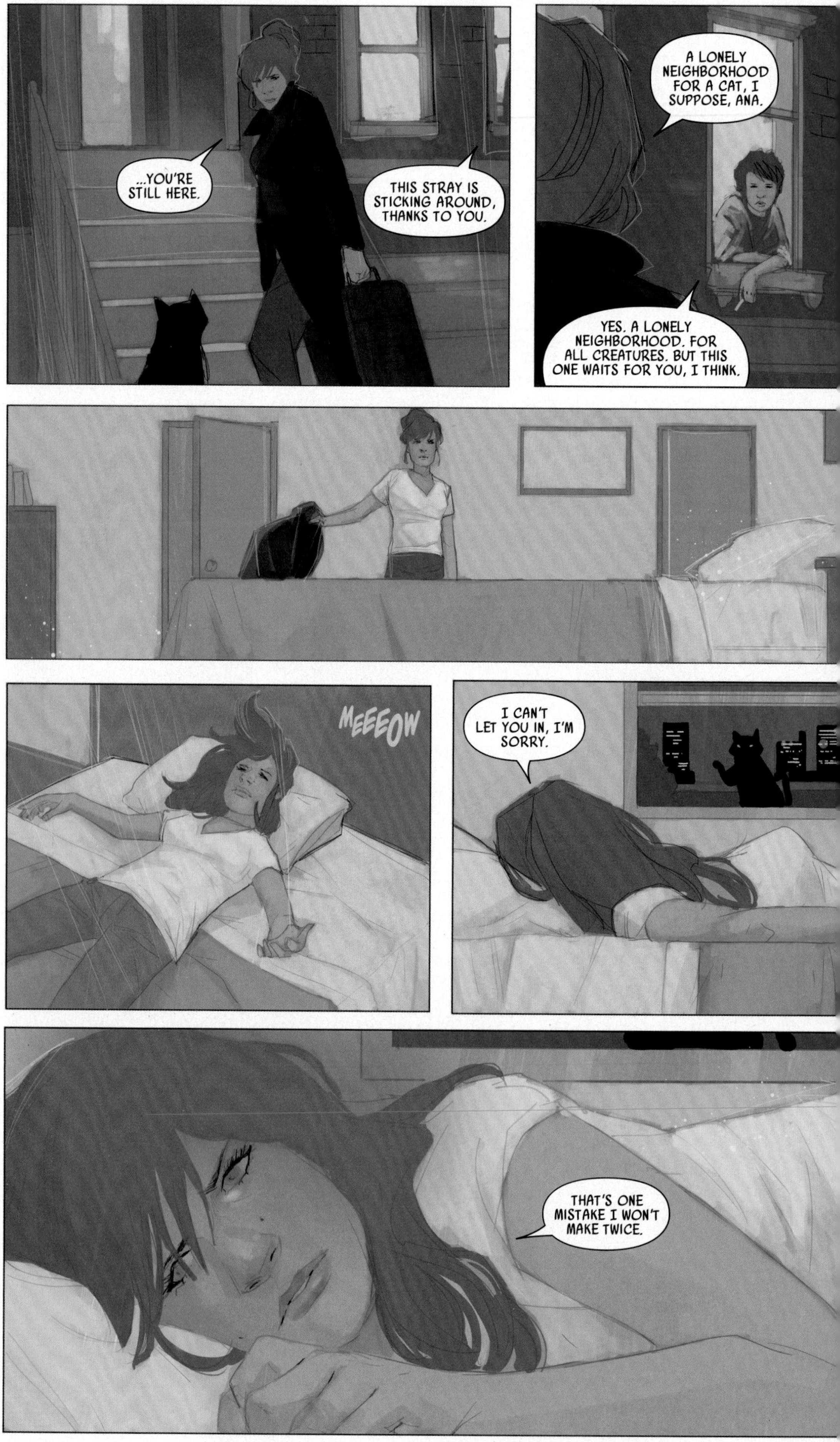
...YOU'RE STILL HERE.
THIS STRAY IS STICKING AROUND, THANKS TO YOU.
A LONELY NEIGHBORHOOD FOR A CAT, I SUPPOSE, ANA.
YES. A LONELY NEIGHBORHOOD. FOR ALL CREATURES. BUT THIS ONE WAITS FOR YOU, I THINK.
MEEEOW
I CAN'T LET YOU IN, I'M SORRY.
THAT'S ONE MISTAKE I WON'T MAKE TWICE.

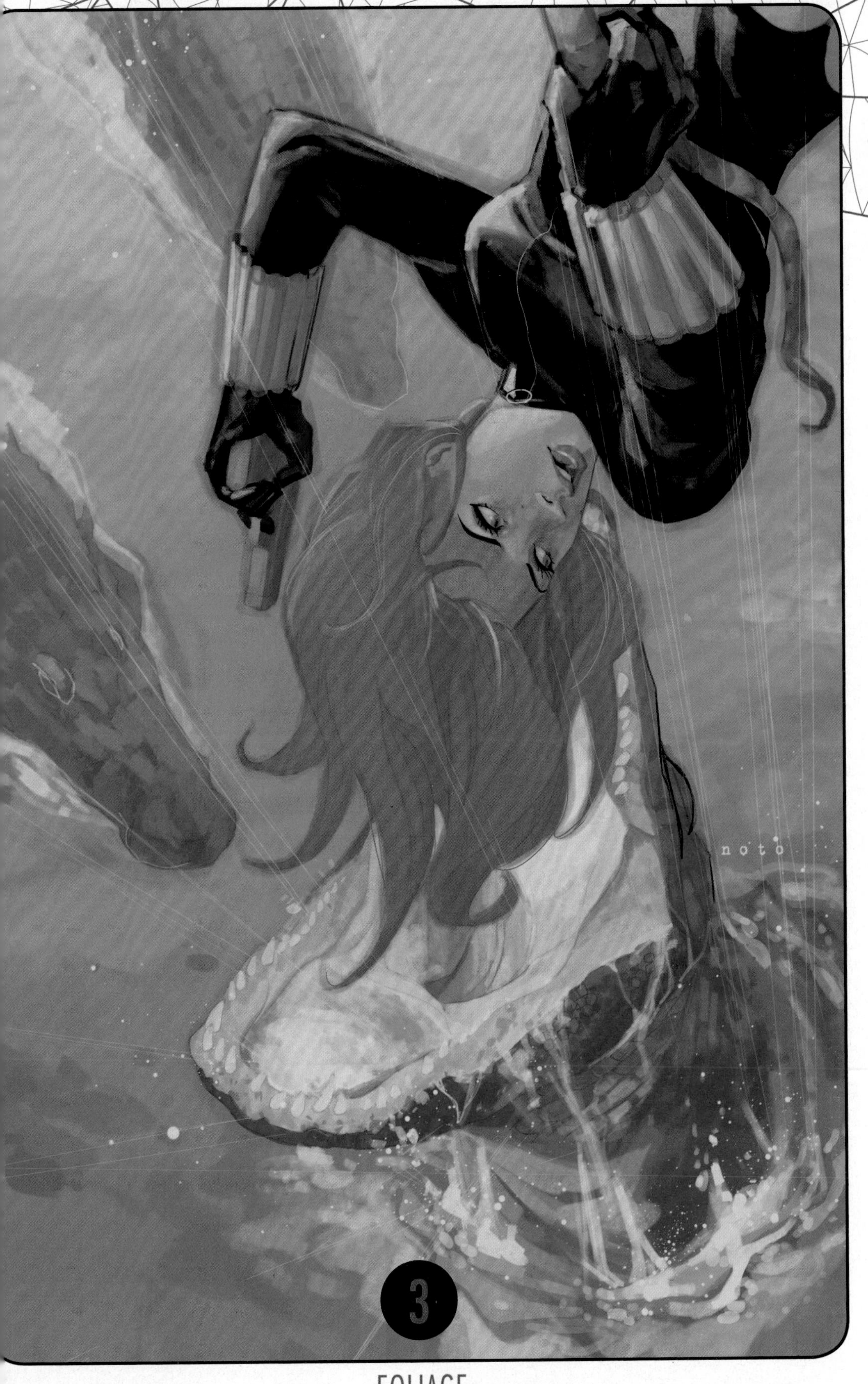
noto
3

FOLIAGE

I DON'T HAVE A HOME.

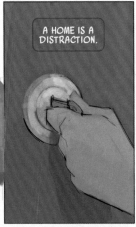

A HOME IS A DISTRACTION.

TRAVELING AGAIN? MORE OVERSEAS CONSULTS?

IN MY WORK ONE CANNOT HAVE DISTRACTIONS.

CONSULTING, YES, OFF TO CATCH THE REDEYE, ANA.

WHAT ARE YOU DOING OUT SO LATE?

I WOULDN'T NECESSARILY KNOW A HOME IF I HAD ONE, THOUGH.

I HEAR YOUR CAT LIHO. SHE WHINES AT DOOR FOR YOU.

SHE'S NOT MY--

ANA. HOW MANY TIMES HAVE I TOLD YOU TO *LEAVE* HIM?

EH, LEAVE TO GO WHERE?

THIS IS HOME.

GOOD NIGHT, NATASHA. I HOPE YOU HAVE GOOD FLIGHT.

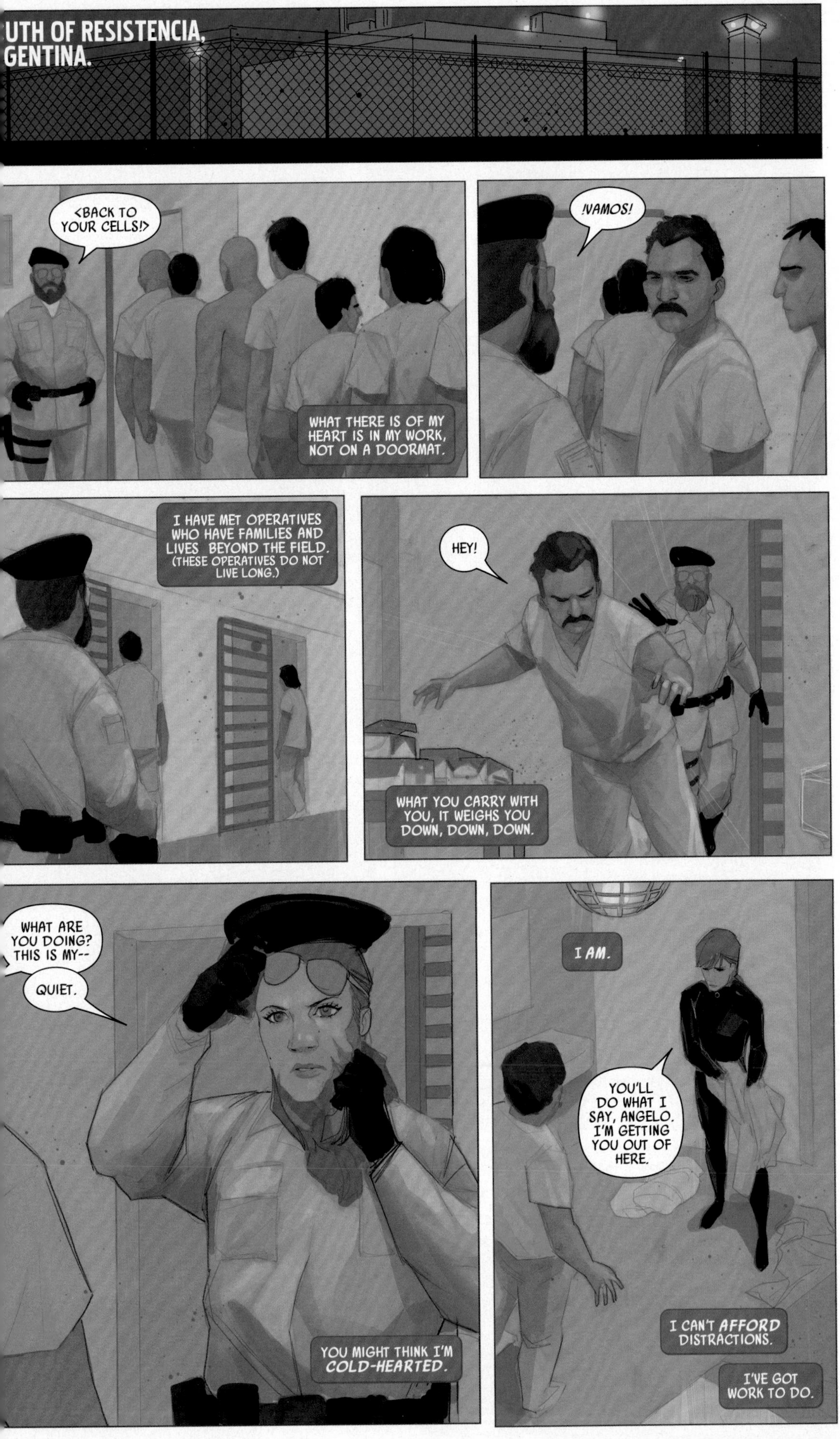
UTH OF RESISTENCIA,
GENTINA.
<BACK TO YOUR CELLS!>
WHAT THERE IS OF MY HEART IS IN MY WORK, NOT ON A DOORMAT.
¡VAMOS!
I HAVE MET OPERATIVES WHO HAVE FAMILIES AND LIVES BEYOND THE FIELD. (THESE OPERATIVES DO NOT LIVE LONG.)
HEY!
WHAT YOU CARRY WITH YOU, IT WEIGHS YOU DOWN, DOWN, DOWN.
WHAT ARE YOU DOING? THIS IS MY--
QUIET.
YOU MIGHT THINK I'M COLD-HEARTED.
I AM.
YOU'LL DO WHAT I SAY, ANGELO. I'M GETTING YOU OUT OF HERE.
I CAN'T AFFORD DISTRACTIONS.
I'VE GOT WORK TO DO.

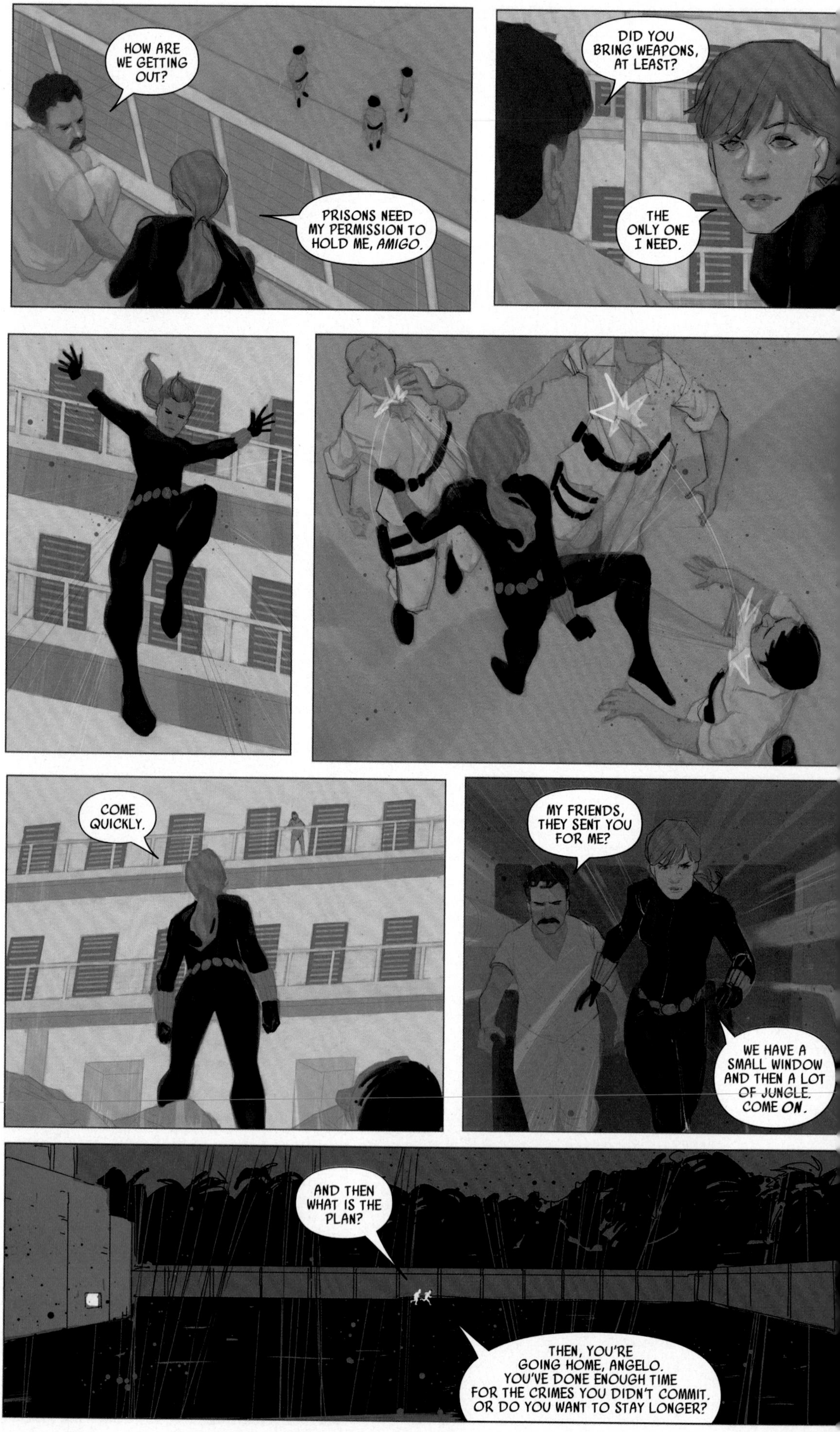
HOW ARE WE GETTING OUT?
PRISONS NEED MY PERMISSION TO HOLD ME, *AMIGO*.
DID YOU BRING WEAPONS, AT LEAST?
THE ONLY ONE I NEED.
COME QUICKLY.
MY FRIENDS, THEY SENT YOU FOR ME?
WE HAVE A SMALL WINDOW AND THEN A LOT OF JUNGLE. COME *ON*.
AND THEN WHAT IS THE PLAN?
THEN, YOU'RE GOING HOME, ANGELO. YOU'VE DONE ENOUGH TIME FOR THE CRIMES YOU DIDN'T COMMIT. OR DO YOU WANT TO STAY LONGER?

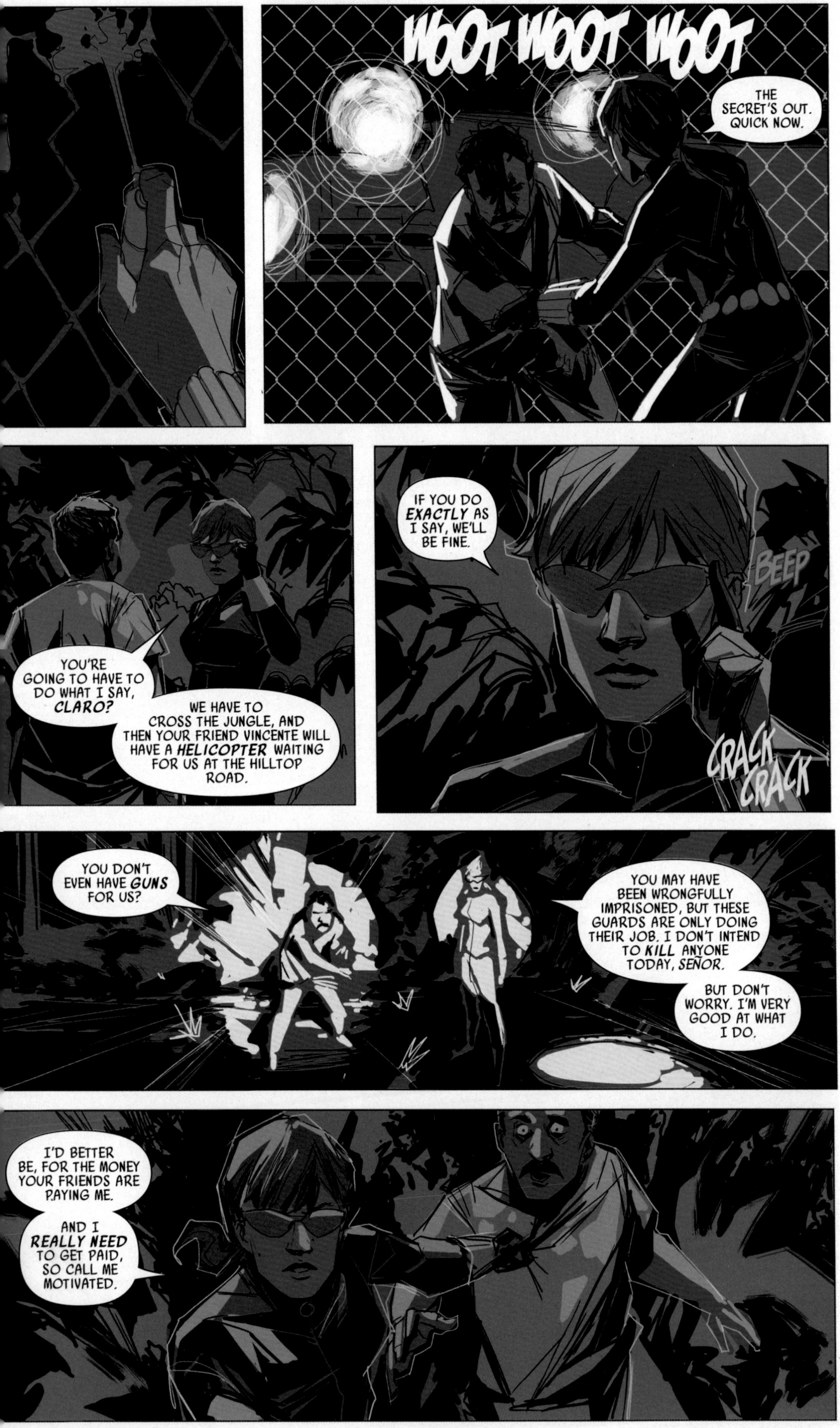
WOOT WOOT WOOT
THE SECRET'S OUT. QUICK NOW.
YOU'RE GOING TO HAVE TO DO WHAT I SAY, CLARO?
WE HAVE TO CROSS THE JUNGLE, AND THEN YOUR FRIEND VINCENTE WILL HAVE A HELICOPTER WAITING FOR US AT THE HILLTOP ROAD.
IF YOU DO EXACTLY AS I SAY, WE'LL BE FINE.
BEEP
CRACK CRACK
YOU DON'T EVEN HAVE GUNS FOR US?
YOU MAY HAVE BEEN WRONGFULLY IMPRISONED, BUT THESE GUARDS ARE ONLY DOING THEIR JOB. I DON'T INTEND TO KILL ANYONE TODAY, SEÑOR.
BUT DON'T WORRY. I'M VERY GOOD AT WHAT I DO.
I'D BETTER BE, FOR THE MONEY YOUR FRIENDS ARE PAYING ME.
AND I REALLY NEED TO GET PAID, SO CALL ME MOTIVATED.

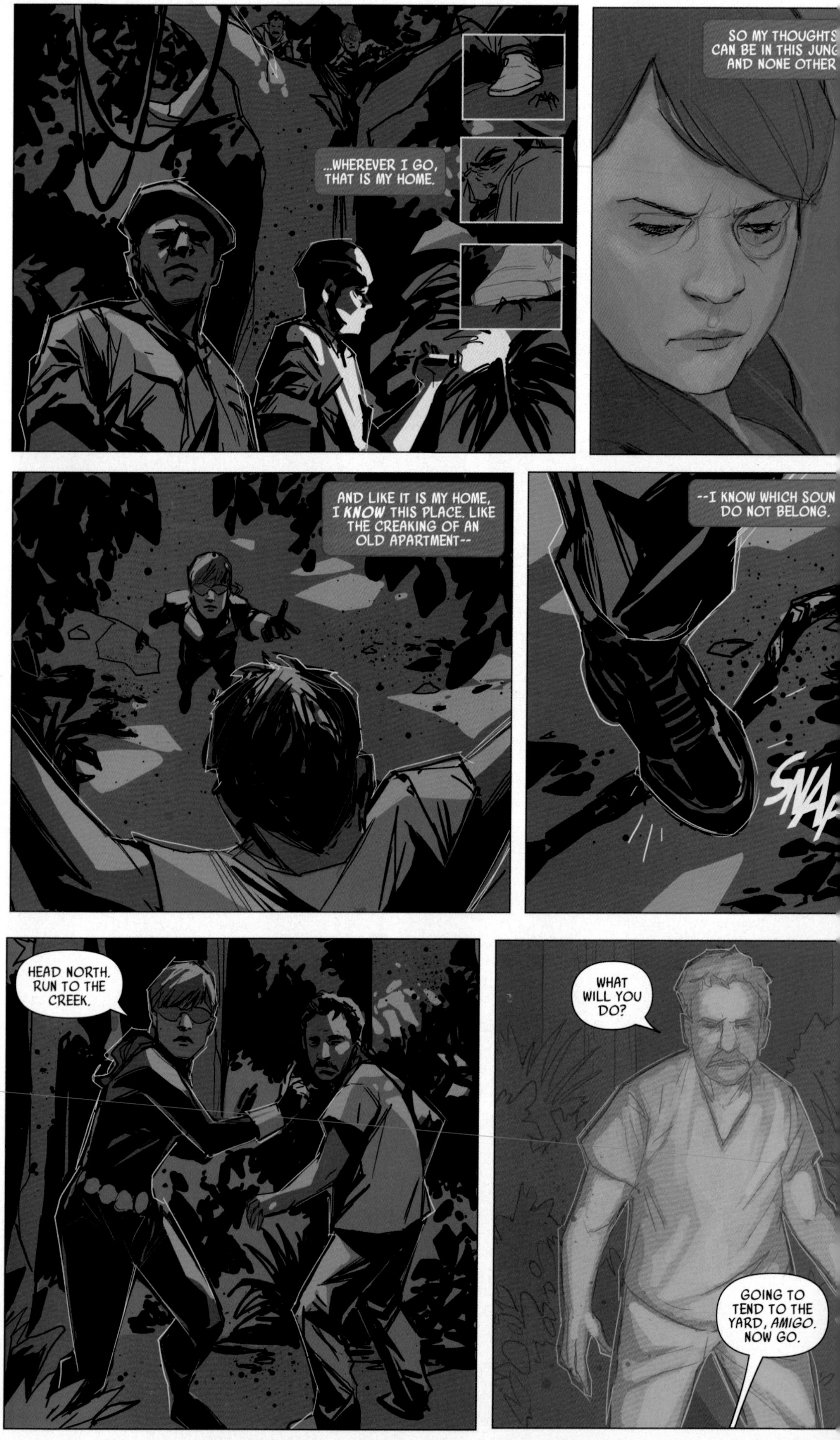
...WHEREVER I GO, THAT IS MY HOME.
SO MY THOUGHTS CAN BE IN THIS JUNG AND NONE OTHER
AND LIKE IT IS MY HOME, I *KNOW* THIS PLACE. LIKE THE CREAKING OF AN OLD APARTMENT--
--I KNOW WHICH SOUN DO NOT BELONG.
SNAP
HEAD NORTH. RUN TO THE CREEK.
WHAT WILL YOU DO?
GOING TO TEND TO THE YARD, *AMIGO.* NOW GO.

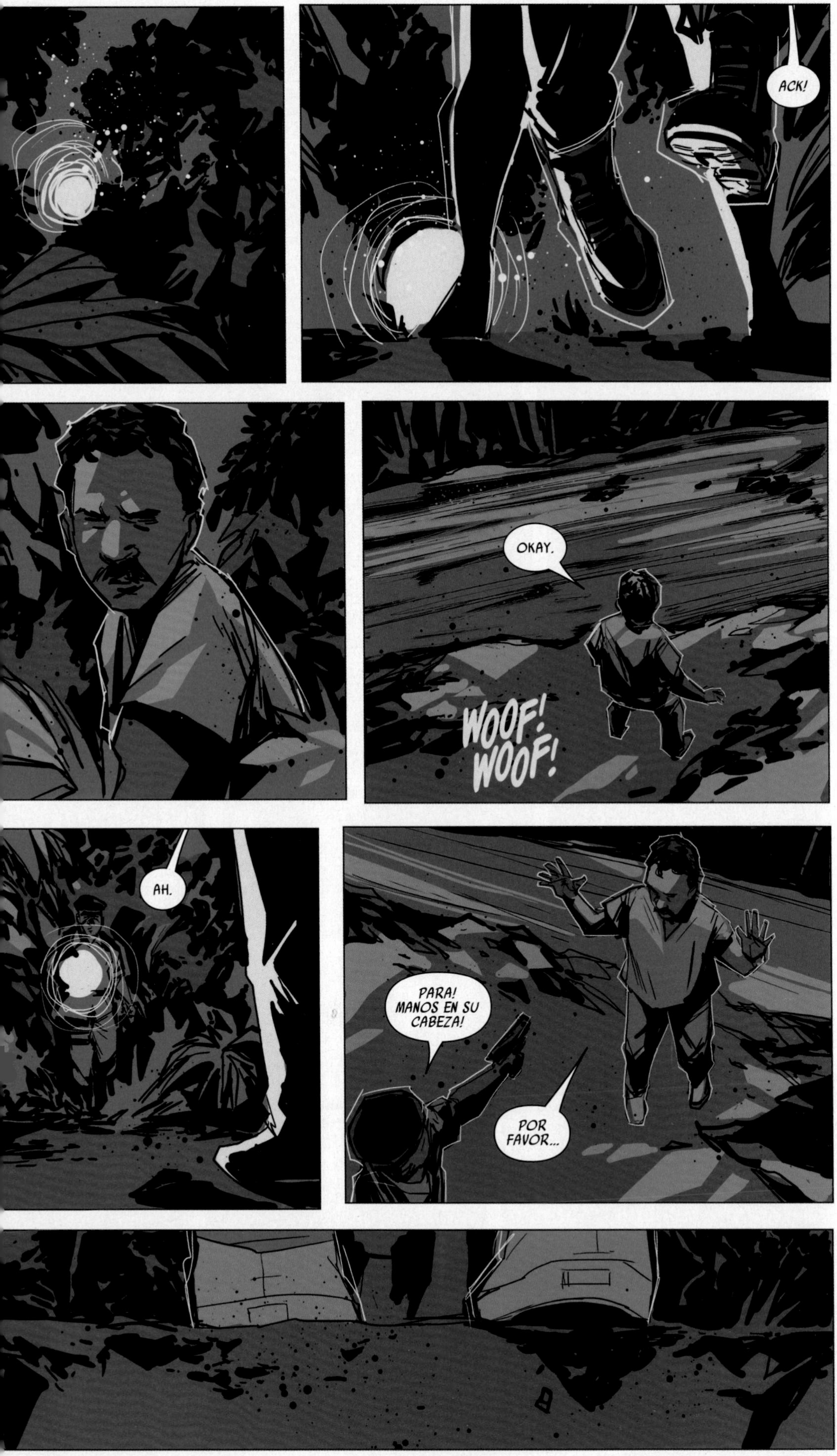
ACK!
OKAY.
WOOF! WOOF!
AH.
PARA! MANOS EN SU CABEZA!
POR FAVOR...

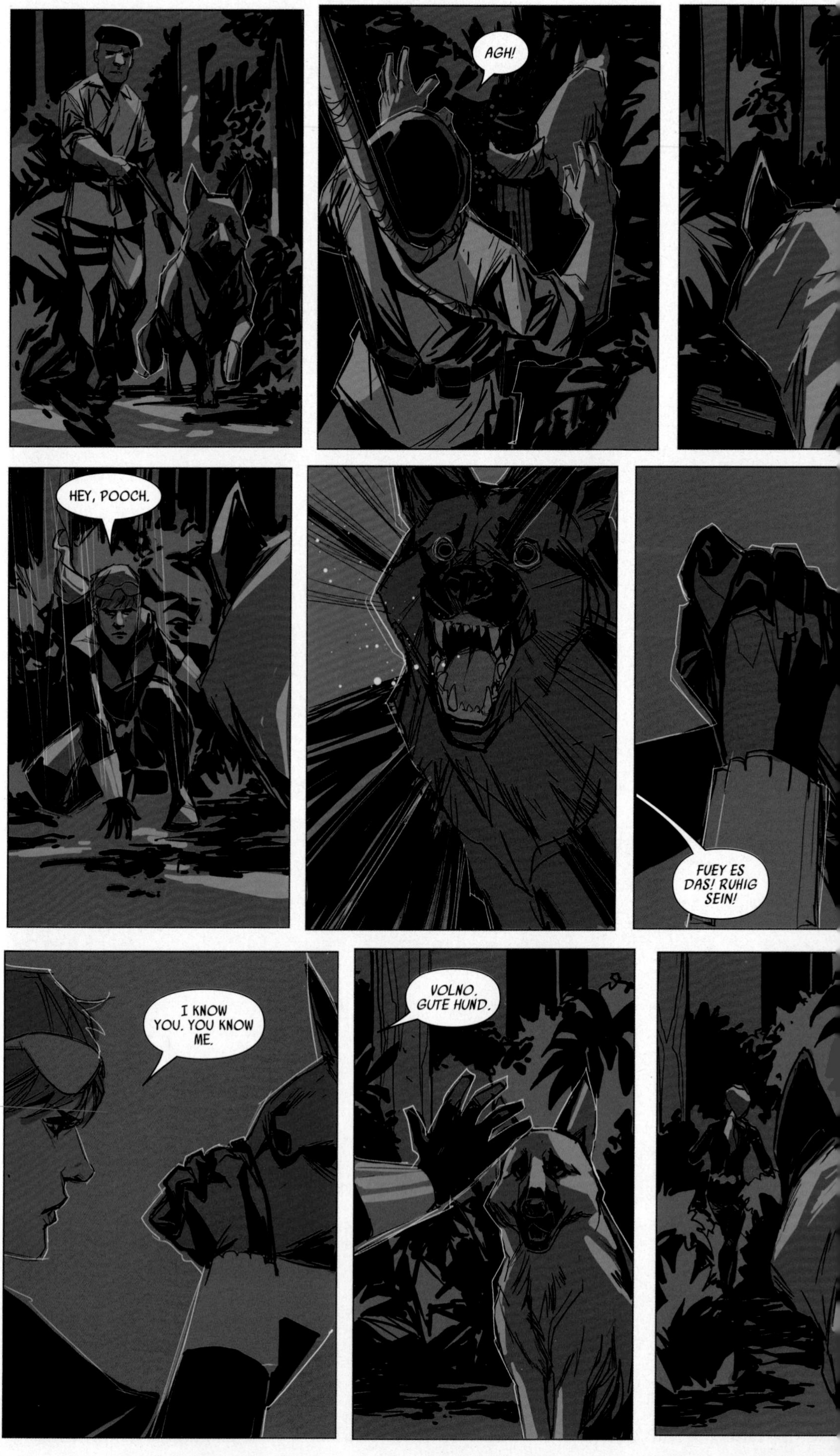
AGH!
HEY, POOCH.
FUEY ES DAS! RUHIG SEIN!
I KNOW YOU. YOU KNOW ME.
VOLNO. GUTE HUND.

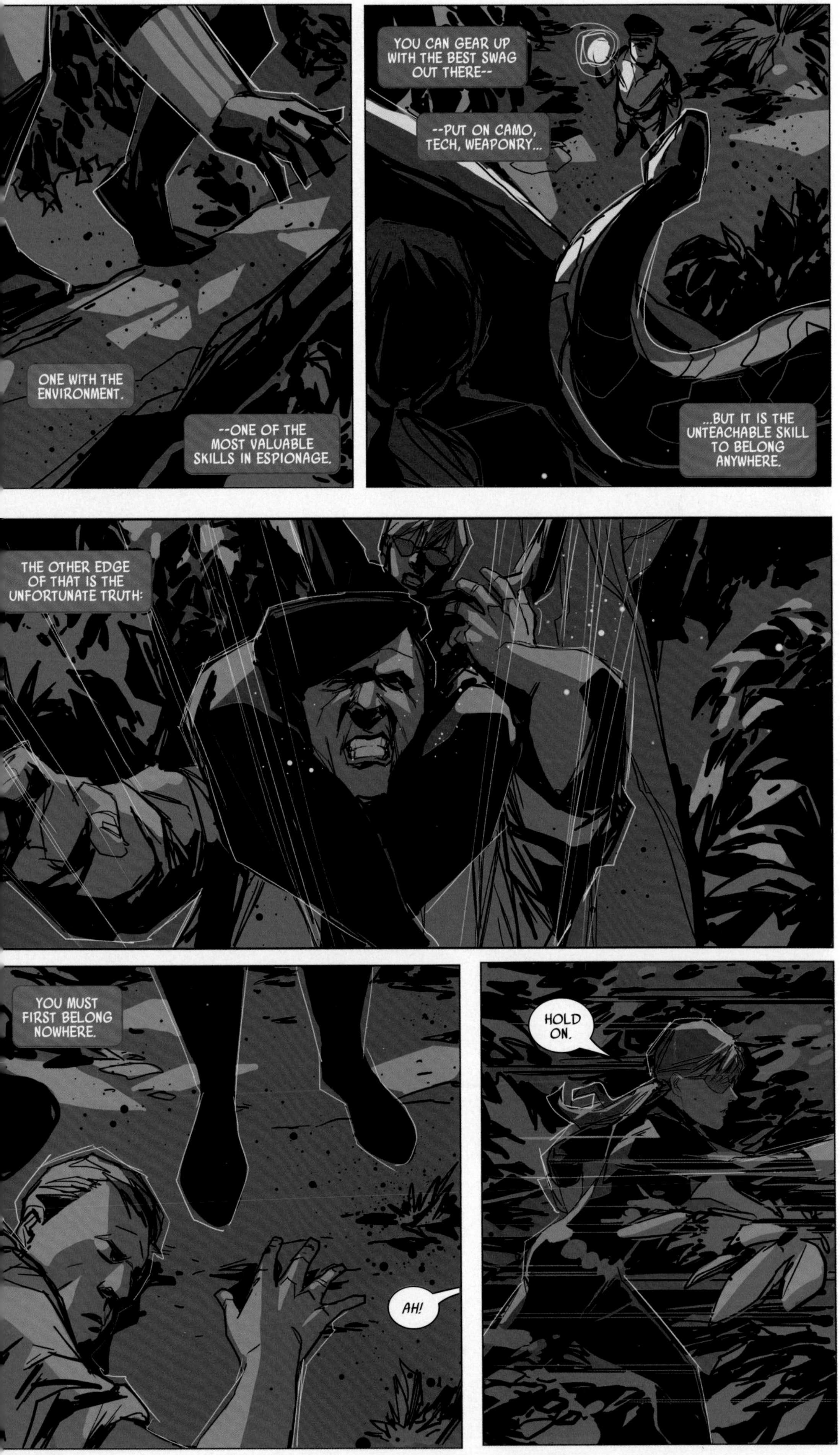
ONE WITH THE ENVIRONMENT.
--ONE OF THE MOST VALUABLE SKILLS IN ESPIONAGE.
YOU CAN GEAR UP WITH THE BEST SWAG OUT THERE--
--PUT ON CAMO, TECH, WEAPONRY...
...BUT IT IS THE UNTEACHABLE SKILL TO BELONG ANYWHERE.
THE OTHER EDGE OF THAT IS THE UNFORTUNATE TRUTH:
YOU MUST FIRST BELONG NOWHERE.
AH!
HOLD ON.

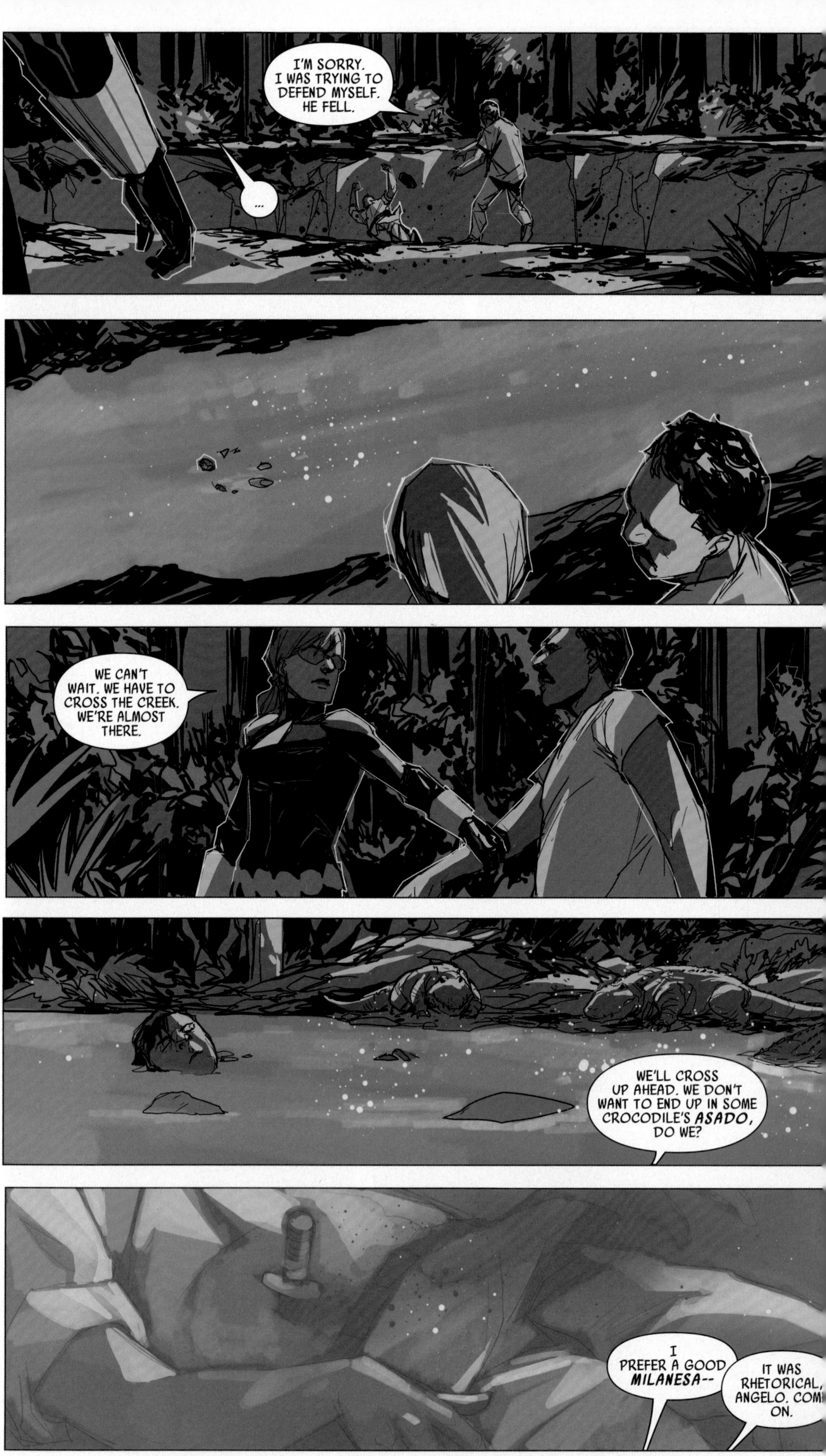
I'M SORRY. I WAS TRYING TO DEFEND MYSELF. HE FELL.
...
WE CAN'T WAIT. WE HAVE TO CROSS THE CREEK. WE'RE ALMOST THERE.
WE'LL CROSS UP AHEAD. WE DON'T WANT TO END UP IN SOME CROCODILE'S ASADO, DO WE?
I PREFER A GOOD MILANESA--
IT WAS RHETORICAL, ANGELO. COM ON.

THAT'S OUR CONTACT, HE'S--

I KNOW HIM. YES.

VINCENTE, OLD FRIEND.

LOBO BLANCO, HEMOS ENTUSIASMO QUE ESPERABA.

HY DO NOW THIS AME?

THE WHITE WOLF...

SEÑOR, THE MEN ARE--

YES, YES YES. PLENTY OF TIME TO TALK ABOUT THAT LATER.

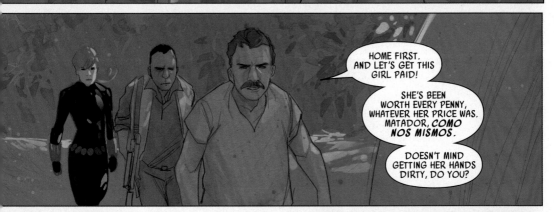

HOME FIRST. AND LET'S GET THIS GIRL PAID!

SHE'S BEEN WORTH EVERY PENNY, WHATEVER HER PRICE WAS. MATADOR, *COMO NOS MISMOS.*

DOESN'T MIND GETTING HER HANDS DIRTY, DO YOU?

VINCENTE, RADIO AHEAD, WHEN WE GET HOME I WOULD LIKE SOME GIRLS WAITING. LET'S MAKE THEM YOUNG. ALSO, SOME CHICKEN WINGS AND... MAYBE SOMETHING SWEET FOR DESSERT?

SÍ, SEÑOR.

COME ON NOW. THE GUARDS AREN'T FAR BEHIND US, AS YOU KNOW.

LOBO BLANCO...

HOW DID I MISS IT?

THE SIGNS WERE THERE.

A DESK OF TRIBUTES FROM OTHER INMATES... PROTECTION PAY.

A DISREGARD FOR LIFE... A DISINTEREST IN DANGER...

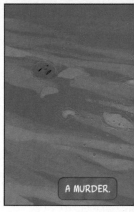

A MURDER.

I MAY NOT HAVE KNOWN WHO HE WAS, BUT I WOULD HAVE KNOWN HE IS NOT WHO THE CLIENT CLAIMED.

AT LEAST, THAT IS NOT ALL HE IS.

YES, HE WAS IMPRISONED ILLEGALLY FOR A CRIME HE DID NOT COMMIT...

BUT BEFORE THAT, LOBO BLANCO, THE BUTCHER OF ARGENTINA...

...I MISSED DISTRACTE

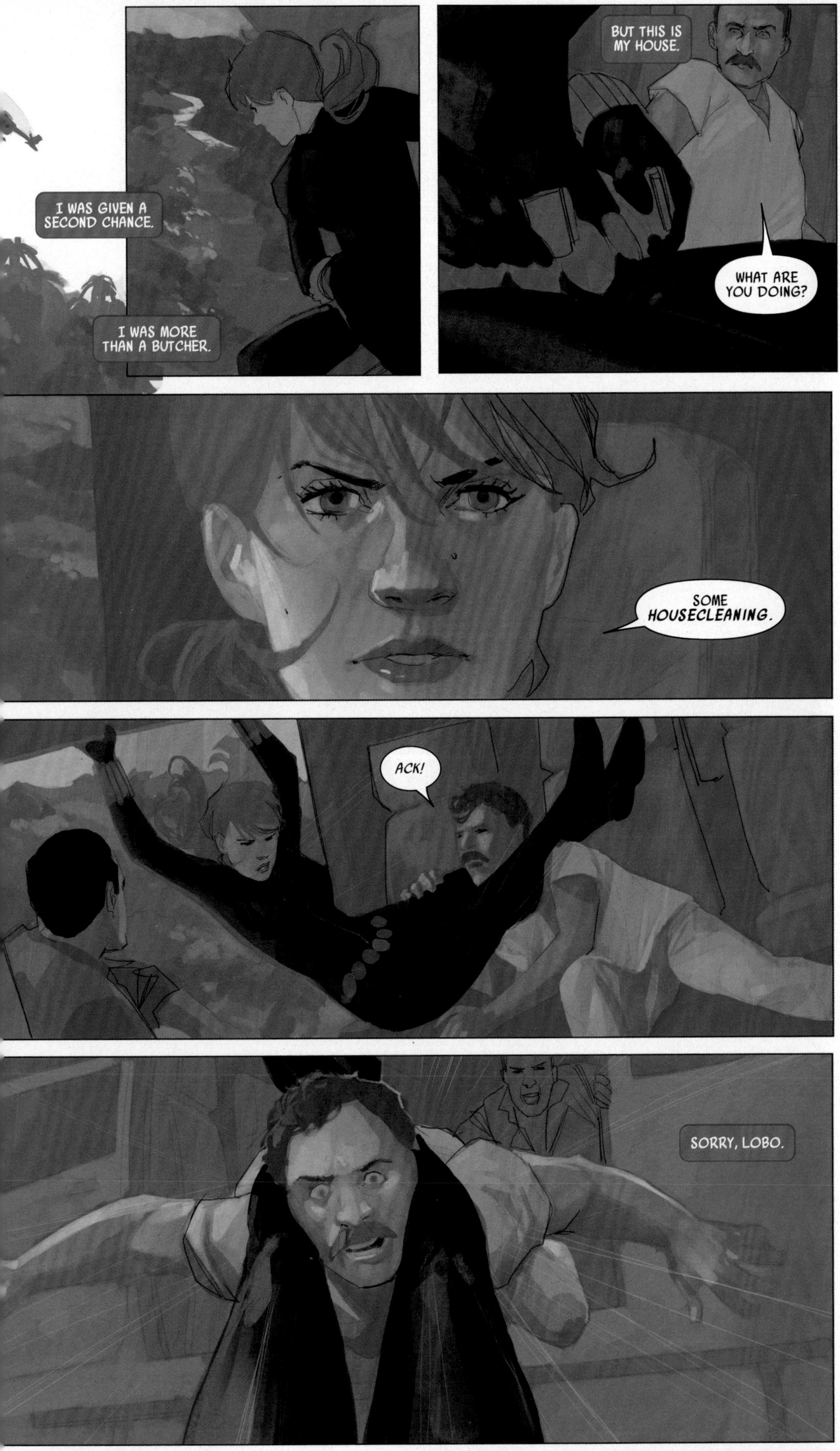
I WAS GIVEN A SECOND CHANCE.
I WAS MORE THAN A BUTCHER.
BUT THIS IS MY HOUSE.
WHAT ARE YOU DOING?
SOME HOUSECLEANING.
ACK!
SORRY, LOBO.

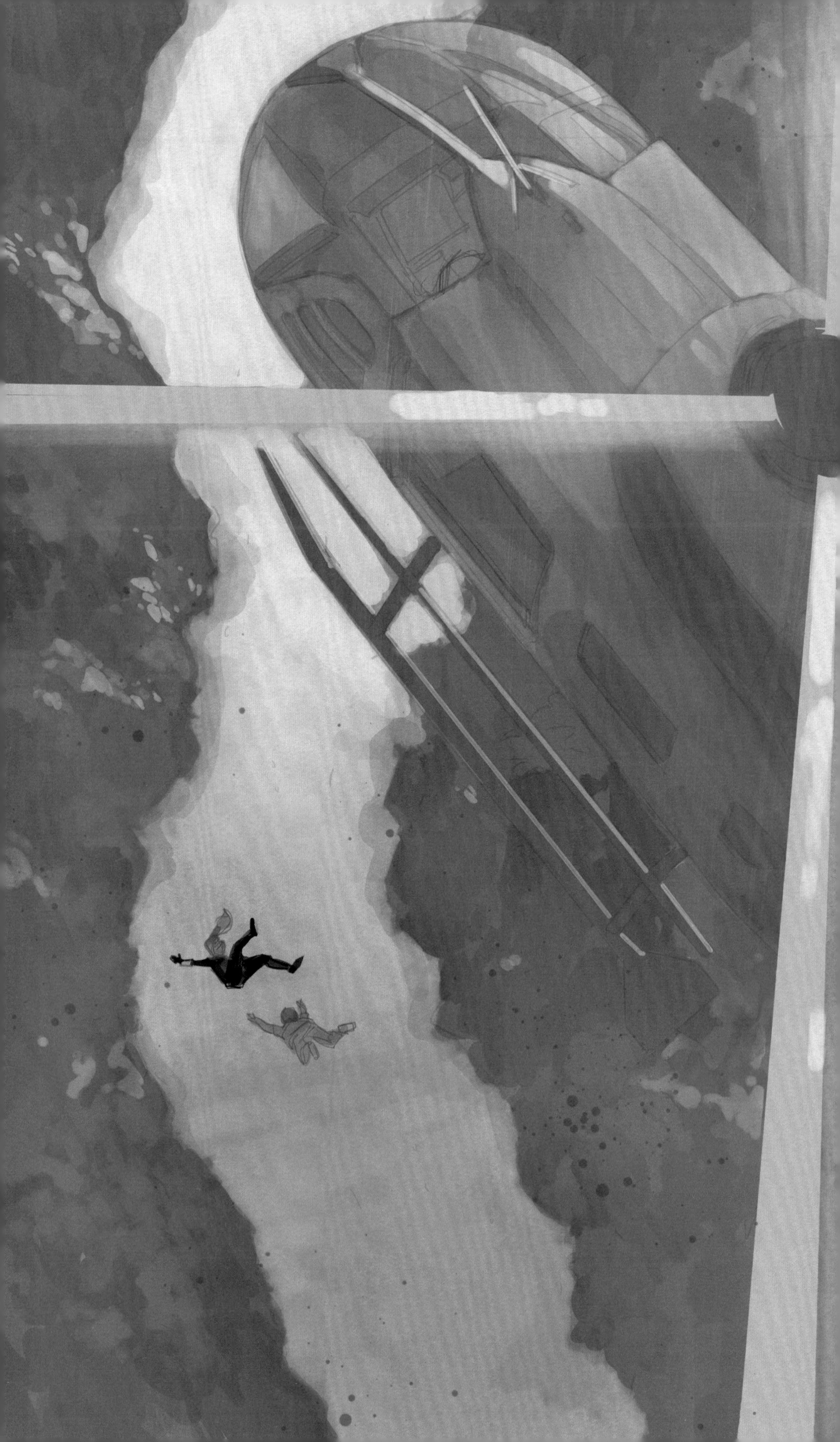

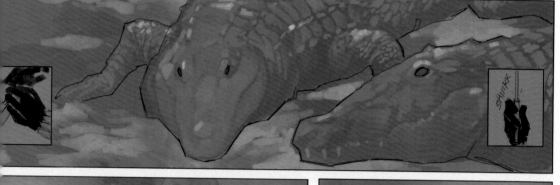

A GOOD OPERATIVE KNOWS HIS ENVIRONMENT-- HIS *HOME.*

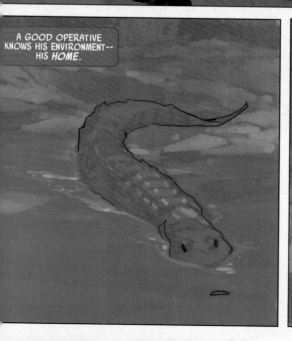

HE KNOWS WHICH CREATURES ARE DOCILE--

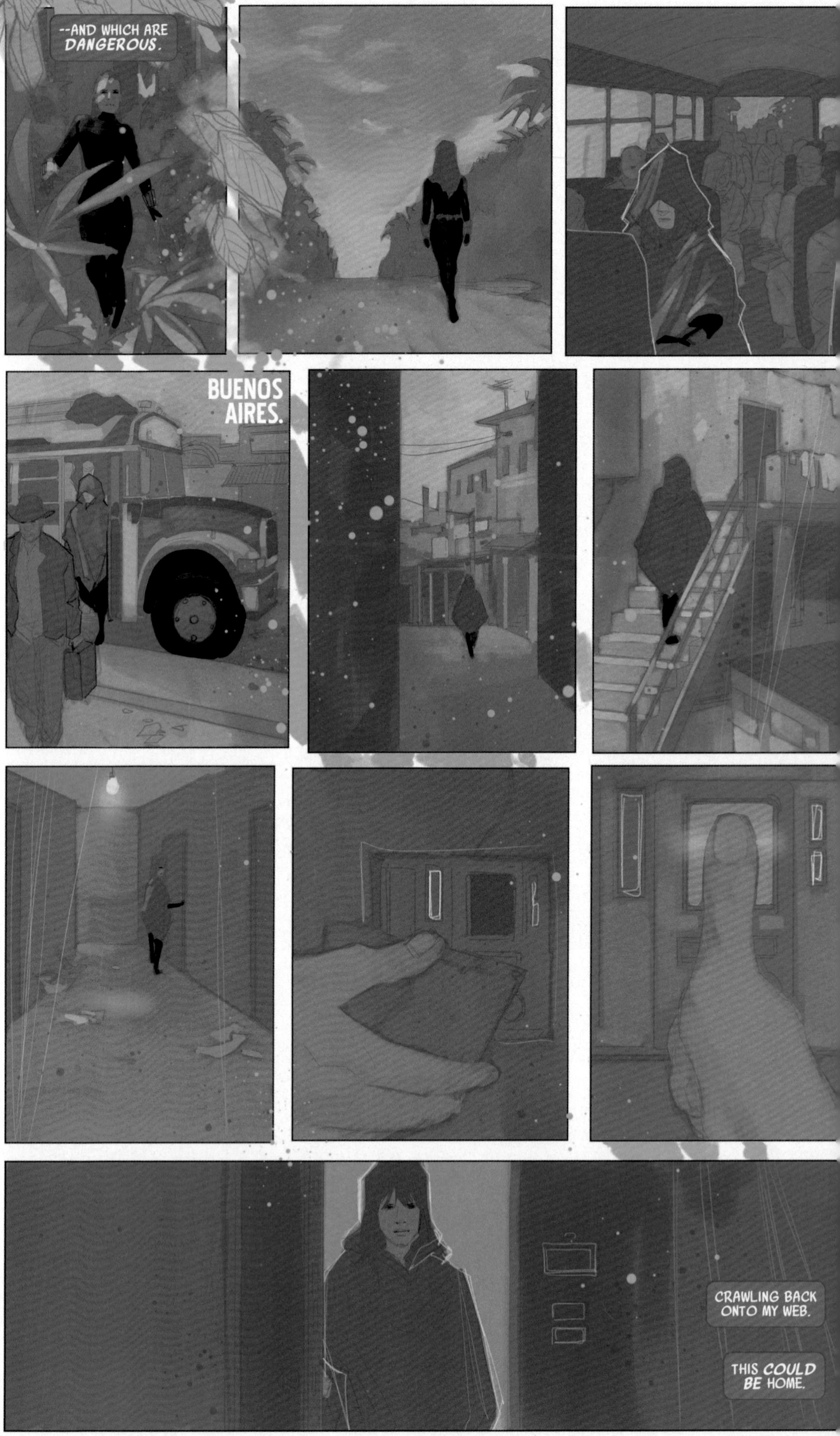
--AND WHICH ARE DANGEROUS.
BUENOS AIRES.
CRAWLING BACK ONTO MY WEB.
THIS COULD BE HOME.

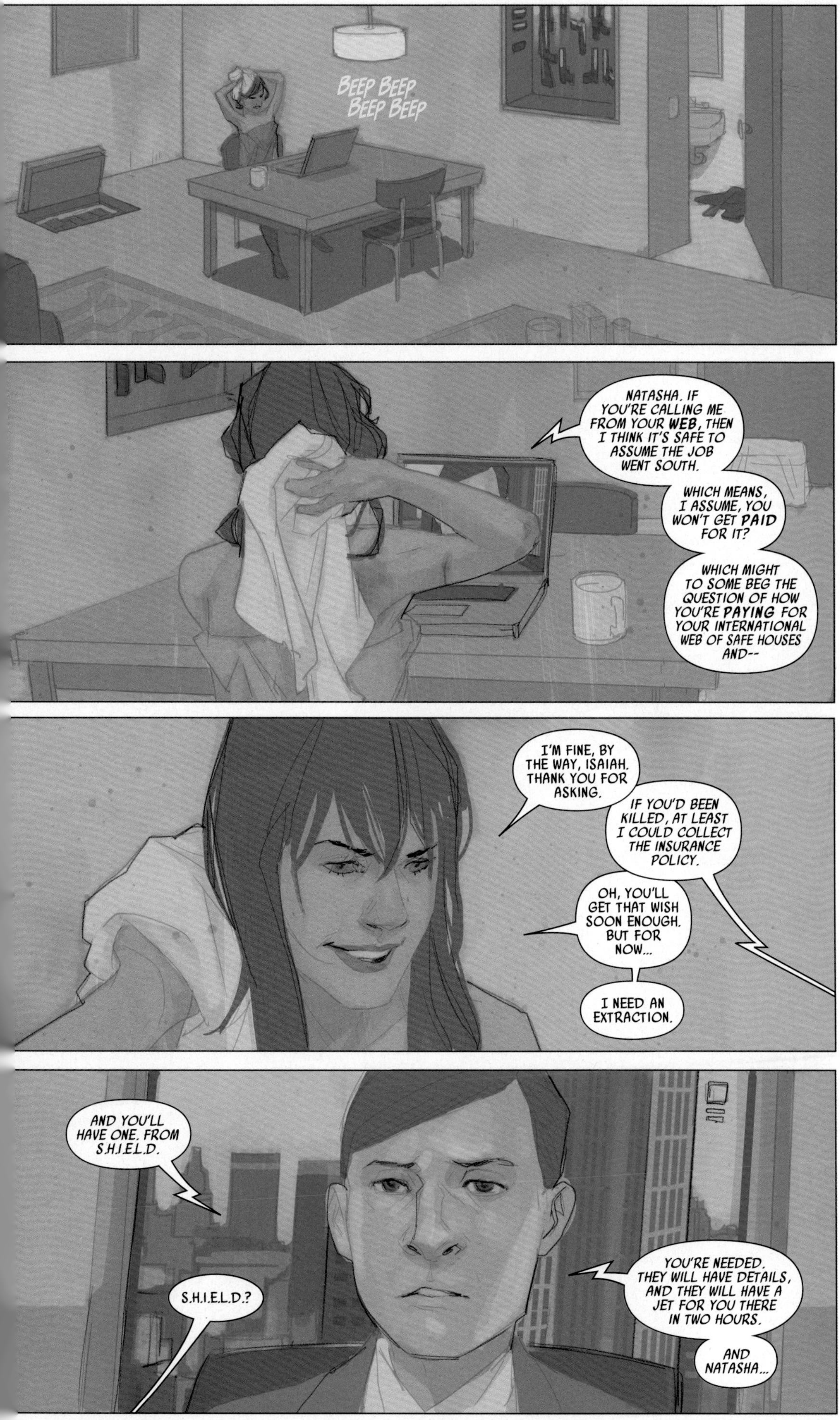
BEEP BEEP BEEP BEEP
NATASHA. IF YOU'RE CALLING ME FROM YOUR WEB, THEN I THINK IT'S SAFE TO ASSUME THE JOB WENT SOUTH.
WHICH MEANS, I ASSUME, YOU WON'T GET PAID FOR IT?
WHICH MIGHT TO SOME BEG THE QUESTION OF HOW YOU'RE PAYING FOR YOUR INTERNATIONAL WEB OF SAFE HOUSES AND--
I'M FINE, BY THE WAY, ISAIAH. THANK YOU FOR ASKING.
IF YOU'D BEEN KILLED, AT LEAST I COULD COLLECT THE INSURANCE POLICY.
OH, YOU'LL GET THAT WISH SOON ENOUGH. BUT FOR NOW...
I NEED AN EXTRACTION.
AND YOU'LL HAVE ONE. FROM S.H.I.E.L.D.
S.H.I.E.L.D.?
YOU'RE NEEDED. THEY WILL HAVE DETAILS, AND THEY WILL HAVE A JET FOR YOU THERE IN TWO HOURS.
AND NATASHA...

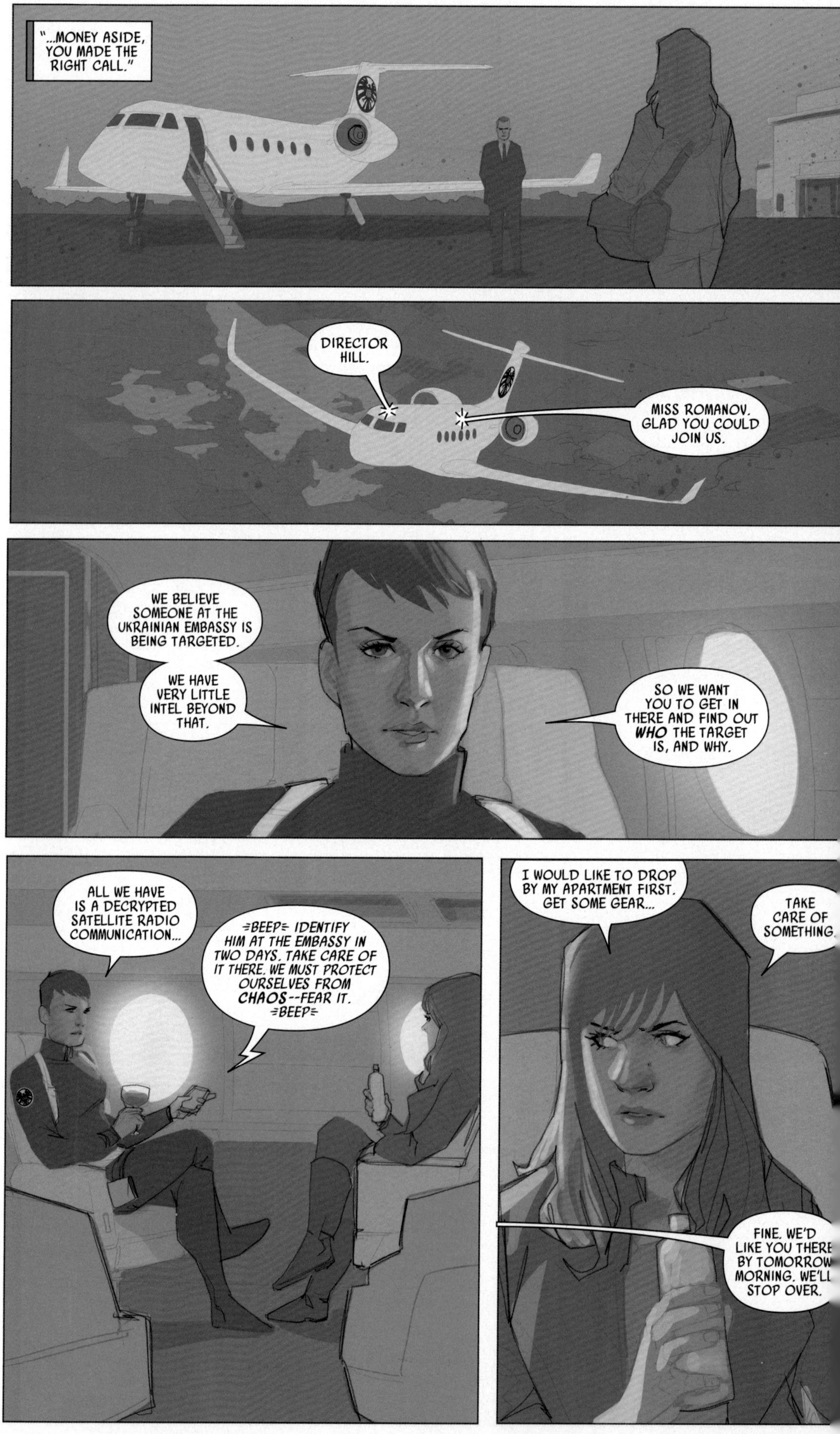
"...MONEY ASIDE, YOU MADE THE RIGHT CALL."
DIRECTOR HILL.
MISS ROMANOV. GLAD YOU COULD JOIN US.
WE BELIEVE SOMEONE AT THE UKRAINIAN EMBASSY IS BEING TARGETED.
WE HAVE VERY LITTLE INTEL BEYOND THAT.
SO WE WANT YOU TO GET IN THERE AND FIND OUT WHO THE TARGET IS, AND WHY.
ALL WE HAVE IS A DECRYPTED SATELLITE RADIO COMMUNICATION...
=BEEP= IDENTIFY HIM AT THE EMBASSY IN TWO DAYS. TAKE CARE OF IT THERE. WE MUST PROTECT OURSELVES FROM CHAOS--FEAR IT. =BEEP=
I WOULD LIKE TO DROP BY MY APARTMENT FIRST. GET SOME GEAR...
TAKE CARE OF SOMETHING.
FINE. WE'D LIKE YOU THERE BY TOMORROW MORNING. WE'LL STOP OVER.

UNFORTUNATELY, I ADMIT, I *DO* HAVE A HOME. I HAVE ALWAYS HAD A HOME.

EVEN IF IT IS NOT APPARENT TO ME OR ANYONE ELSE.

HOME IS WHERE THE *HURT* IS.

THAT MIGHT BE THE JUNGLE. IT MIGHT BE BACK ON THE STREETS OF MY BIRTH CITY. IT MIGHT BE HERE.

AND EVERY HOME...

...HAS DANGEROUS PREDATORS OF ITS OWN.

KNOCK

NATASHA, I--

MOVE ASIDE, ANA.

WHAT DO YOU DO IN MY--

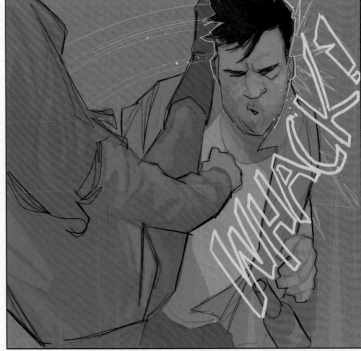

WHACK!

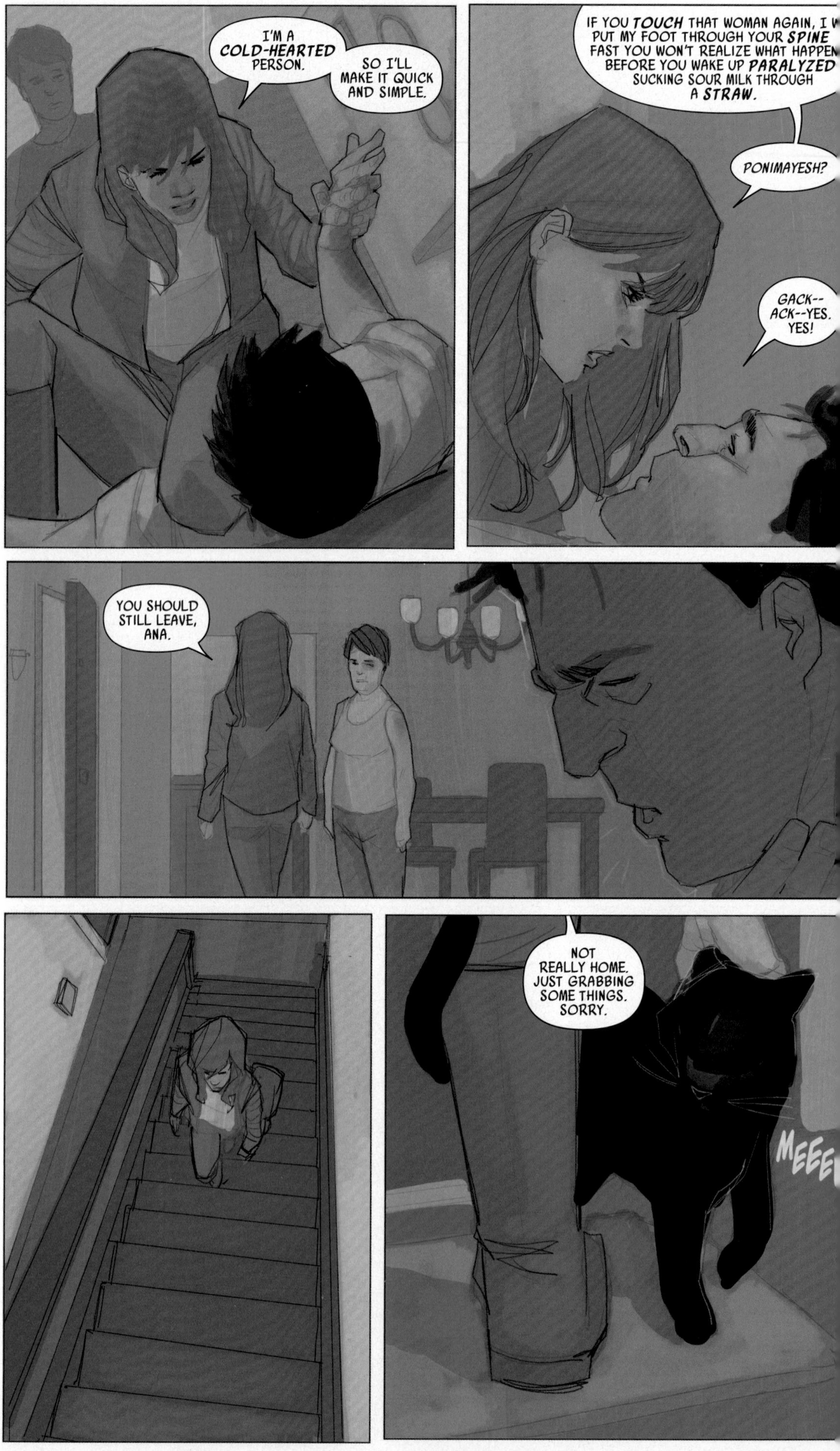
I'M A COLD-HEARTED PERSON.
SO I'LL MAKE IT QUICK AND SIMPLE.
IF YOU TOUCH THAT WOMAN AGAIN, I
PUT MY FOOT THROUGH YOUR SPINE
FAST YOU WON'T REALIZE WHAT HAPPEN
BEFORE YOU WAKE UP PARALYZED
SUCKING SOUR MILK THROUGH A STRAW.
PONIMAYESH?
GACK-- ACK--YES. YES!
YOU SHOULD STILL LEAVE, ANA.
NOT REALLY HOME. JUST GRABBING SOME THINGS. SORRY.
MEEE

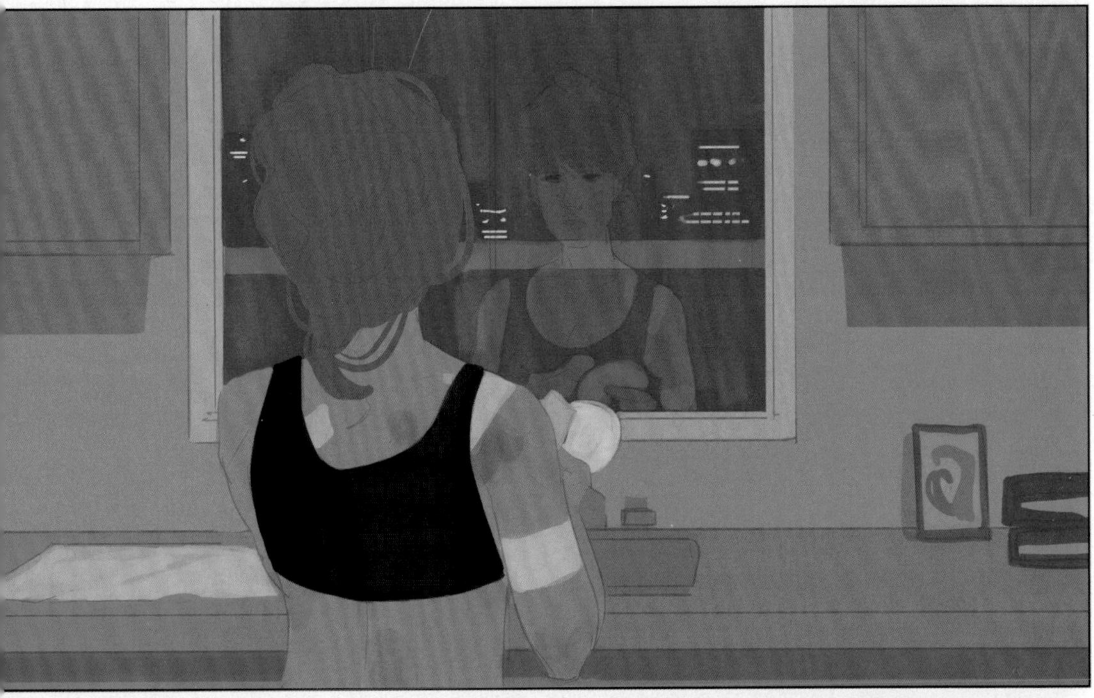

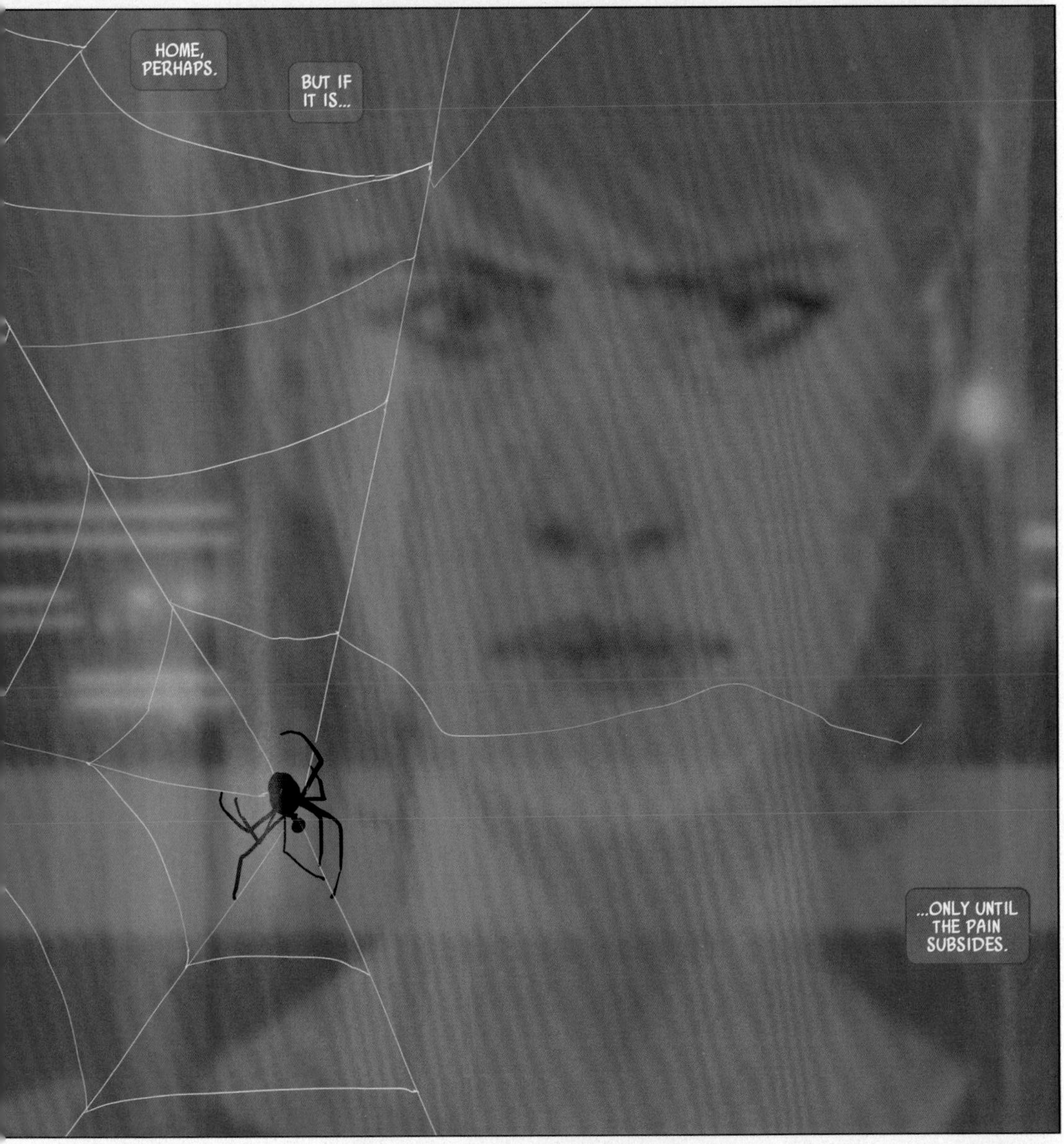
HOME, PERHAPS.
BUT IF IT IS...
...ONLY UNTIL THE PAIN SUBSIDES.

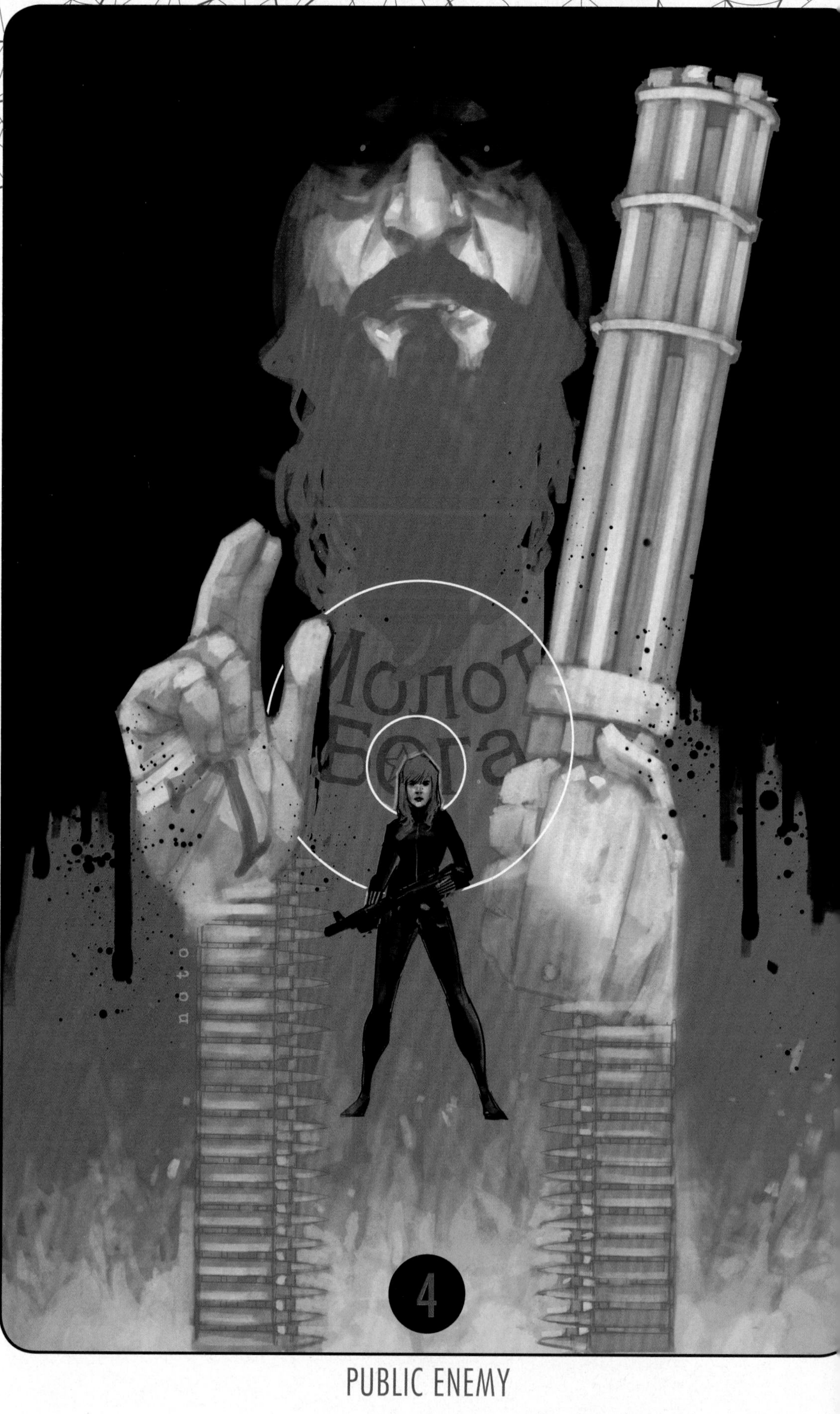
Молот
Бога
noto
4

PUBLIC ENEMY

THEY ARE DANGEROUS.

WE HAVE TO TAKE CARE OF THEM BEFORE IT'S TOO LATE.

THEY HAVE *SINNED*.

THEY ARE-- YES, SURE, THEY HAVE.

THEY ARE SINNERS. THEY'VE SINNED. AND THEY HAVE TO BE *PUNISHED*, MOLOT.

YOUR WORD IS LIKE *FIRE* TO ME. I SHALL BE YOUR *HAMMER* THAT BREAKS THE ROCK INTO PIECES.

...

OKAY. GOOD. JUST, MOLOT...

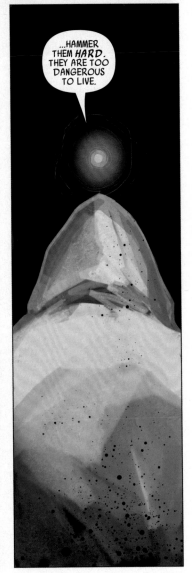

...HAMMER THEM *HARD*. THEY ARE TOO DANGEROUS TO LIVE.

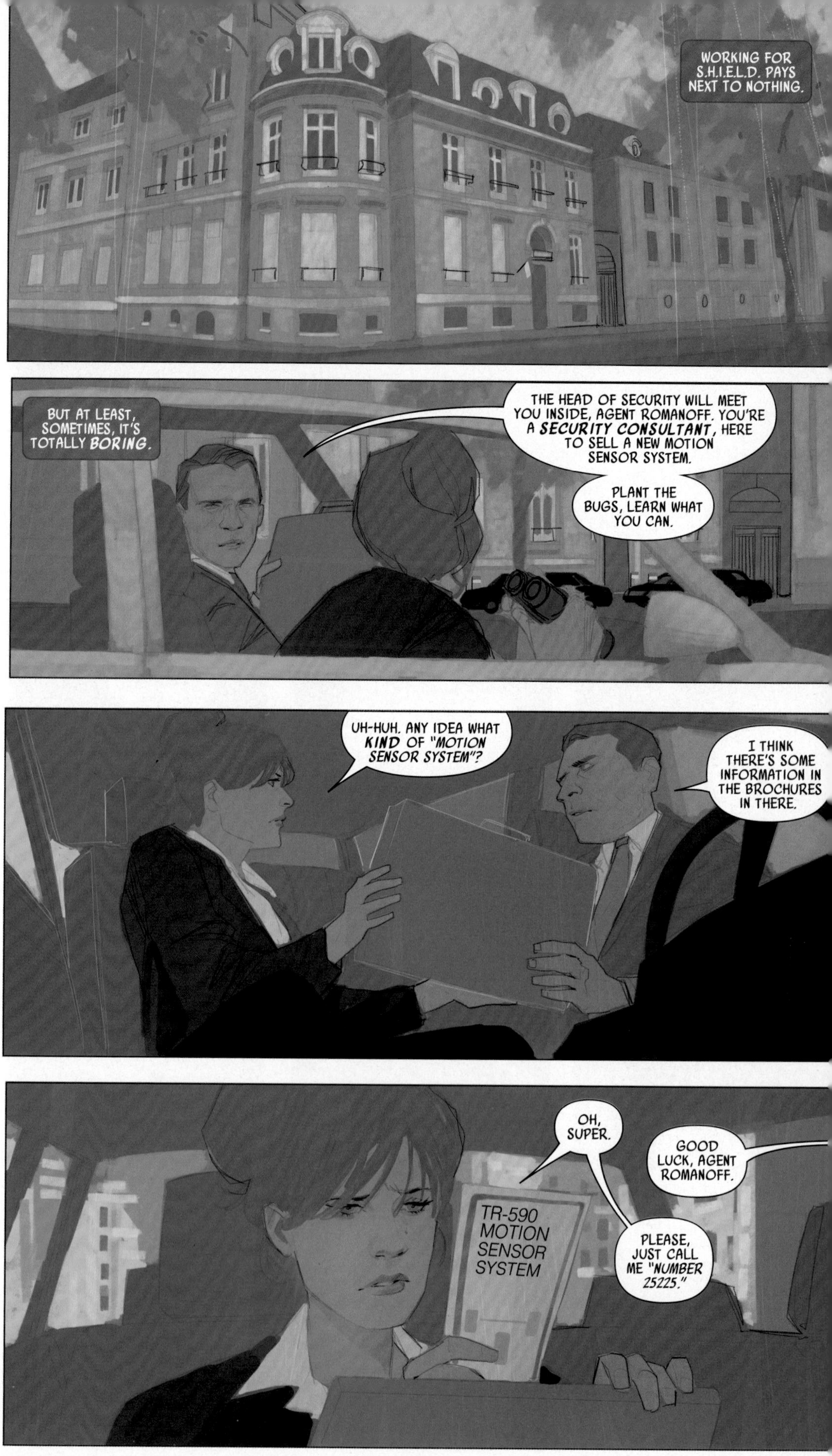
WORKING FOR S.H.I.E.L.D. PAYS NEXT TO NOTHING.
BUT AT LEAST, SOMETIMES, IT'S TOTALLY BORING.
THE HEAD OF SECURITY WILL MEET YOU INSIDE, AGENT ROMANOFF. YOU'RE A SECURITY CONSULTANT, HERE TO SELL A NEW MOTION SENSOR SYSTEM.
PLANT THE BUGS, LEARN WHAT YOU CAN.
UH-HUH. ANY IDEA WHAT KIND OF "MOTION SENSOR SYSTEM"?
I THINK THERE'S SOME INFORMATION IN THE BROCHURES IN THERE.
TR-590 MOTION SENSOR SYSTEM
OH, SUPER.
GOOD LUCK, AGENT ROMANOFF.
PLEASE, JUST CALL ME "NUMBER 25225."

BORING.

BEST TO REMEMBER THAT S.H.I.E.L.D. IS A BUREAUCRACY. WHEN YOU START TO ARGUE, YOU ONLY GET TANGLED UP IN RED TAPE.

BUT THEY'RE BETTER THAN THE *OTHER* DIRECT-ACTION, COVERT-INTEL BUREAUCRACIES. USUALLY.

ONCE YOU'VE FOUGHT OFF INVADING ALIENS FOR THEM, SOMETIMES DOING S.H.I.E.L.D.'S GROUND-LEVEL WORK CAN BE TEDIOUS.

BUT THE TRUTH ABOUT INTELLIGENCE GATHERING? THE DEVIL IS IN THE DETAILS.

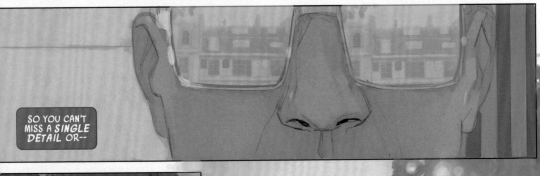

SO YOU CAN'T MISS A *SINGLE* DETAIL OR--

YOU MIGHT MISS THE DEVIL HIMSELF...

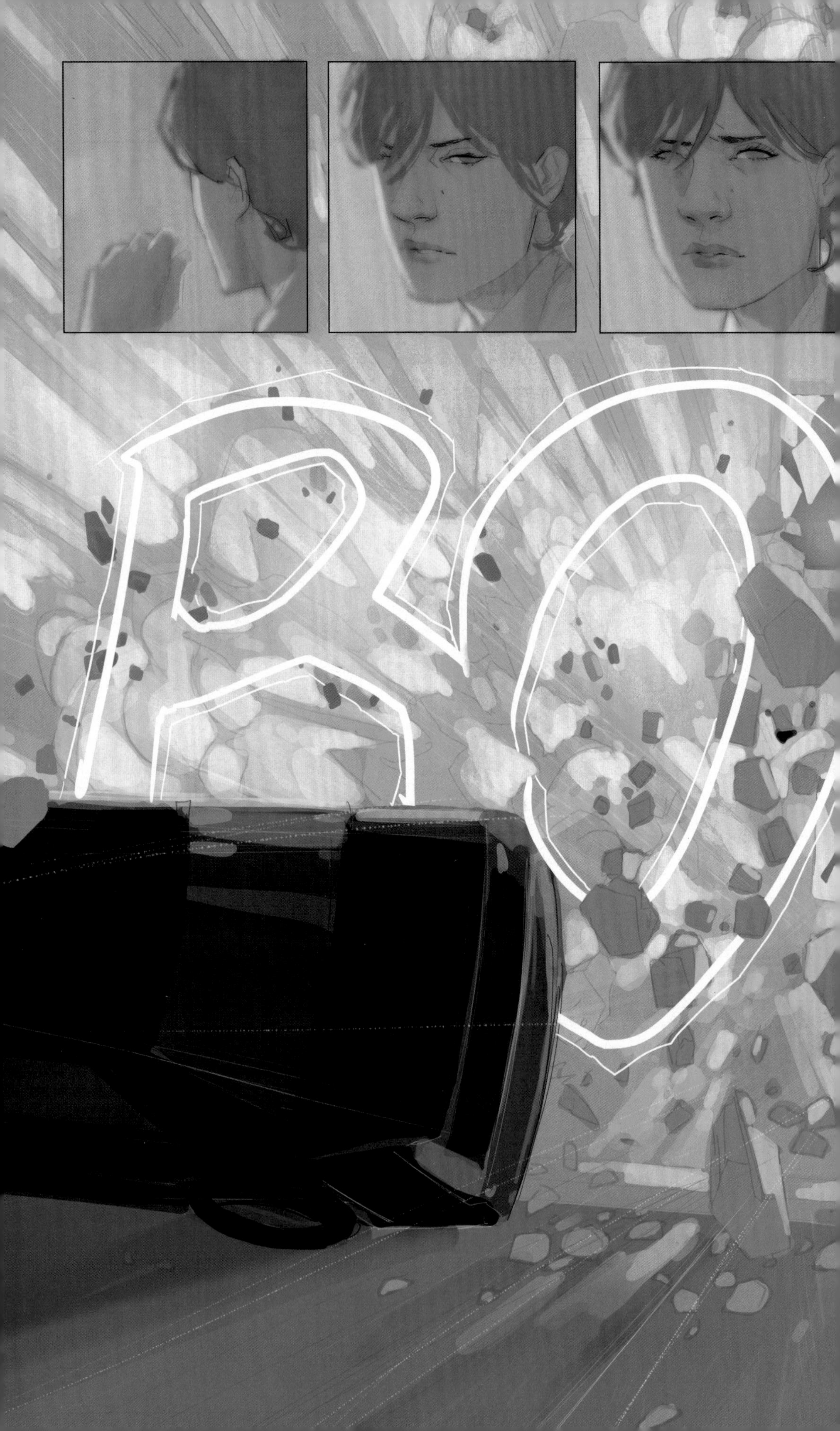
RO

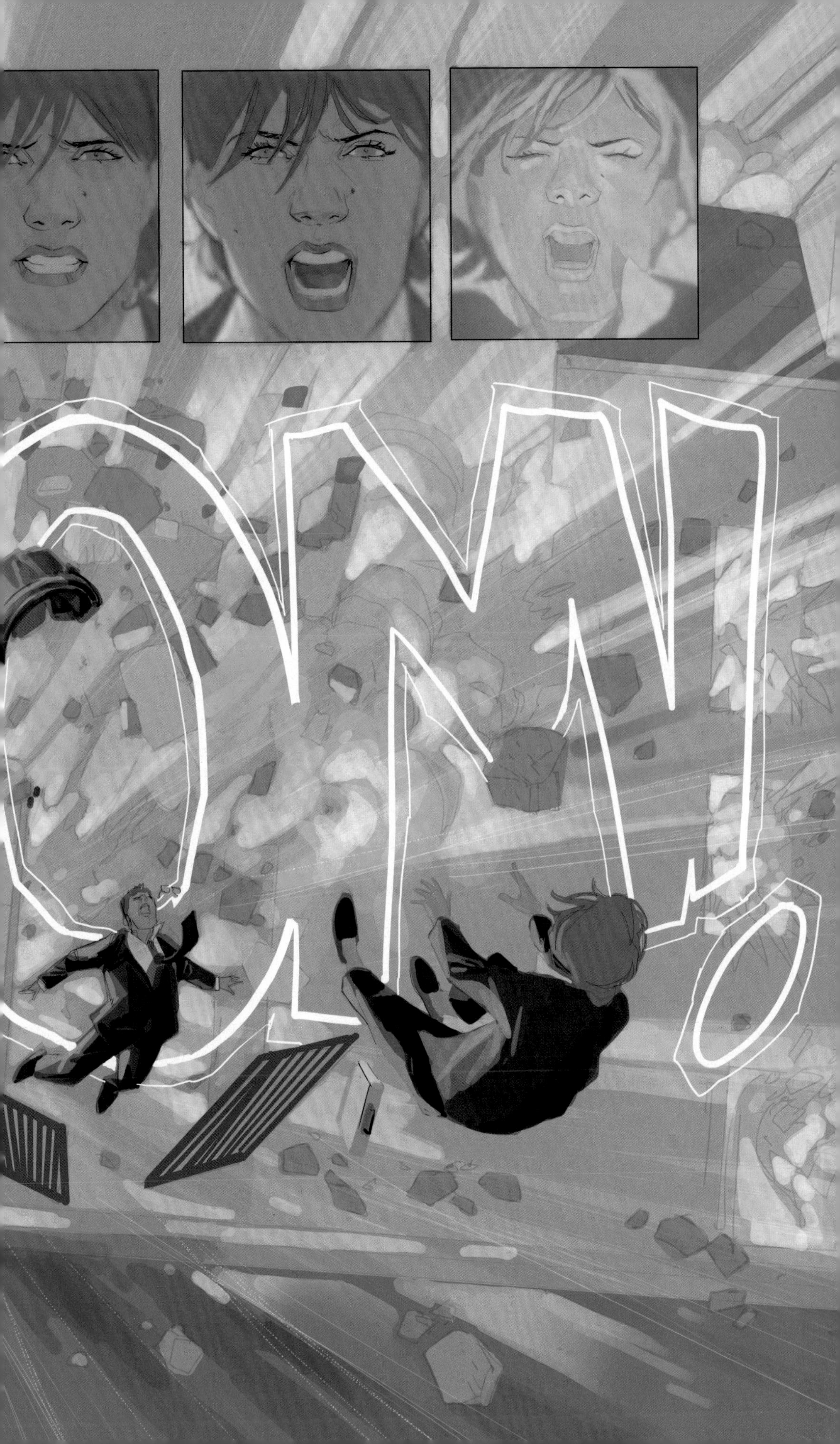
OM!

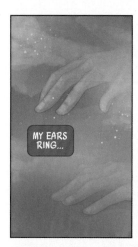

MY EARS RING...

MY BODY IS NUMB...

BUT IMMEDIATELY I WONDER...

DID THEY KNOW?

AGENT ROMANOFF!

CALL DIRECTOR HILL! *I'M IN PURSUIT.*

WHOEVER HE IS, HE'S A *COWARD.*

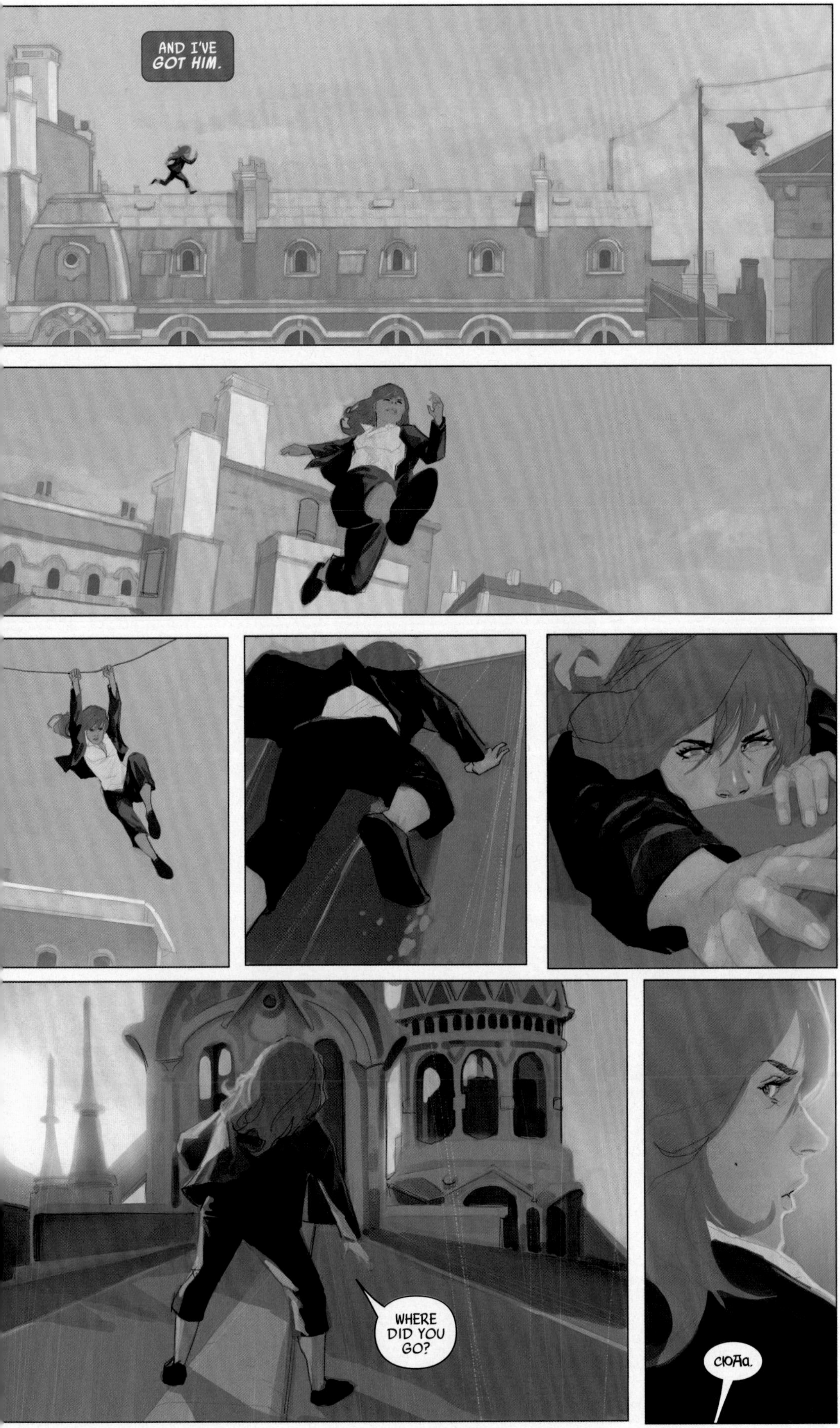
AND I'VE GOT HIM.
WHERE DID YOU GO?
сюда.

KKKKRRR A AA CCK
BAM!
"WHO
HE? WHO
WORK

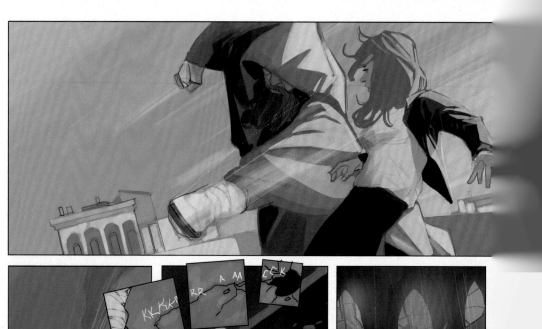

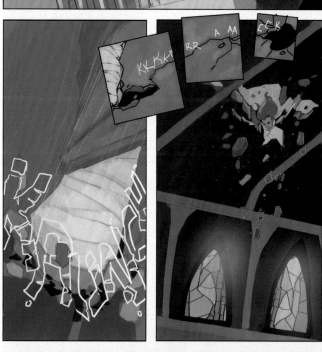

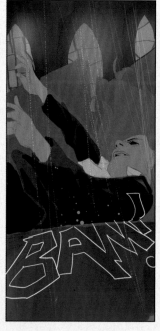

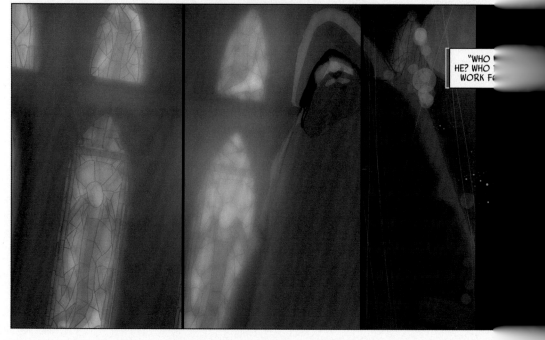

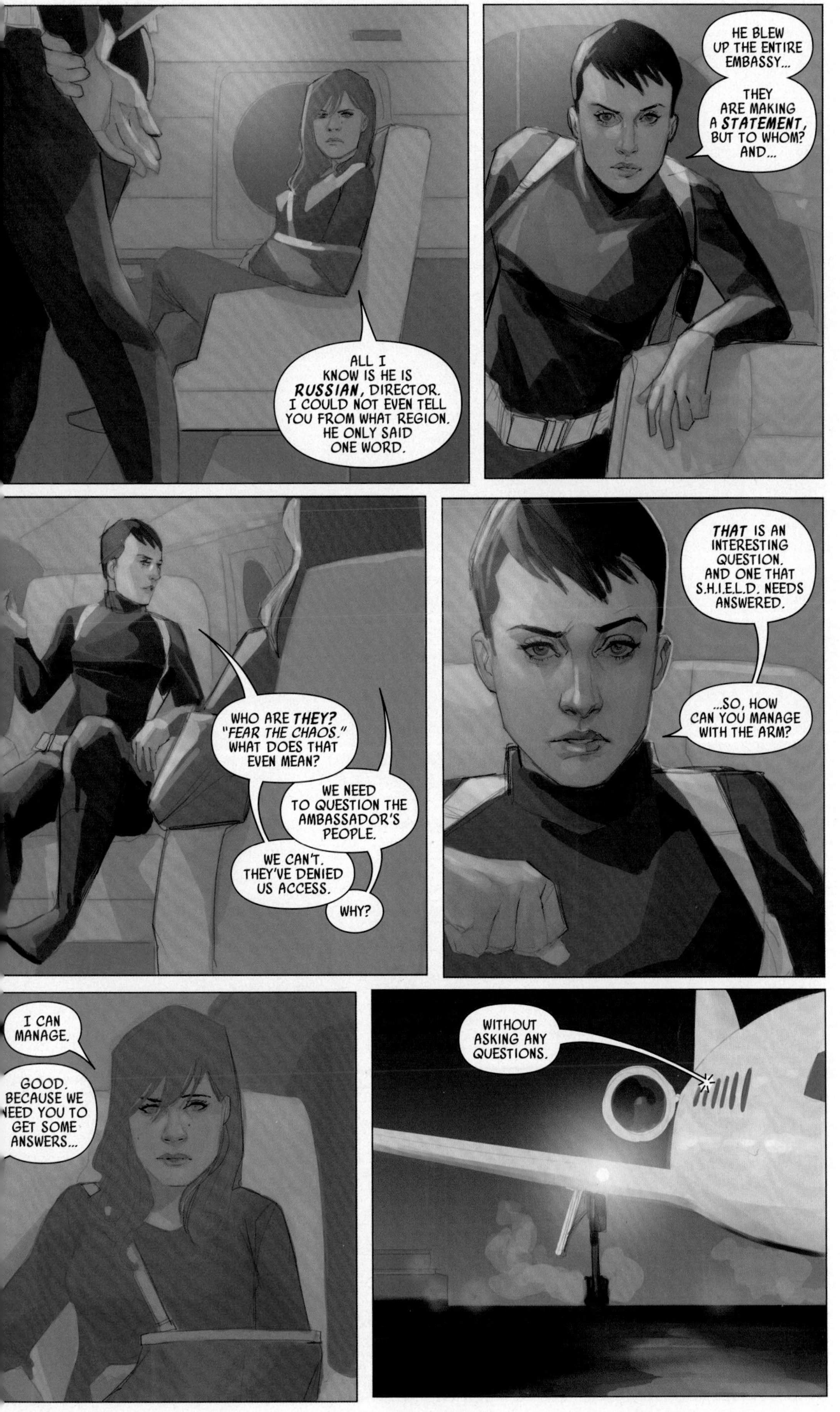
ALL I KNOW IS HE IS RUSSIAN, DIRECTOR. I COULD NOT EVEN TELL YOU FROM WHAT REGION. HE ONLY SAID ONE WORD.
HE BLEW UP THE ENTIRE EMBASSY...
THEY ARE MAKING A STATEMENT, BUT TO WHOM? AND...
WHO ARE THEY? "FEAR THE CHAOS." WHAT DOES THAT EVEN MEAN?
WE NEED TO QUESTION THE AMBASSADOR'S PEOPLE.
WE CAN'T. THEY'VE DENIED US ACCESS.
WHY?
THAT IS AN INTERESTING QUESTION. AND ONE THAT S.H.I.E.L.D. NEEDS ANSWERED.
...SO, HOW CAN YOU MANAGE WITH THE ARM?
I CAN MANAGE.
GOOD. BECAUSE WE NEED YOU TO GET SOME ANSWERS...
WITHOUT ASKING ANY QUESTIONS.

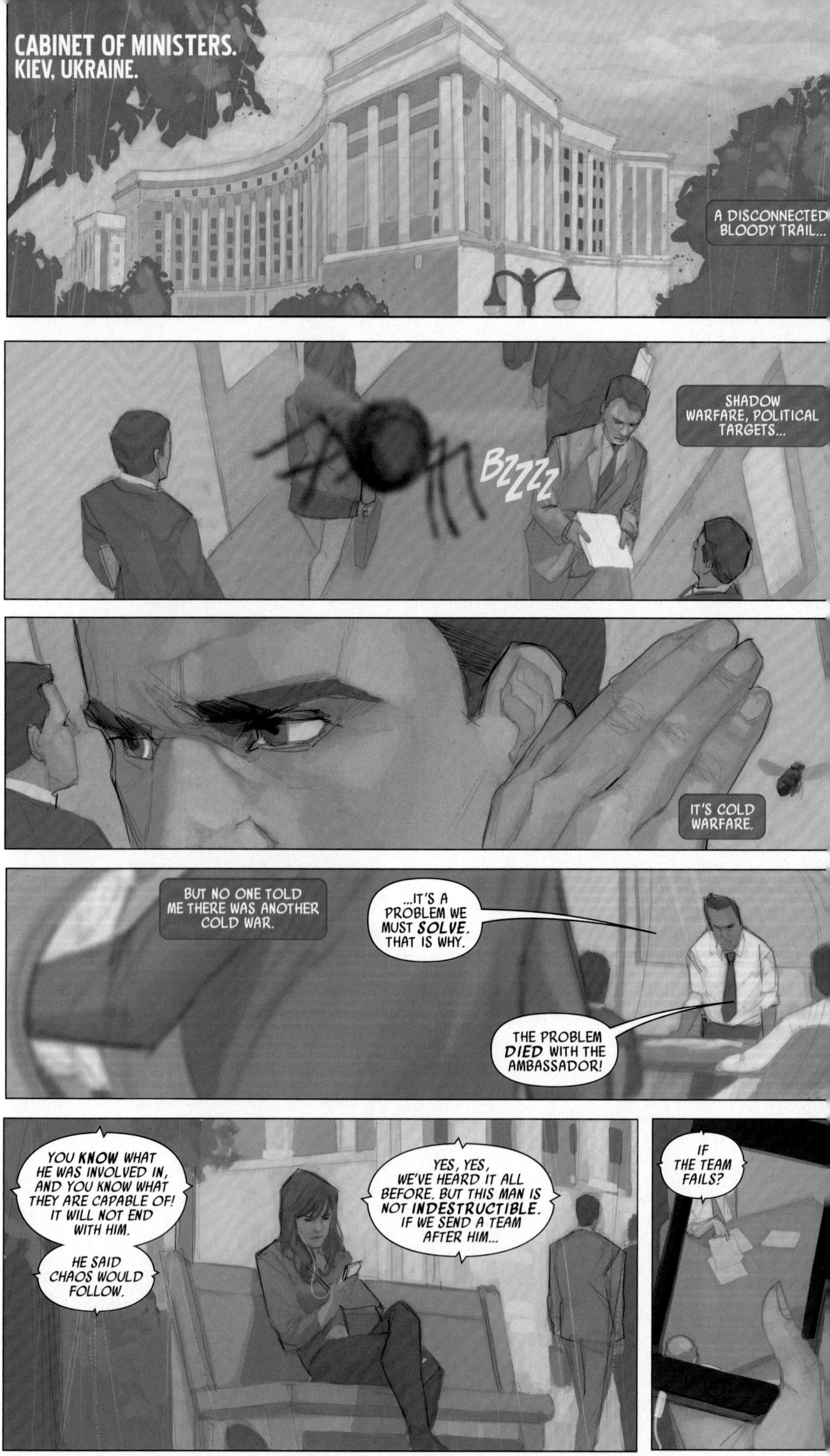
CABINET OF MINISTERS.
KIEV, UKRAINE.
A DISCONNECTED BLOODY TRAIL...
SHADOW WARFARE, POLITICAL TARGETS...
BZZZZ
IT'S COLD WARFARE.
BUT NO ONE TOLD ME THERE WAS ANOTHER COLD WAR.
...IT'S A PROBLEM WE MUST SOLVE. THAT IS WHY.
THE PROBLEM DIED WITH THE AMBASSADOR!
YOU KNOW WHAT HE WAS INVOLVED IN, AND YOU KNOW WHAT THEY ARE CAPABLE OF! IT WILL NOT END WITH HIM.
HE SAID CHAOS WOULD FOLLOW.
YES, YES, WE'VE HEARD IT ALL BEFORE. BUT THIS MAN IS NOT INDESTRUCTIBLE. IF WE SEND A TEAM AFTER HIM...
IF THE TEAM FAILS?

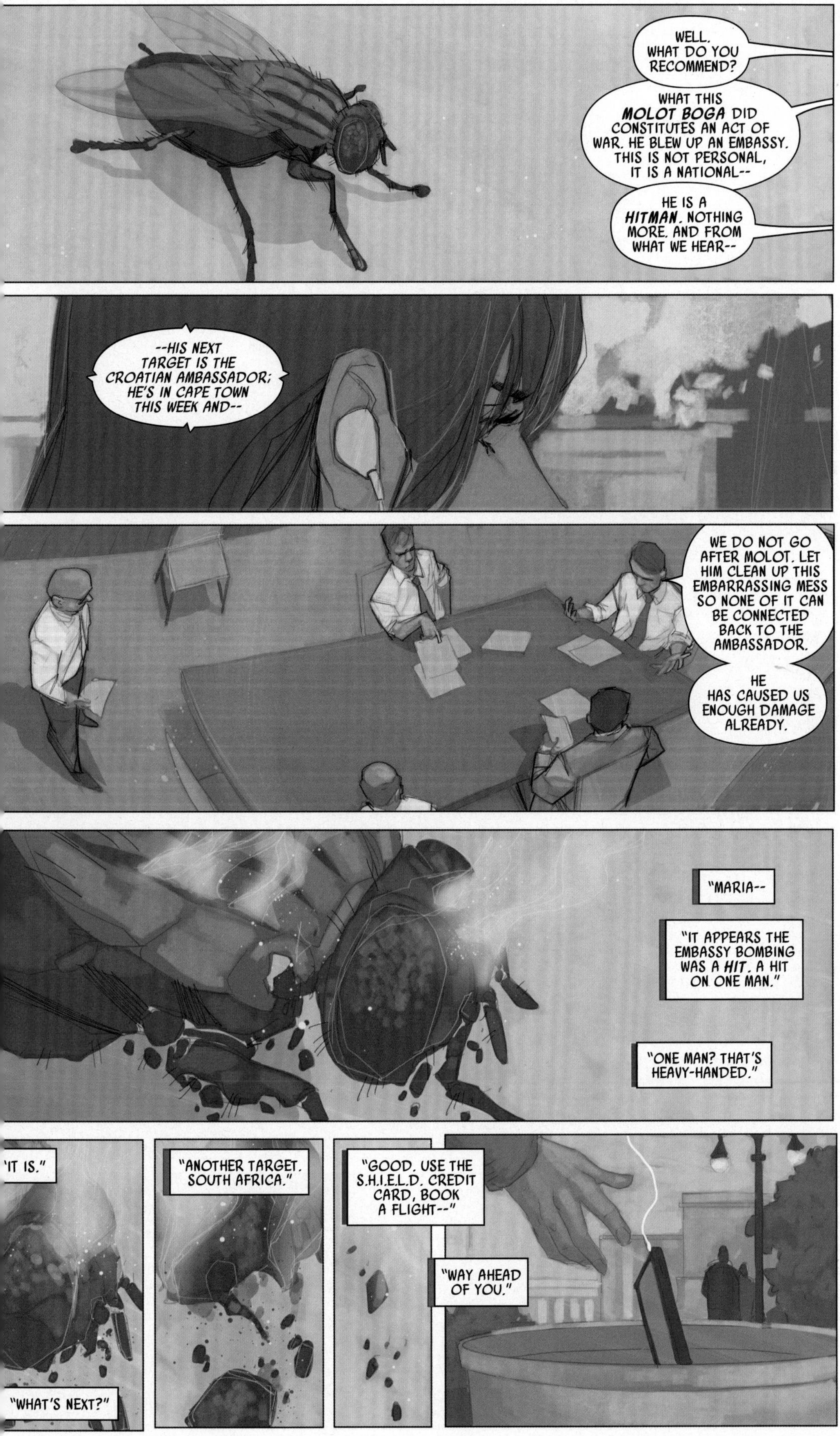

WELL. WHAT DO YOU RECOMMEND?
WHAT THIS MOLOT BOGA DID CONSTITUTES AN ACT OF WAR. HE BLEW UP AN EMBASSY. THIS IS NOT PERSONAL, IT IS A NATIONAL--
HE IS A HITMAN. NOTHING MORE. AND FROM WHAT WE HEAR--
--HIS NEXT TARGET IS THE CROATIAN AMBASSADOR; HE'S IN CAPE TOWN THIS WEEK AND--
WE DO NOT GO AFTER MOLOT. LET HIM CLEAN UP THIS EMBARRASSING MESS SO NONE OF IT CAN BE CONNECTED BACK TO THE AMBASSADOR.
HE HAS CAUSED US ENOUGH DAMAGE ALREADY.
"MARIA--
"IT APPEARS THE EMBASSY BOMBING WAS A HIT. A HIT ON ONE MAN."
"ONE MAN? THAT'S HEAVY-HANDED."
"IT IS."
"WHAT'S NEXT?"
"ANOTHER TARGET. SOUTH AFRICA."
"GOOD. USE THE S.H.I.E.L.D. CREDIT CARD, BOOK A FLIGHT--"
"WAY AHEAD OF YOU."

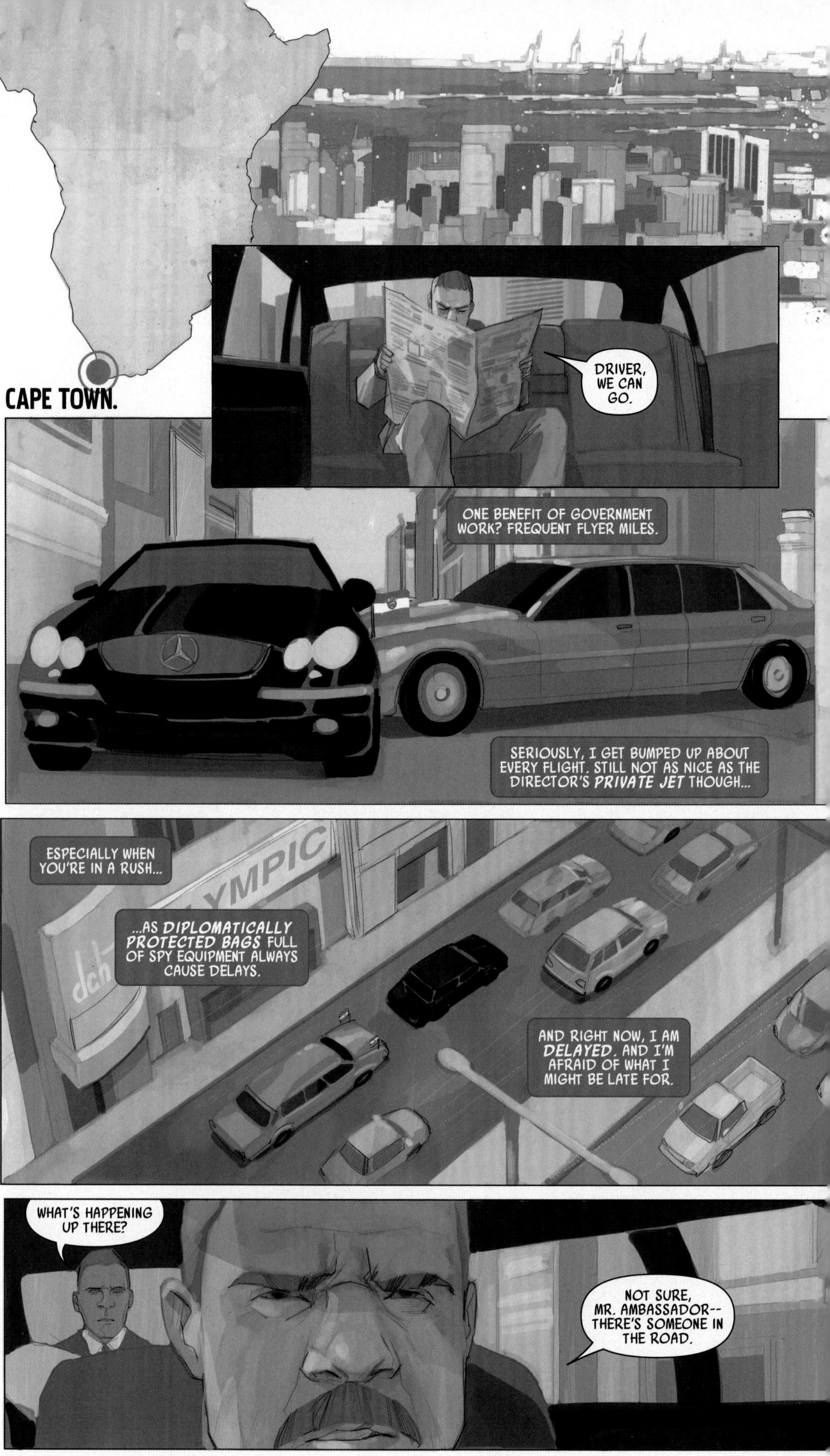
CAPE TOWN.
DRIVER, WE CAN GO.
ONE BENEFIT OF GOVERNMENT WORK? FREQUENT FLYER MILES.
SERIOUSLY, I GET BUMPED UP ABOUT EVERY FLIGHT. STILL NOT AS NICE AS THE DIRECTOR'S PRIVATE JET THOUGH...
ESPECIALLY WHEN YOU'RE IN A RUSH...
...AS DIPLOMATICALLY PROTECTED BAGS FULL OF SPY EQUIPMENT ALWAYS CAUSE DELAYS.
AND RIGHT NOW, I AM DELAYED. AND I'M AFRAID OF WHAT I MIGHT BE LATE FOR.
WHAT'S HAPPENING UP THERE?
NOT SURE, MR. AMBASSADOR-- THERE'S SOMEONE IN THE ROAD.

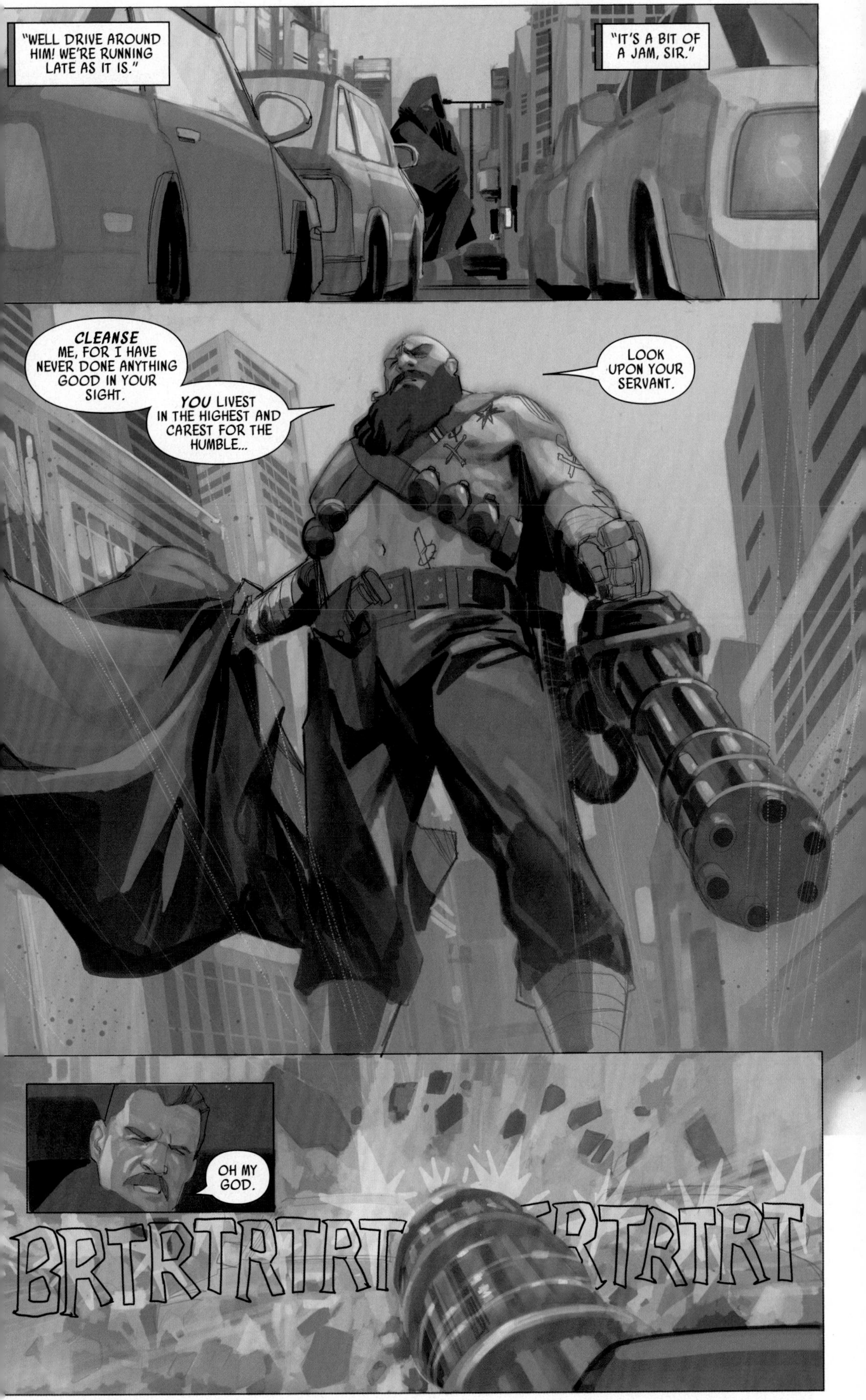
"WELL DRIVE AROUND HIM! WE'RE RUNNING LATE AS IT IS."
"IT'S A BIT OF A JAM, SIR."
CLEANSE ME, FOR I HAVE NEVER DONE ANYTHING GOOD IN YOUR SIGHT.
YOU LIVEST IN THE HIGHEST AND CAREST FOR THE HUMBLE...
LOOK UPON YOUR SERVANT.
OH MY GOD.
BRTRTRTRT
RTRTRT

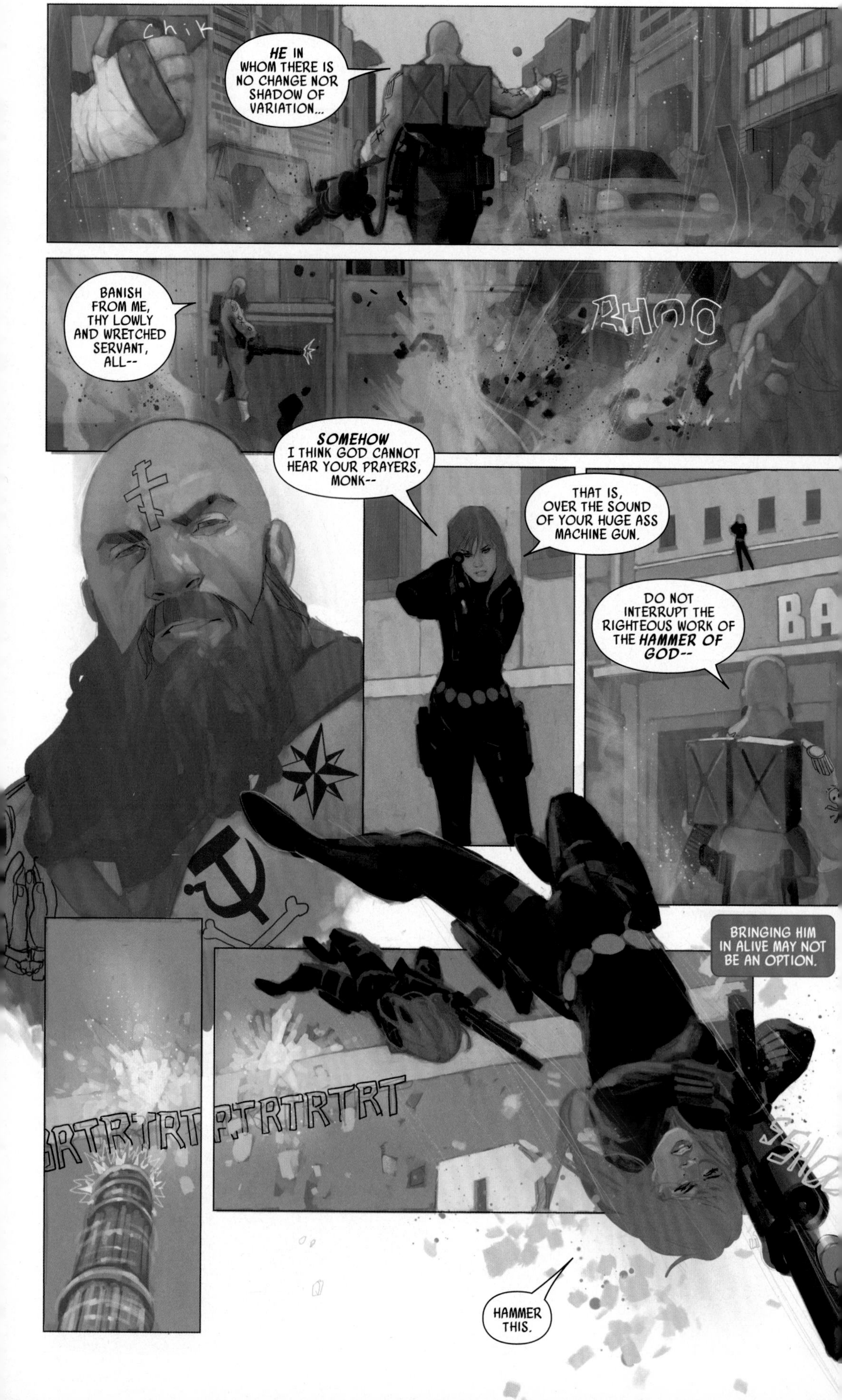
Chik
HE IN WHOM THERE IS NO CHANGE NOR SHADOW OF VARIATION...
BANISH FROM ME, THY LOWLY AND WRETCHED SERVANT, ALL--
BHOO
SOMEHOW I THINK GOD CANNOT HEAR YOUR PRAYERS, MONK--
THAT IS, OVER THE SOUND OF YOUR HUGE ASS MACHINE GUN.
DO NOT INTERRUPT THE RIGHTEOUS WORK OF THE HAMMER OF GOD--
BRINGING HIM IN ALIVE MAY NOT BE AN OPTION.
BRTRTRTRT
RTRTRTRTRT
HAMMER THIS.

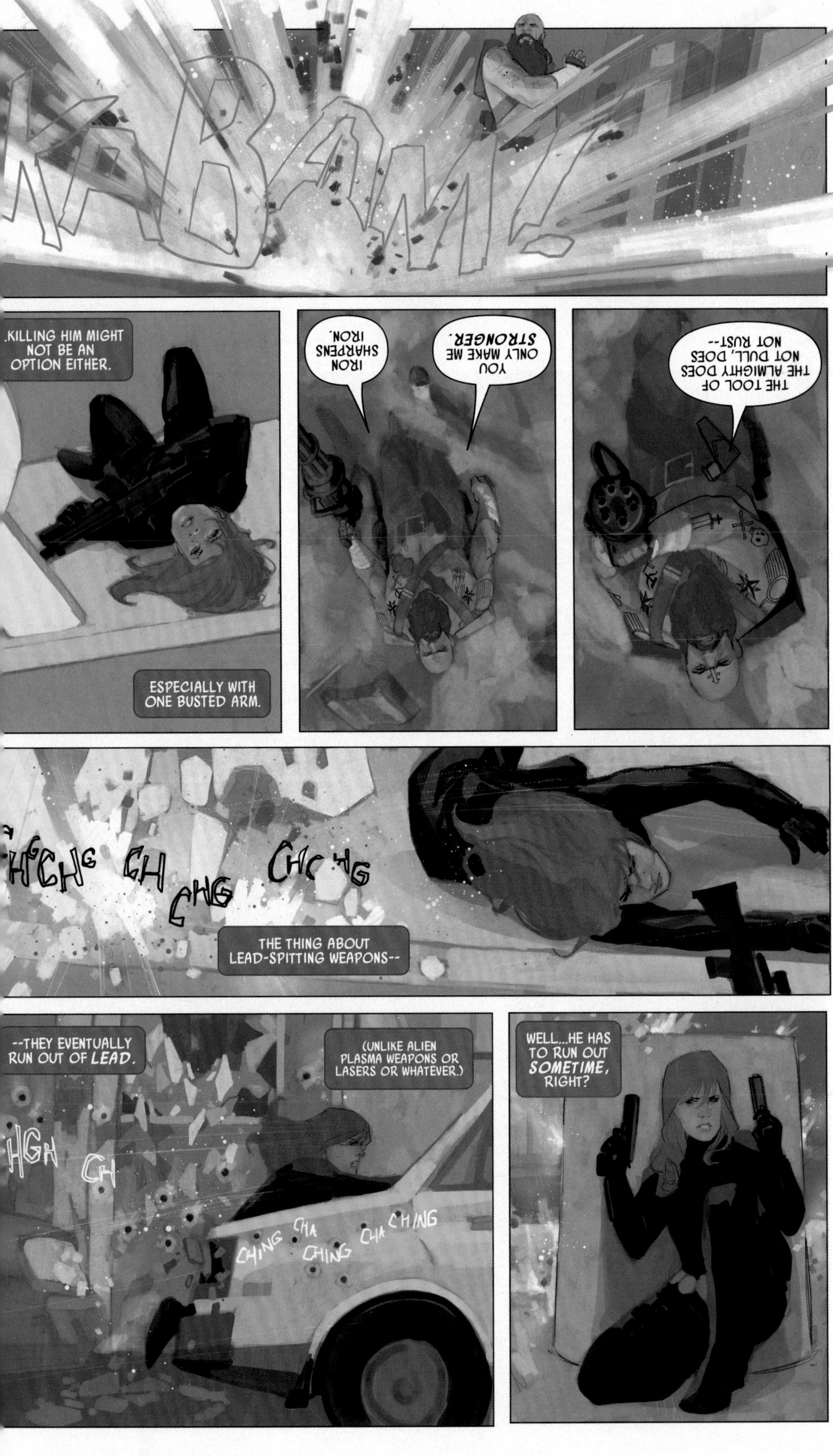
KABAM!
..KILLING HIM MIGHT NOT BE AN OPTION EITHER.
ESPECIALLY WITH ONE BUSTED ARM.
YOU ONLY MAKE ME STRONGER.
IRON SHARPENS IRON.
THE TOOL OF THE ALMIGHTY DOES NOT DULL, DOES NOT RUST--
CHGCHG CHG CHG CHCHG
THE THING ABOUT LEAD-SPITTING WEAPONS--
--THEY EVENTUALLY RUN OUT OF LEAD.
(UNLIKE ALIEN PLASMA WEAPONS OR LASERS OR WHATEVER.)
CHGH CH
CHING CHA CHING CHA CHING
WELL...HE HAS TO RUN OUT SOMETIME, RIGHT?

CLIK
CLIK

AH, THERE WE GO.

BLAM
BLAM
BLAM

BLAM
BLAM
BLAM

IT'S TWO AGAINST NONE NOW, PAL. STAND DOWN OR I SHOOT--

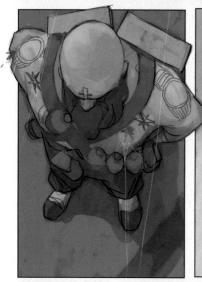

TWO AND ALSO TWO.

BLAM

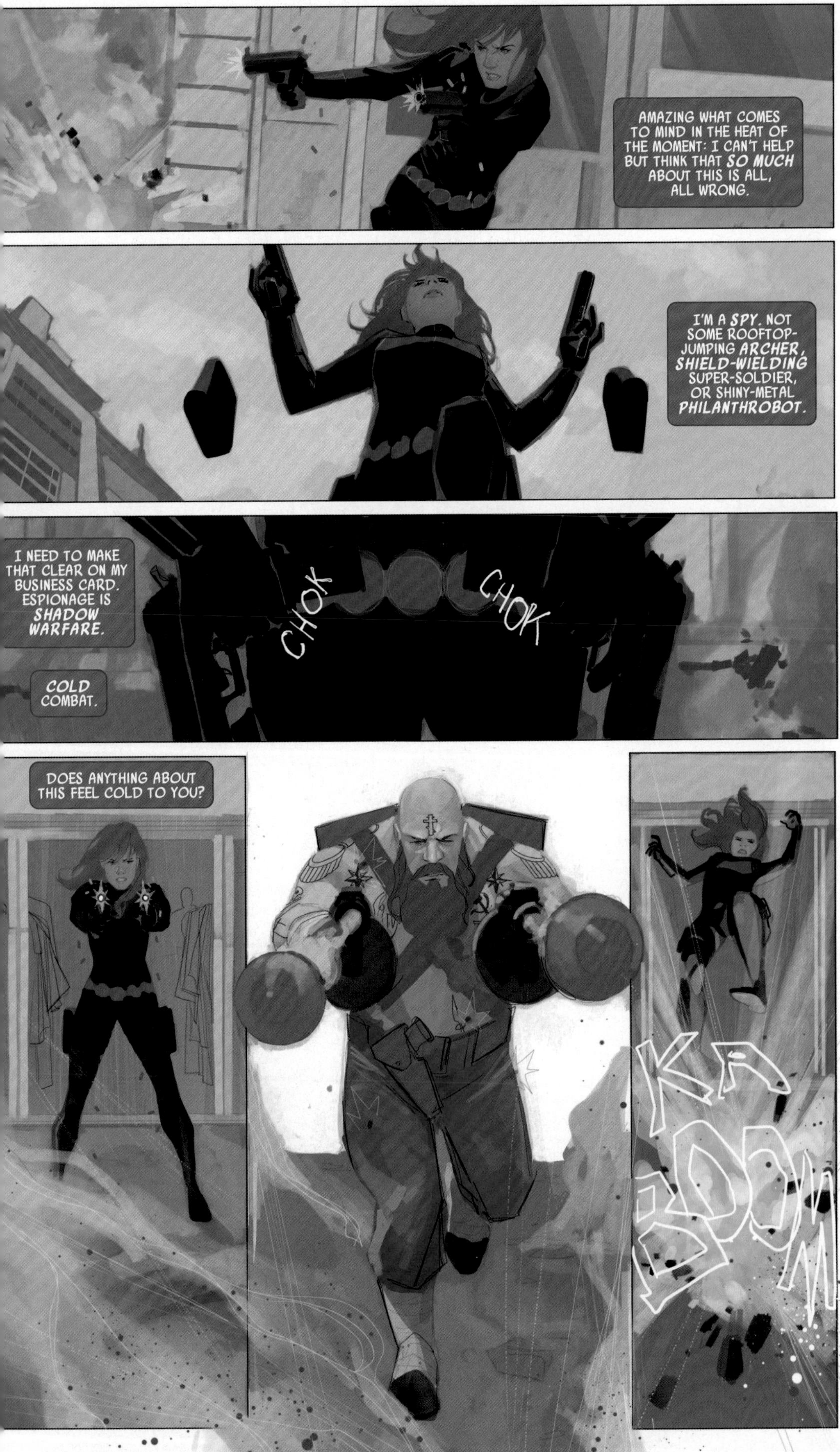
AMAZING WHAT COMES TO MIND IN THE HEAT OF THE MOMENT: I CAN'T HELP BUT THINK THAT SO MUCH ABOUT THIS IS ALL, ALL WRONG.
I'M A SPY. NOT SOME ROOFTOP-JUMPING ARCHER, SHIELD-WIELDING SUPER-SOLDIER, OR SHINY-METAL PHILANTHROBOT.
I NEED TO MAKE THAT CLEAR ON MY BUSINESS CARD. ESPIONAGE IS SHADOW WARFARE.
CHOK
CHOK
COLD COMBAT.
DOES ANYTHING ABOUT THIS FEEL COLD TO YOU?
KA BOOM

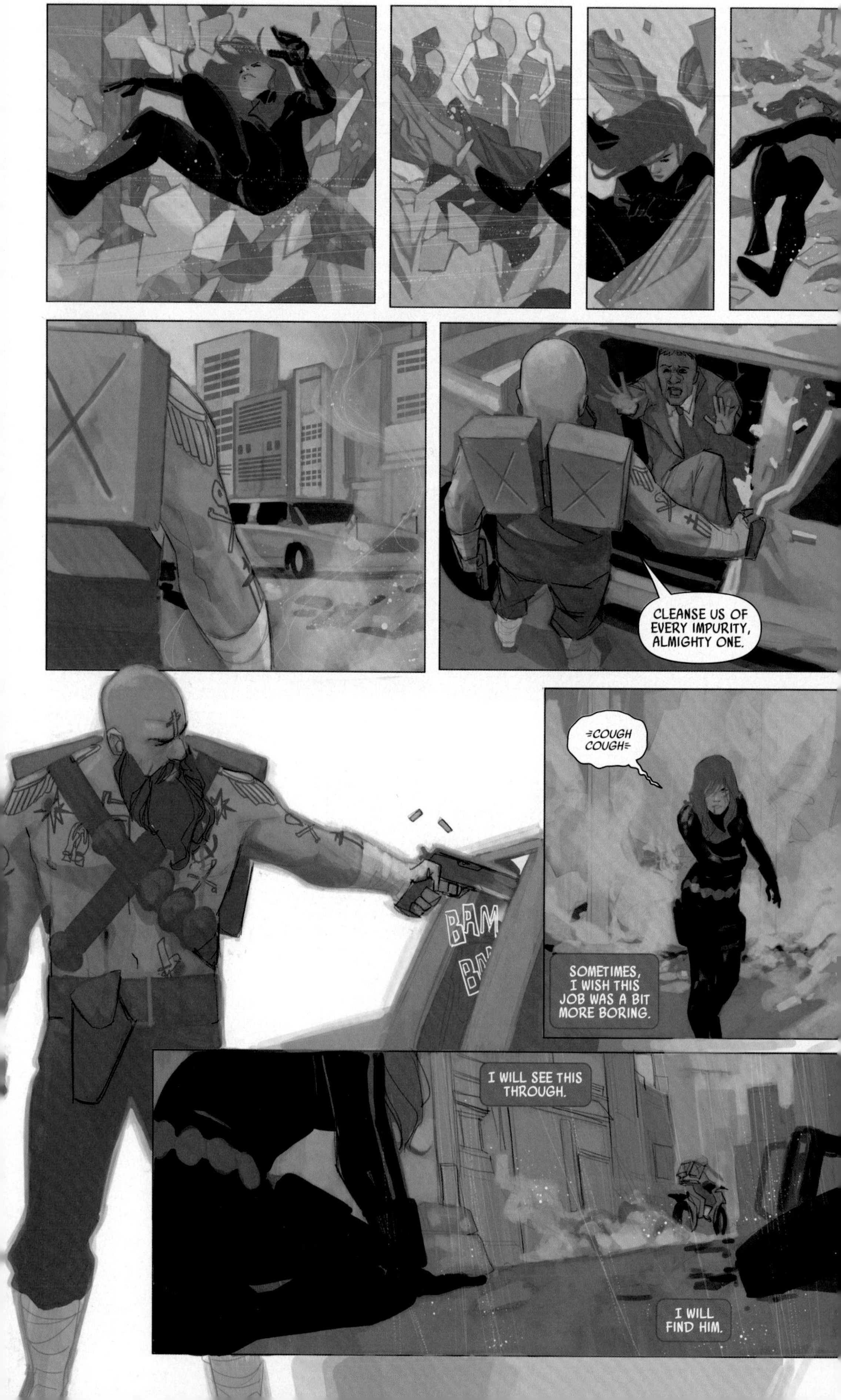
CLEANSE US OF EVERY IMPURITY, ALMIGHTY ONE.
BAM
BA
=COUGH COUGH=
SOMETIMES, I WISH THIS JOB WAS A BIT MORE BORING.
I WILL SEE THIS THROUGH.
I WILL FIND HIM.

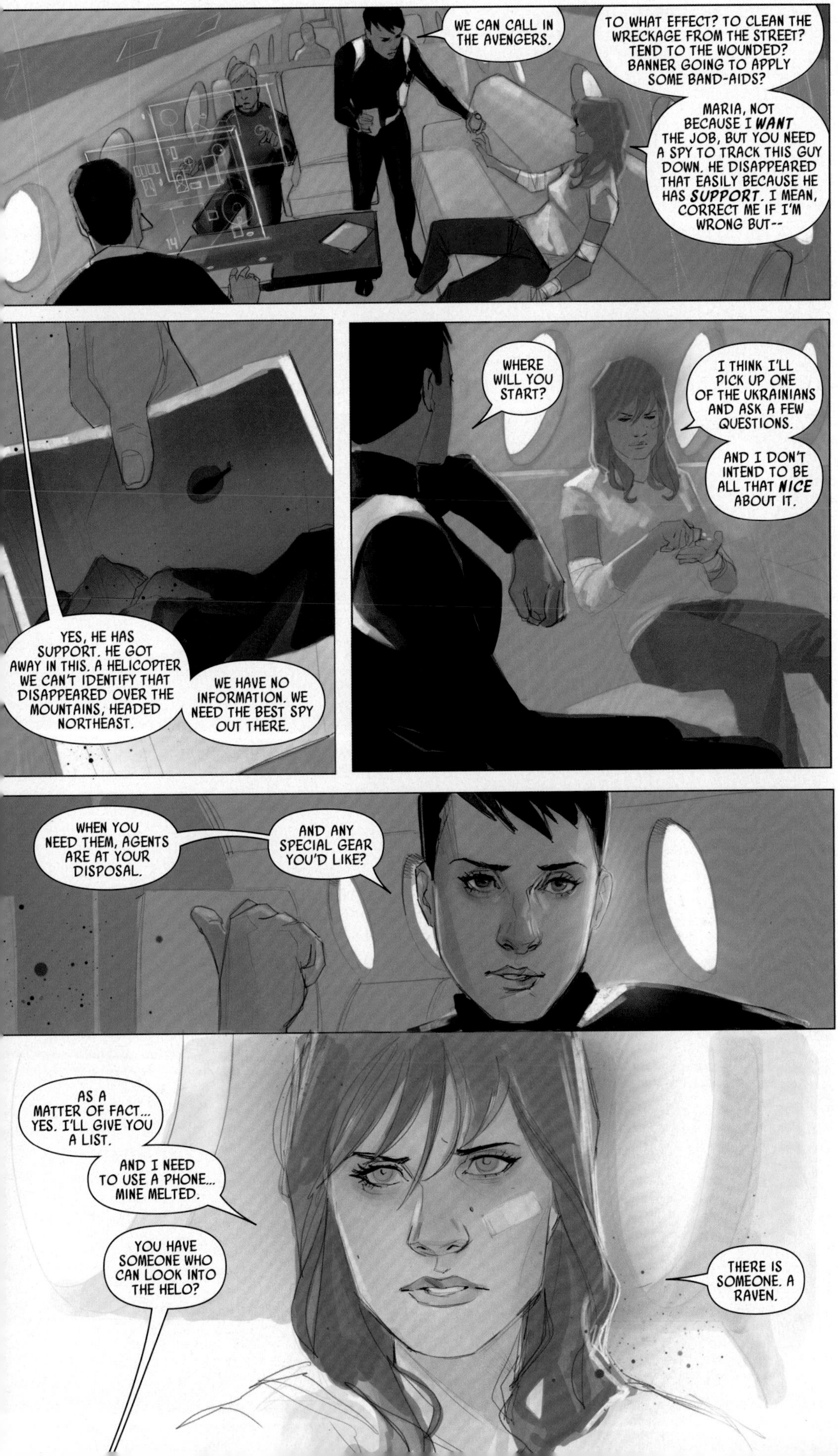
WE CAN CALL IN THE AVENGERS.
TO WHAT EFFECT? TO CLEAN THE WRECKAGE FROM THE STREET? TEND TO THE WOUNDED? BANNER GOING TO APPLY SOME BAND-AIDS?
MARIA, NOT BECAUSE I WANT THE JOB, BUT YOU NEED A SPY TO TRACK THIS GUY DOWN. HE DISAPPEARED THAT EASILY BECAUSE HE HAS SUPPORT. I MEAN, CORRECT ME IF I'M WRONG BUT--
YES, HE HAS SUPPORT. HE GOT AWAY IN THIS. A HELICOPTER WE CAN'T IDENTIFY THAT DISAPPEARED OVER THE MOUNTAINS, HEADED NORTHEAST.
WE HAVE NO INFORMATION. WE NEED THE BEST SPY OUT THERE.
WHERE WILL YOU START?
I THINK I'LL PICK UP ONE OF THE UKRAINIANS AND ASK A FEW QUESTIONS.
AND I DON'T INTEND TO BE ALL THAT NICE ABOUT IT.
WHEN YOU NEED THEM, AGENTS ARE AT YOUR DISPOSAL.
AND ANY SPECIAL GEAR YOU'D LIKE?
AS A MATTER OF FACT... YES. I'LL GIVE YOU A LIST.
AND I NEED TO USE A PHONE... MINE MELTED.
YOU HAVE SOMEONE WHO CAN LOOK INTO THE HELO?
THERE IS SOMEONE. A RAVEN.

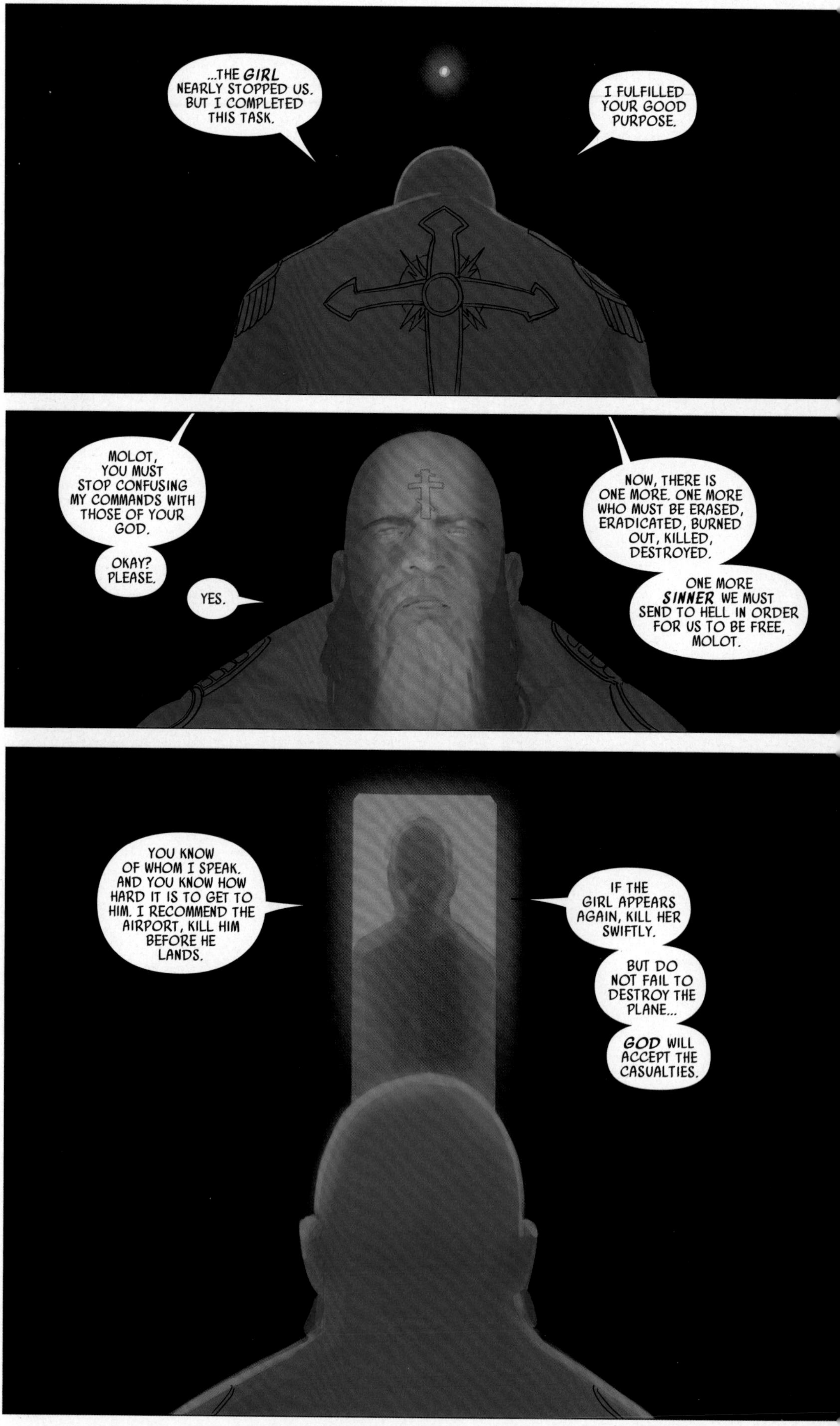
...THE GIRL NEARLY STOPPED US. BUT I COMPLETED THIS TASK.
I FULFILLED YOUR GOOD PURPOSE.
MOLOT, YOU MUST STOP CONFUSING MY COMMANDS WITH THOSE OF YOUR GOD.
OKAY? PLEASE.
YES.
NOW, THERE IS ONE MORE. ONE MORE WHO MUST BE ERASED, ERADICATED, BURNED OUT, KILLED, DESTROYED.
ONE MORE SINNER WE MUST SEND TO HELL IN ORDER FOR US TO BE FREE, MOLOT.
YOU KNOW OF WHOM I SPEAK. AND YOU KNOW HOW HARD IT IS TO GET TO HIM. I RECOMMEND THE AIRPORT, KILL HIM BEFORE HE LANDS.
IF THE GIRL APPEARS AGAIN, KILL HER SWIFTLY.
BUT DO NOT FAIL TO DESTROY THE PLANE...
GOD WILL ACCEPT THE CASUALTIES.

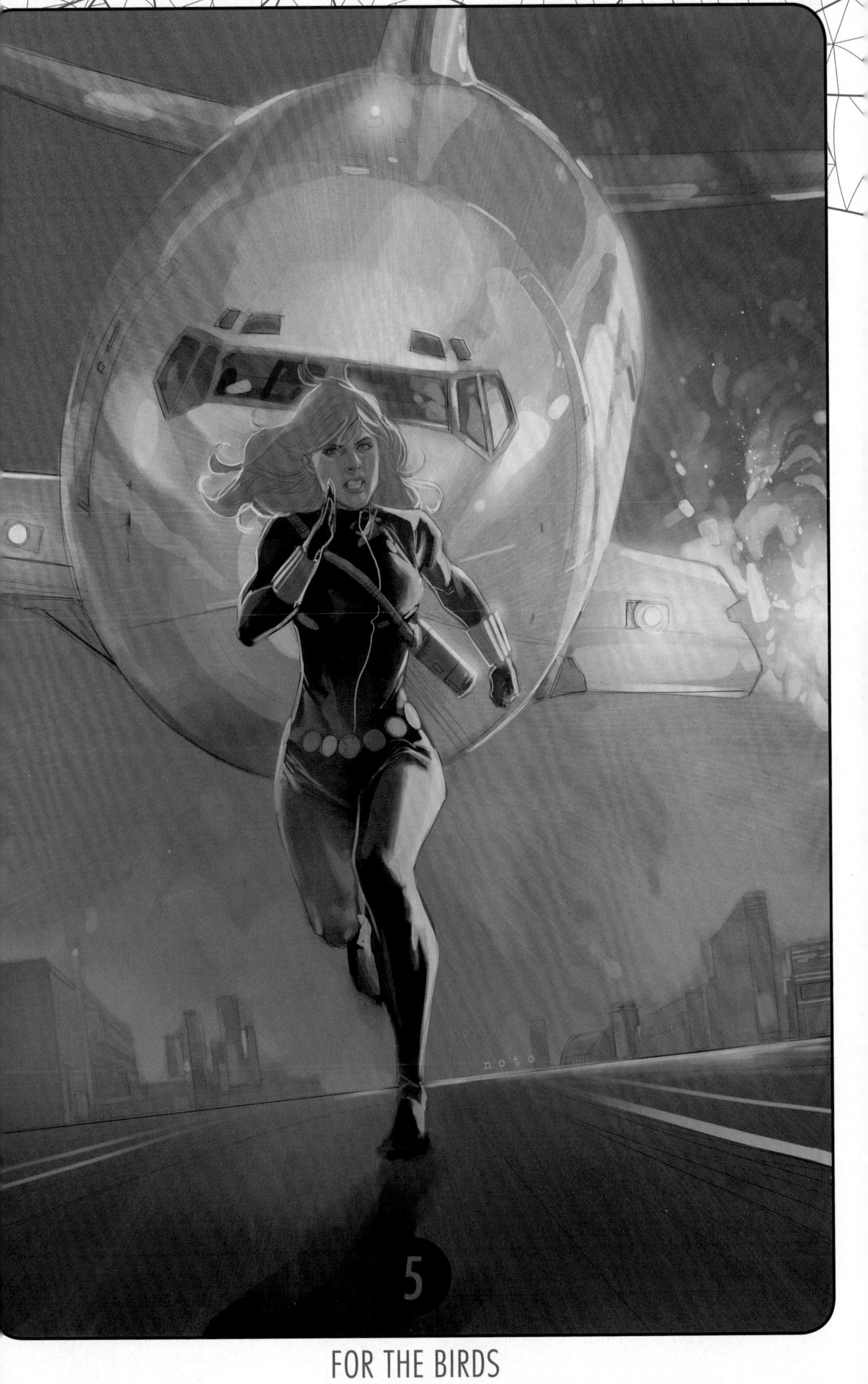
5
noto

FOR THE BIRDS

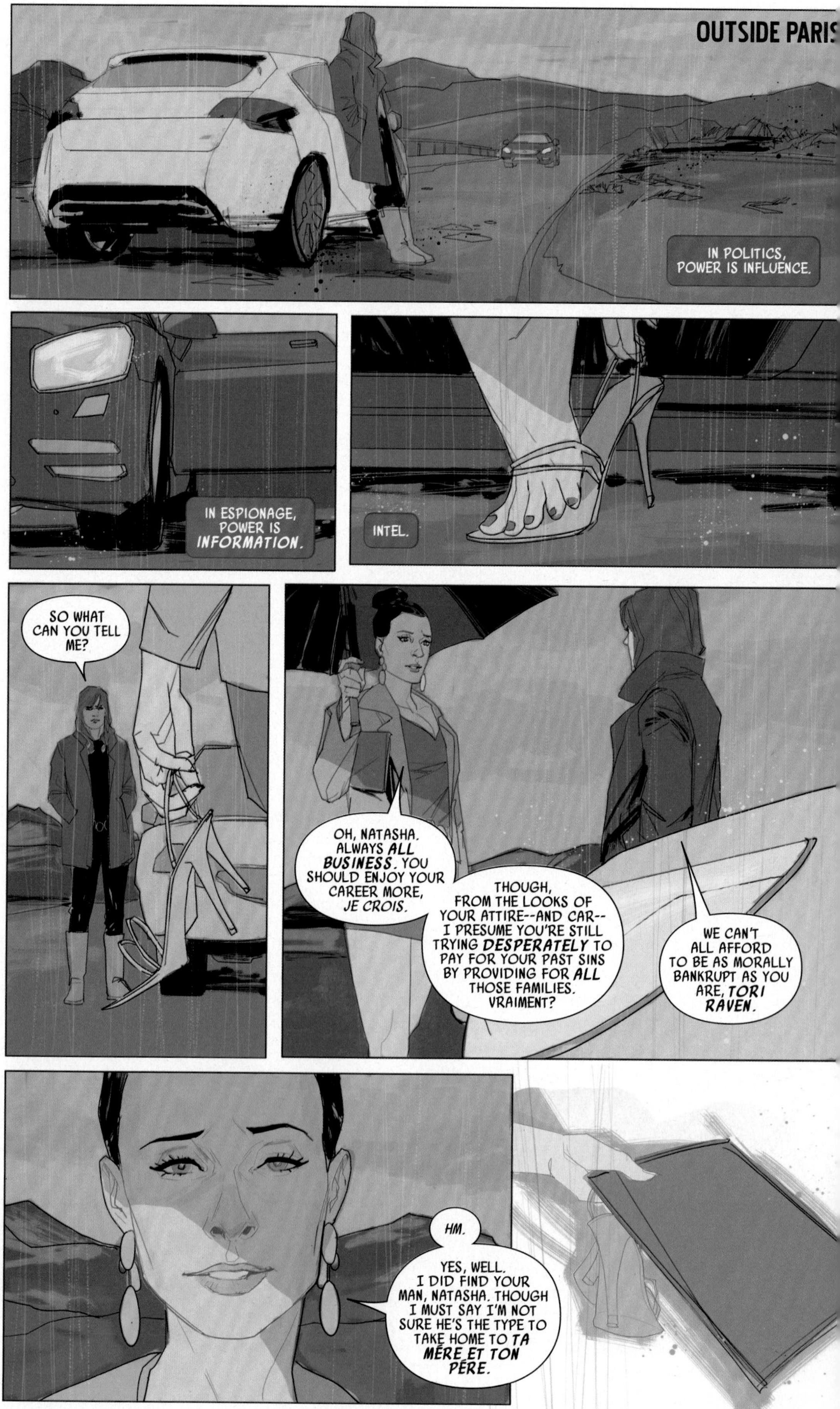
OUTSIDE PARIS
IN POLITICS, POWER IS INFLUENCE.
IN ESPIONAGE, POWER IS INFORMATION.
INTEL.
SO WHAT CAN YOU TELL ME?
OH, NATASHA. ALWAYS ALL BUSINESS. YOU SHOULD ENJOY YOUR CAREER MORE, JE CROIS.
THOUGH, FROM THE LOOKS OF YOUR ATTIRE--AND CAR--I PRESUME YOU'RE STILL TRYING DESPERATELY TO PAY FOR YOUR PAST SINS BY PROVIDING FOR ALL THOSE FAMILIES. VRAIMENT?
WE CAN'T ALL AFFORD TO BE AS MORALLY BANKRUPT AS YOU ARE, TORI RAVEN.
HM.
YES, WELL. I DID FIND YOUR MAN, NATASHA. THOUGH I MUST SAY I'M NOT SURE HE'S THE TYPE TO TAKE HOME TO TA MÉRE ET TON PÉRE.

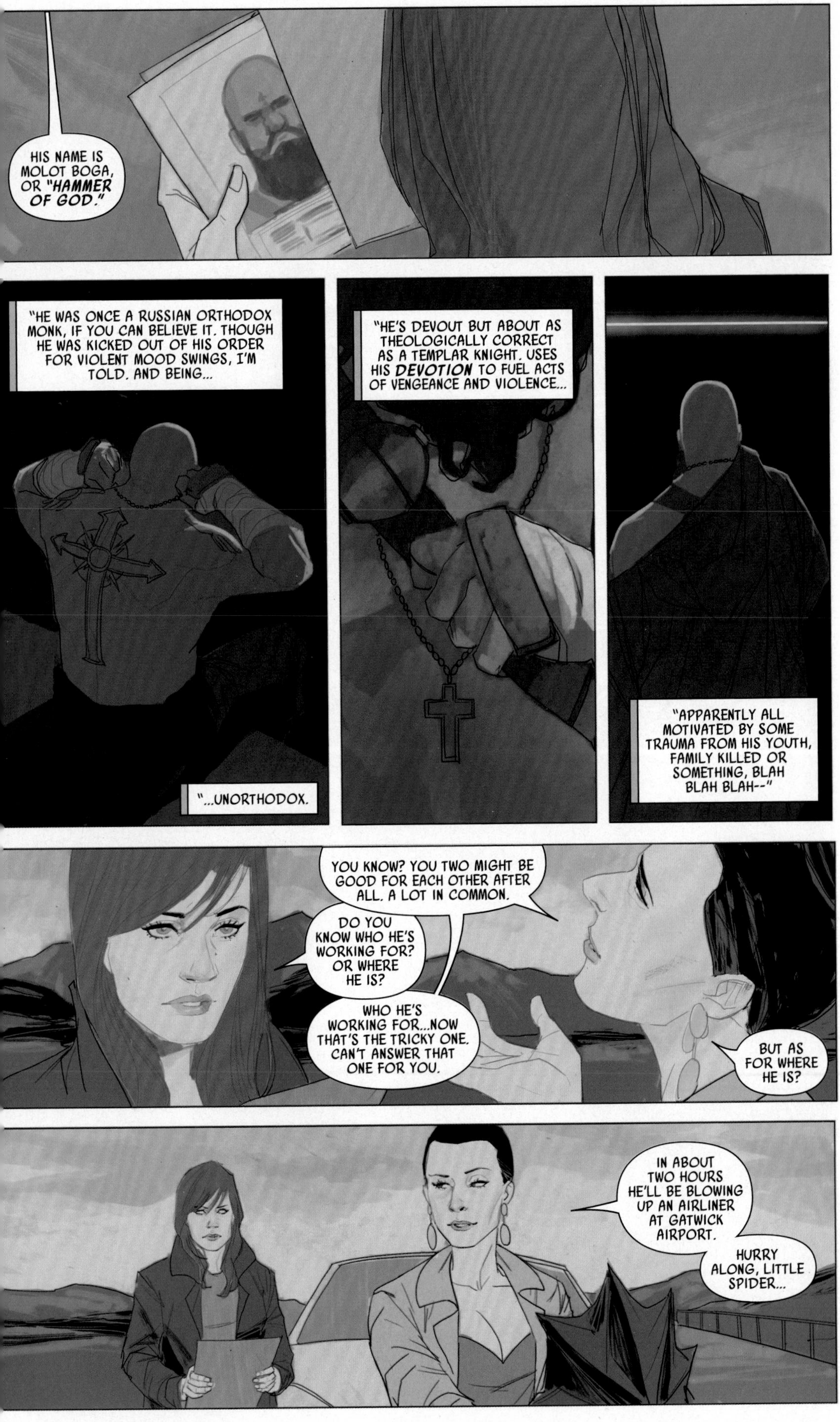

HIS NAME IS MOLOT BOGA, OR "HAMMER OF GOD."
"HE WAS ONCE A RUSSIAN ORTHODOX MONK, IF YOU CAN BELIEVE IT. THOUGH HE WAS KICKED OUT OF HIS ORDER FOR VIOLENT MOOD SWINGS, I'M TOLD. AND BEING...
"...UNORTHODOX.
"HE'S DEVOUT BUT ABOUT AS THEOLOGICALLY CORRECT AS A TEMPLAR KNIGHT. USES HIS DEVOTION TO FUEL ACTS OF VENGEANCE AND VIOLENCE...
"APPARENTLY ALL MOTIVATED BY SOME TRAUMA FROM HIS YOUTH, FAMILY KILLED OR SOMETHING, BLAH BLAH BLAH--"
YOU KNOW? YOU TWO MIGHT BE GOOD FOR EACH OTHER AFTER ALL. A LOT IN COMMON.
DO YOU KNOW WHO HE'S WORKING FOR? OR WHERE HE IS?
WHO HE'S WORKING FOR...NOW THAT'S THE TRICKY ONE. CAN'T ANSWER THAT ONE FOR YOU.
BUT AS FOR WHERE HE IS?
IN ABOUT TWO HOURS HE'LL BE BLOWING UP AN AIRLINER AT GATWICK AIRPORT.
HURRY ALONG, LITTLE SPIDER...

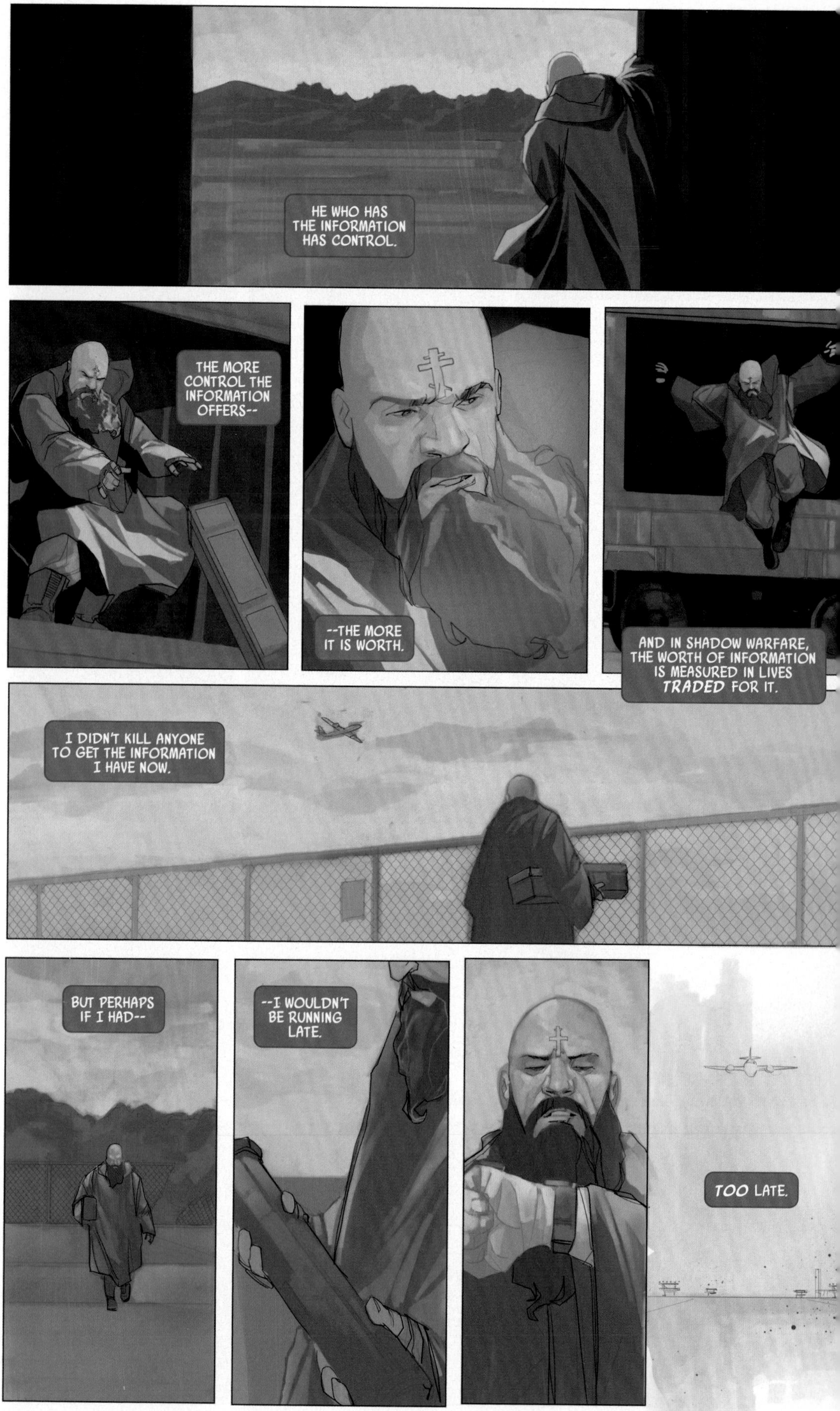

HE WHO HAS THE INFORMATION HAS CONTROL.
THE MORE CONTROL THE INFORMATION OFFERS--
--THE MORE IT IS WORTH.
AND IN SHADOW WARFARE, THE WORTH OF INFORMATION IS MEASURED IN LIVES TRADED FOR IT.
I DIDN'T KILL ANYONE TO GET THE INFORMATION I HAVE NOW.
BUT PERHAPS IF I HAD--
--I WOULDN'T BE RUNNING LATE.
TOO LATE.

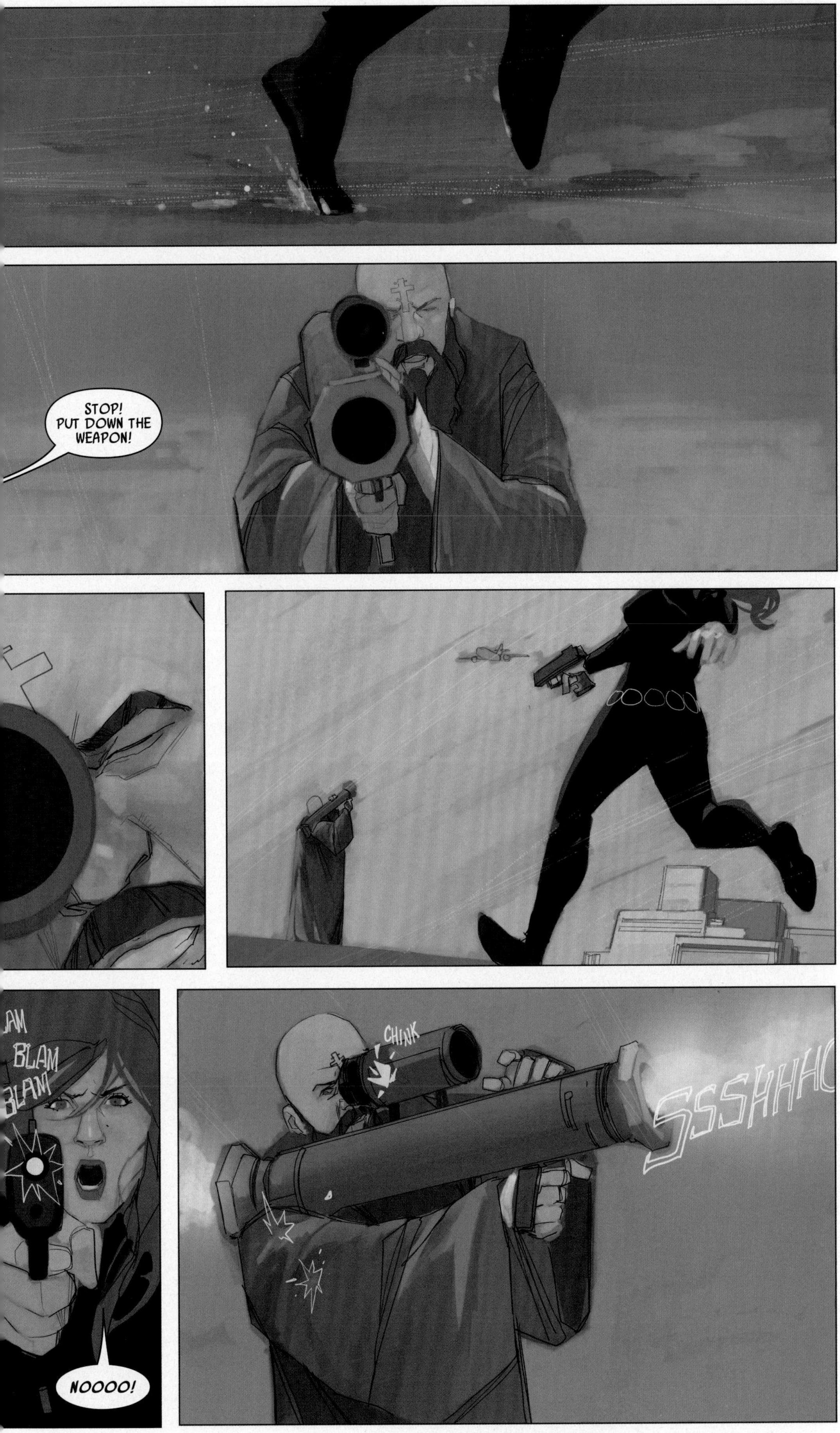
STOP! PUT DOWN THE WEAPON!
BLAM
BLAM
BLAM
CHINK
SSSHHHO
NOOOO!

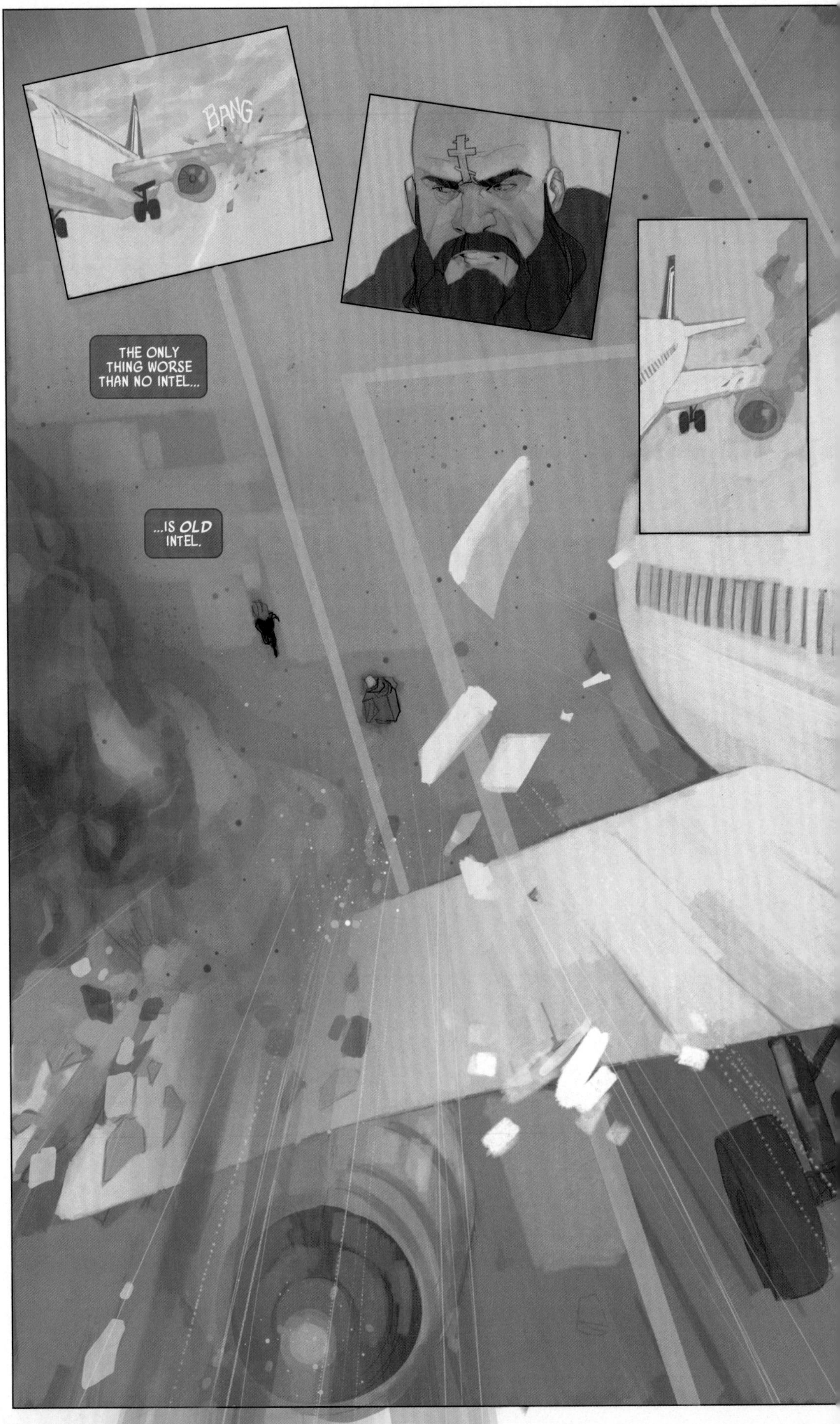
BANG
THE ONLY THING WORSE THAN NO INTEL...
...IS OLD INTEL.

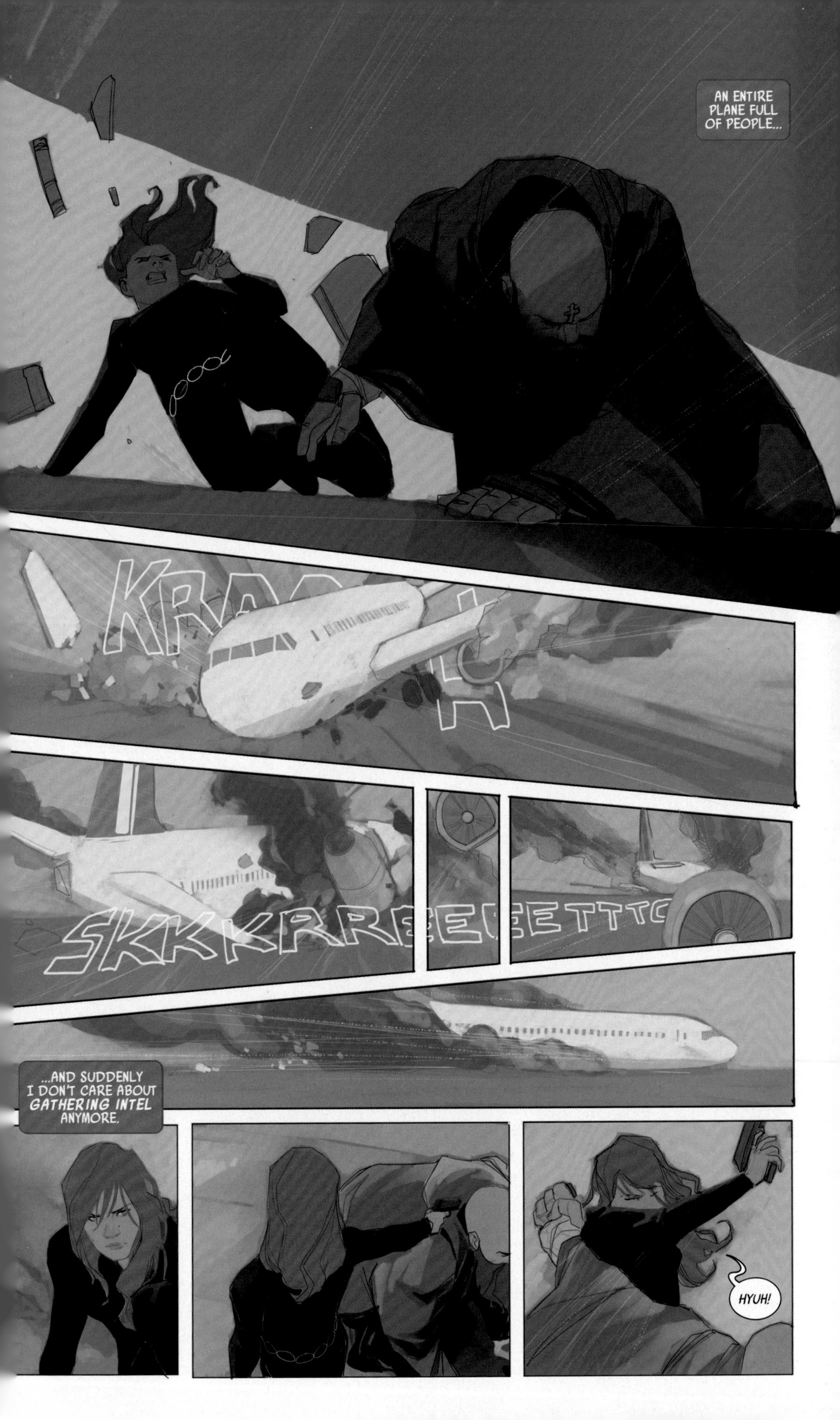

AN ENTIRE PLANE FULL OF PEOPLE...
SKKRREEEETTTC
...AND SUDDENLY I DON'T CARE ABOUT GATHERING INTEL ANYMORE.
HYUH!

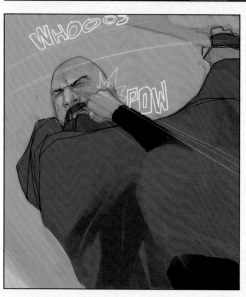

THE INSTRUMENT OF GOD CANNOT BE--

YOU KNOW, MOLOT--

--I'M FAIRLY SURE IT'S NOT *GOD'S* WORK YOU'RE DOING.

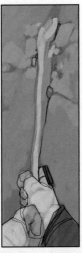

THEY MUST BE PUNISHED FOR THEIR SINS.

PRO TIP: (OFTEN LEARNED TOO LATE) DON'T ARGUE WITH CRAZY.

JUST EXPECT CRAZY...

BAMM

BAMM

...TO BE &@#$%&# INSANE.

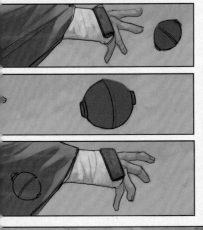

BOOM

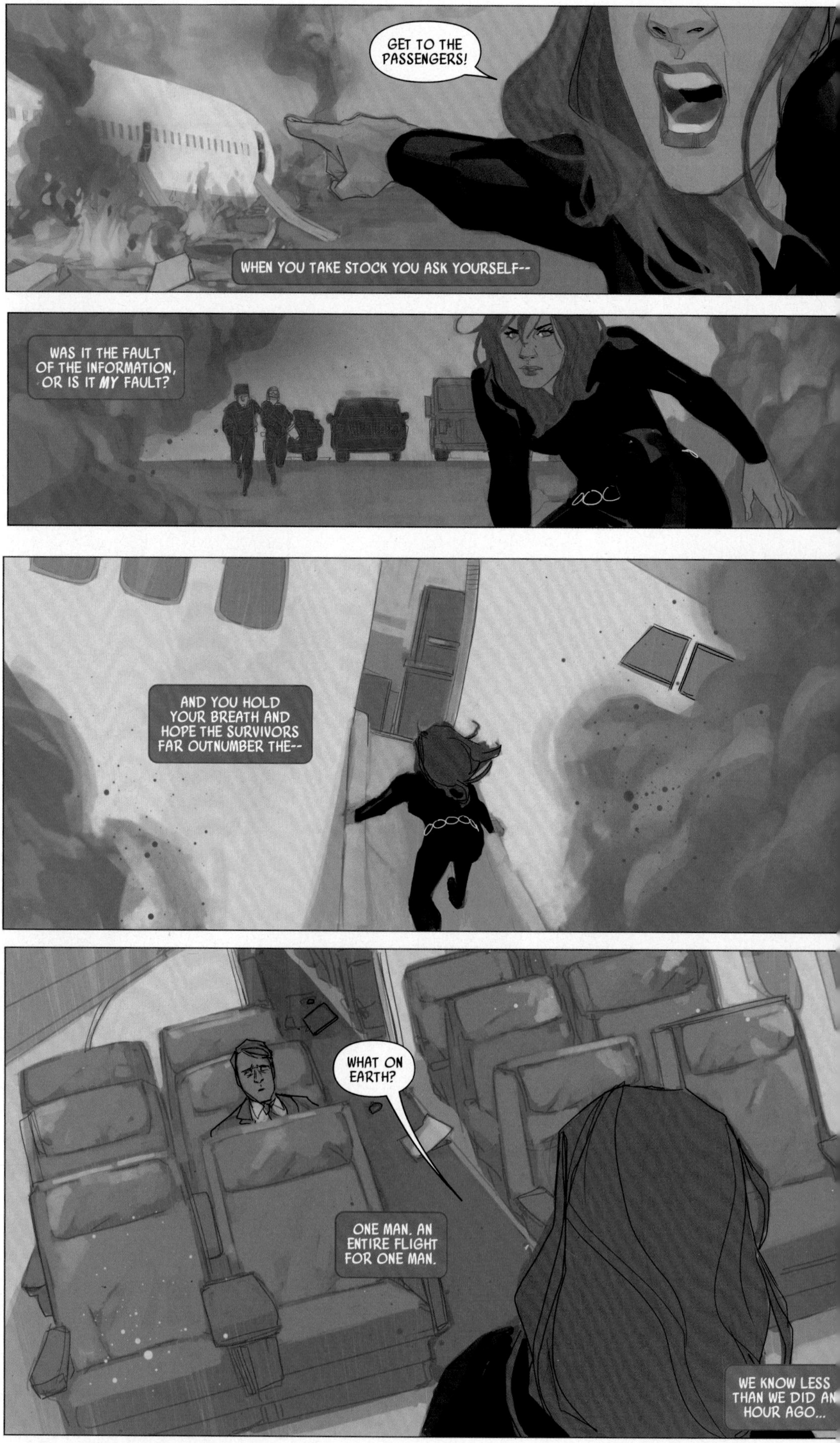
GET TO THE PASSENGERS!
WHEN YOU TAKE STOCK YOU ASK YOURSELF--
WAS IT THE FAULT OF THE INFORMATION, OR IS IT *MY* FAULT?
AND YOU HOLD YOUR BREATH AND HOPE THE SURVIVORS FAR OUTNUMBER THE--
WHAT ON EARTH?
ONE MAN. AN ENTIRE FLIGHT FOR ONE MAN.
WE KNOW LESS THAN WE DID AN HOUR AGO...

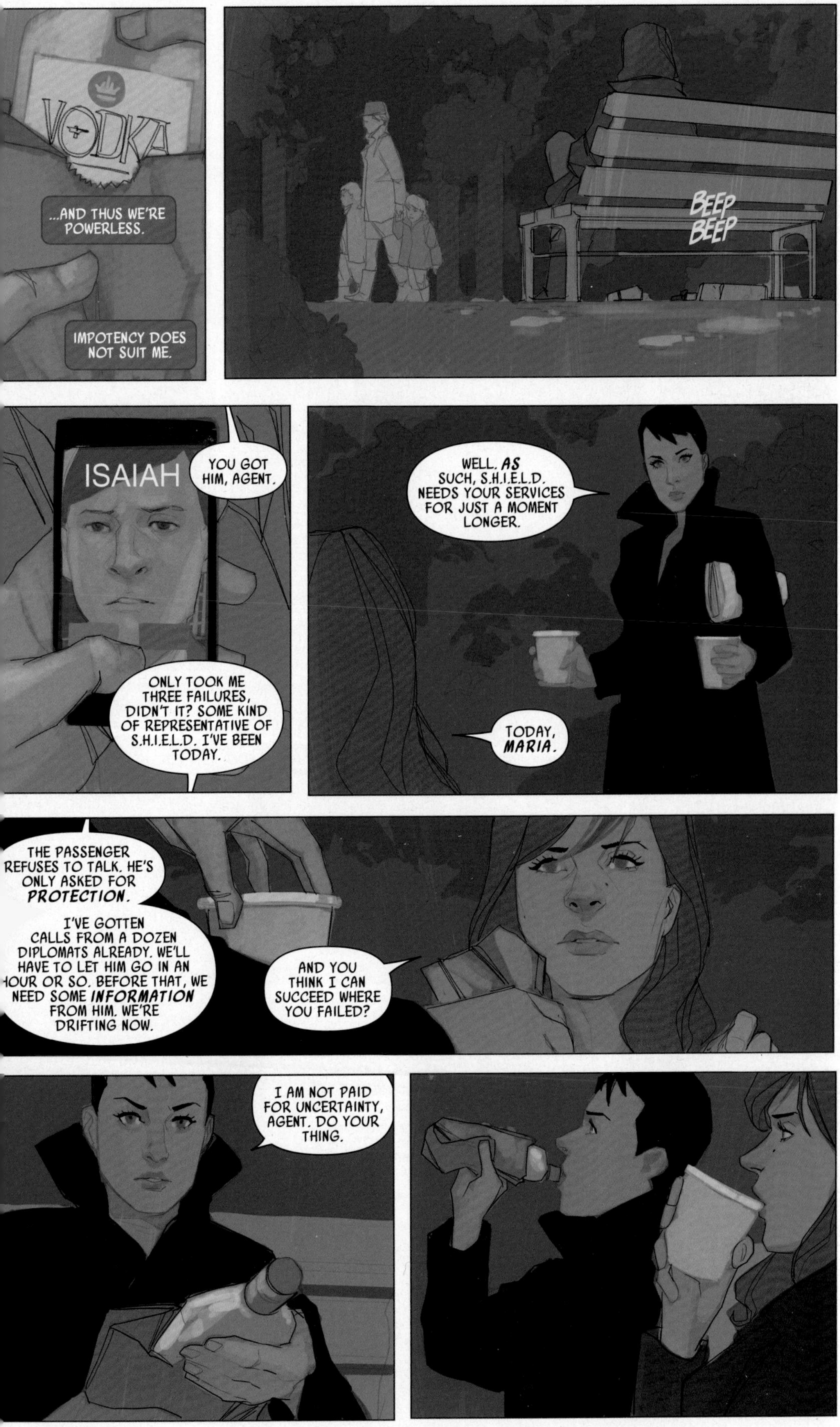

VODKA
...AND THUS WE'RE POWERLESS.
IMPOTENCY DOES NOT SUIT ME.
BEEP BEEP
ISAIAH
YOU GOT HIM, AGENT.
ONLY TOOK ME THREE FAILURES, DIDN'T IT? SOME KIND OF REPRESENTATIVE OF S.H.I.E.L.D. I'VE BEEN TODAY.
WELL. AS SUCH, S.H.I.E.L.D. NEEDS YOUR SERVICES FOR JUST A MOMENT LONGER.
TODAY, MARIA.
THE PASSENGER REFUSES TO TALK. HE'S ONLY ASKED FOR PROTECTION.
I'VE GOTTEN CALLS FROM A DOZEN DIPLOMATS ALREADY. WE'LL HAVE TO LET HIM GO IN AN HOUR OR SO. BEFORE THAT, WE NEED SOME INFORMATION FROM HIM. WE'RE DRIFTING NOW.
AND YOU THINK I CAN SUCCEED WHERE YOU FAILED?
I AM NOT PAID FOR UNCERTAINTY, AGENT. DO YOUR THING.

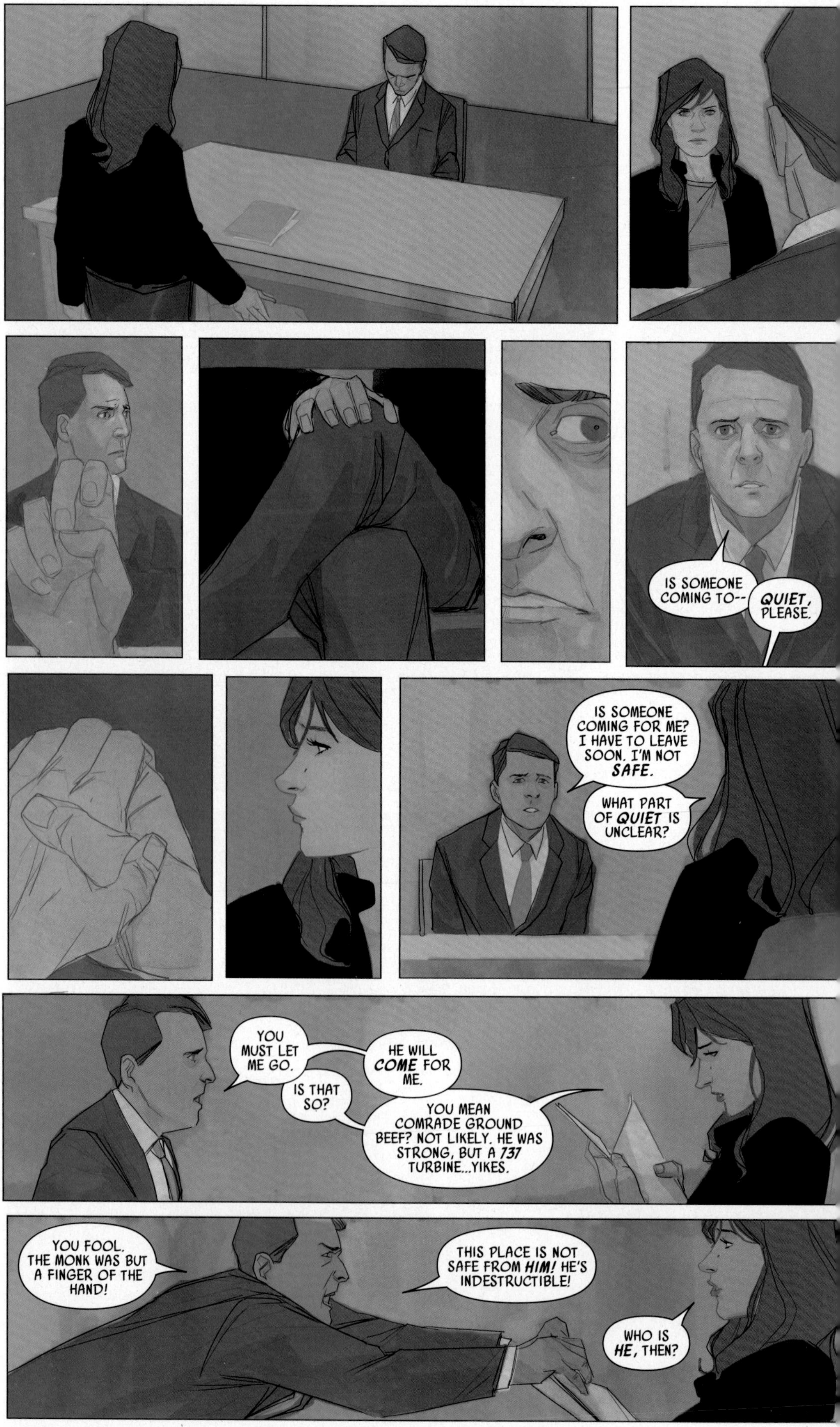
IS SOMEONE COMING TO--
QUIET, PLEASE.
IS SOMEONE COMING FOR ME? I HAVE TO LEAVE SOON. I'M NOT SAFE.
WHAT PART OF QUIET IS UNCLEAR?
YOU MUST LET ME GO.
HE WILL COME FOR ME.
IS THAT SO?
YOU MEAN COMRADE GROUND BEEF? NOT LIKELY. HE WAS STRONG, BUT A 737 TURBINE...YIKES.
YOU FOOL. THE MONK WAS BUT A FINGER OF THE HAND!
THIS PLACE IS NOT SAFE FROM HIM! HE'S INDESTRUCTIBLE!
WHO IS HE, THEN?

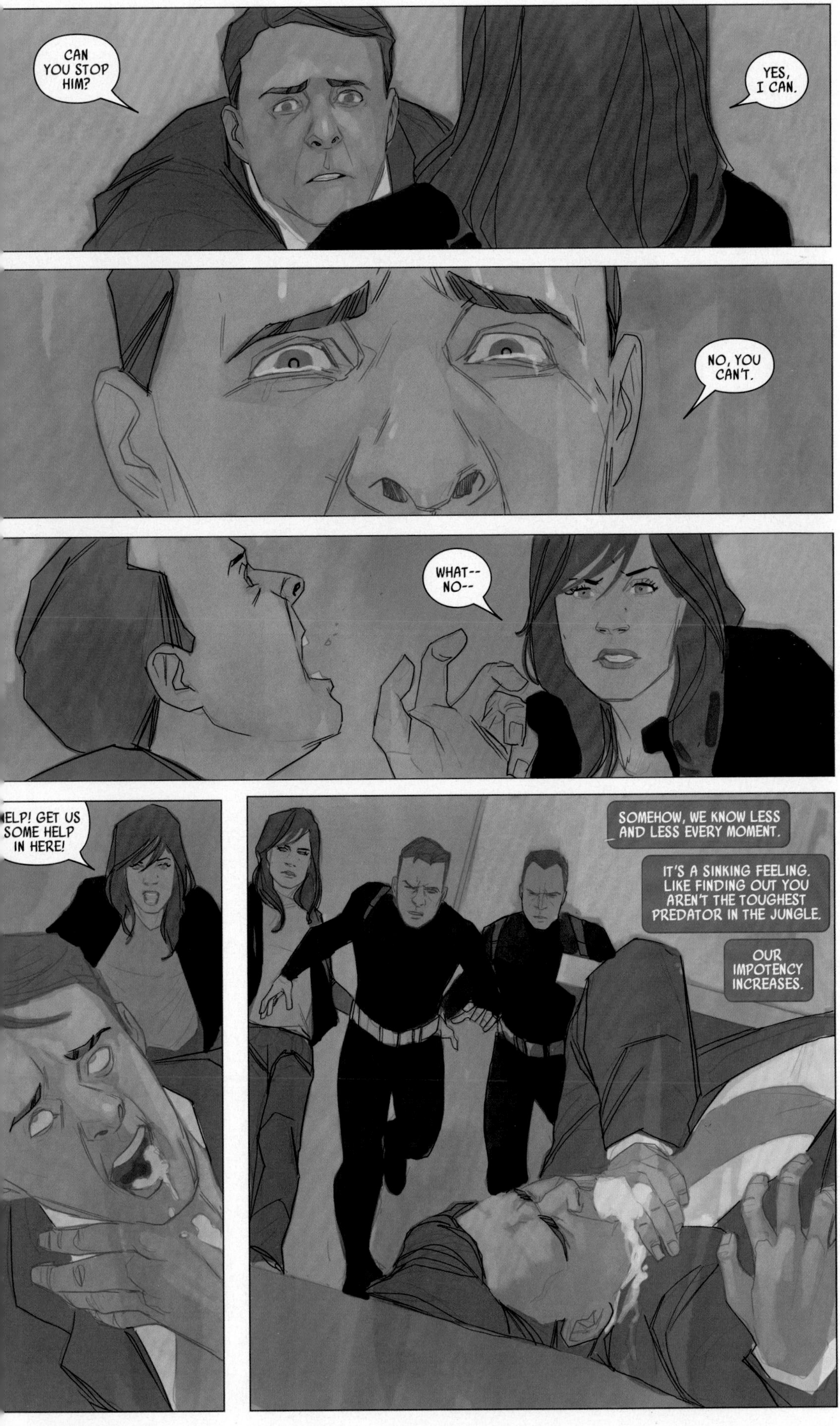
CAN YOU STOP HIM?
YES, I CAN.
NO, YOU CAN'T.
WHAT-- NO--
ELP! GET US SOME HELP IN HERE!
SOMEHOW, WE KNOW LESS AND LESS EVERY MOMENT.
IT'S A SINKING FEELING. LIKE FINDING OUT YOU AREN'T THE TOUGHEST PREDATOR IN THE JUNGLE.
OUR IMPOTENCY INCREASES.

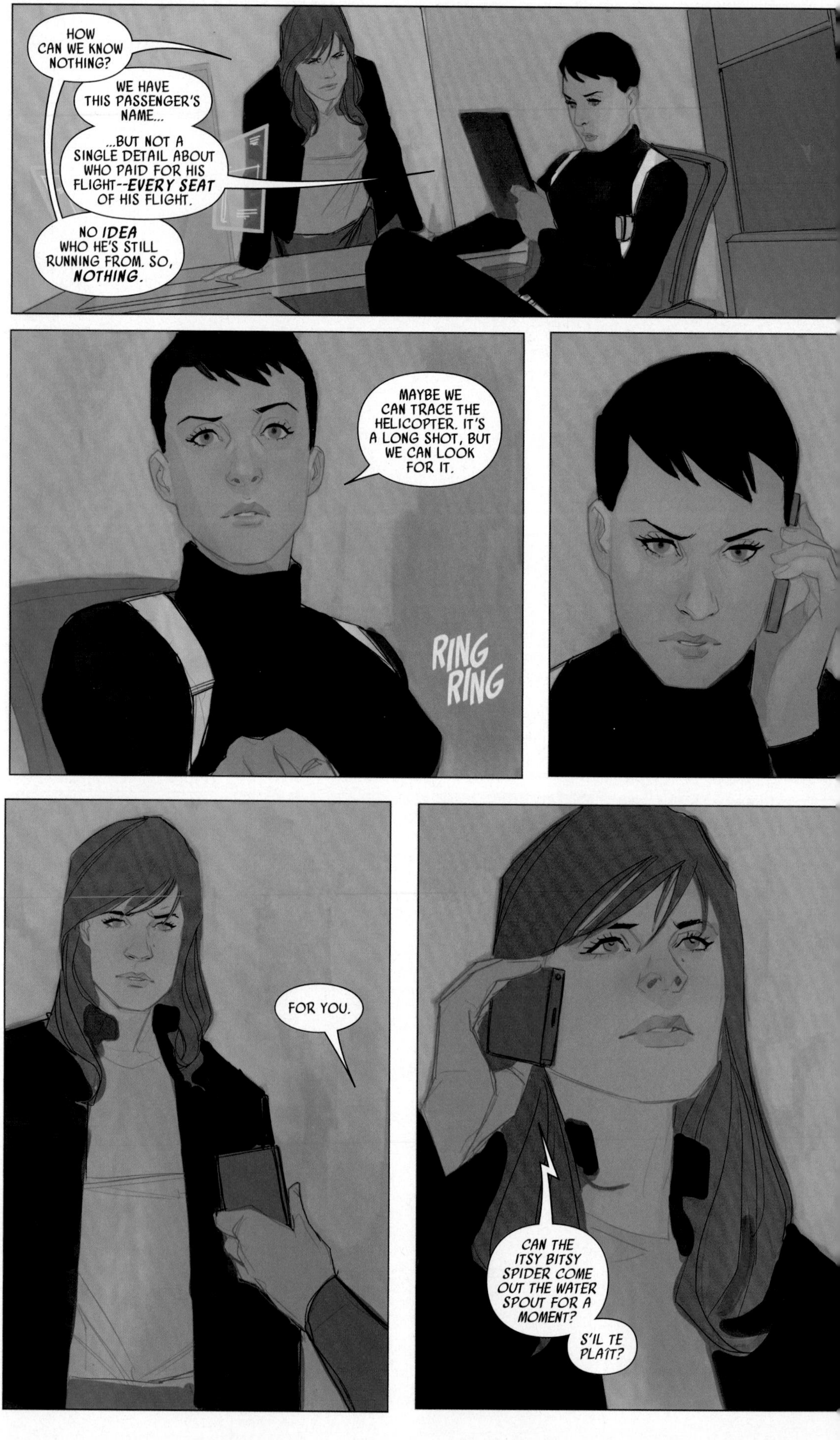
HOW CAN WE KNOW NOTHING?
WE HAVE THIS PASSENGER'S NAME...
...BUT NOT A SINGLE DETAIL ABOUT WHO PAID FOR HIS FLIGHT--EVERY SEAT OF HIS FLIGHT.
NO IDEA WHO HE'S STILL RUNNING FROM. SO, NOTHING.
MAYBE WE CAN TRACE THE HELICOPTER. IT'S A LONG SHOT, BUT WE CAN LOOK FOR IT.
RING RING
FOR YOU.
CAN THE ITSY BITSY SPIDER COME OUT THE WATER SPOUT FOR A MOMENT?
S'IL TE PLAÎT?

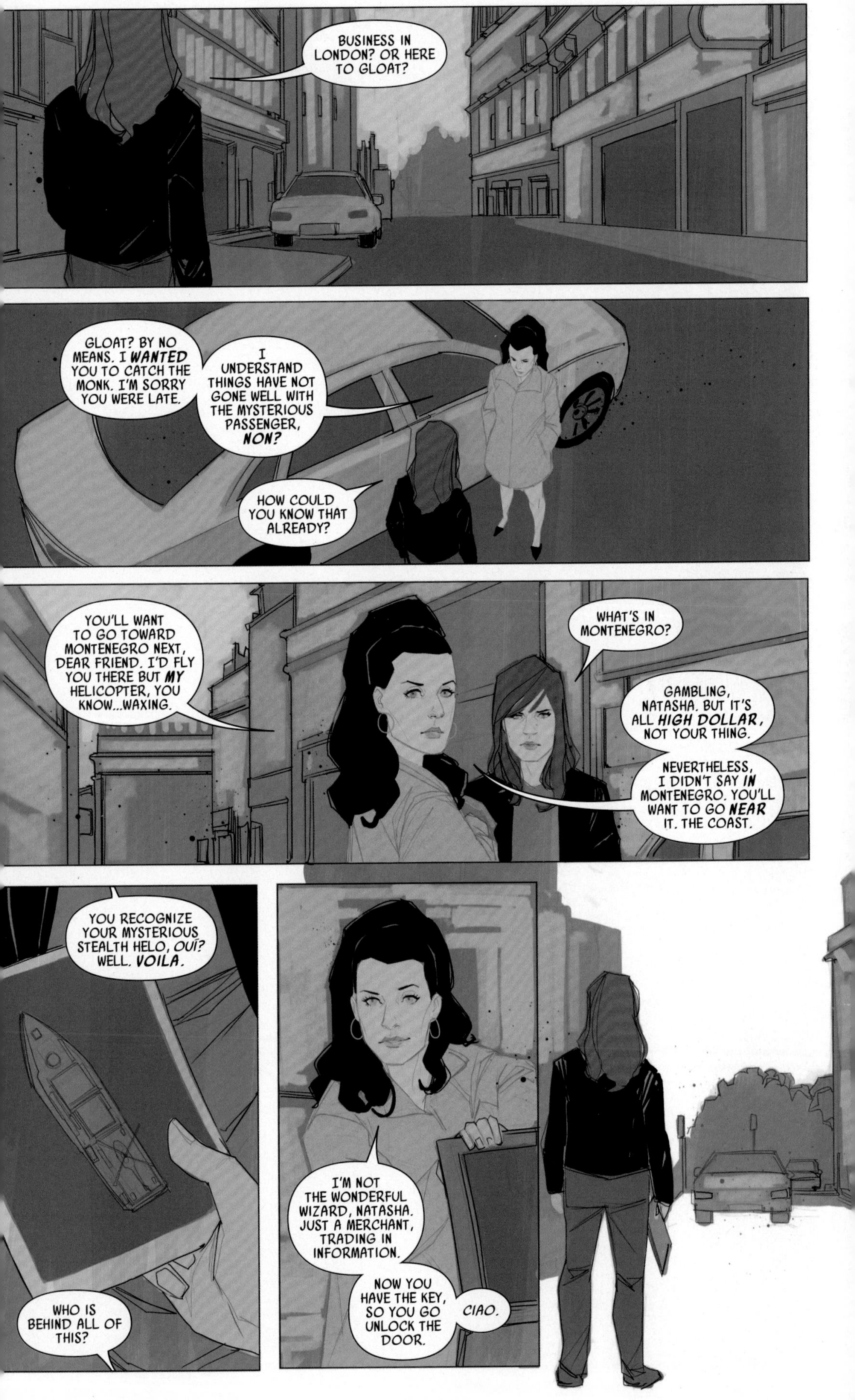
BUSINESS IN LONDON? OR HERE TO GLOAT?
GLOAT? BY NO MEANS. I WANTED YOU TO CATCH THE MONK. I'M SORRY YOU WERE LATE.
I UNDERSTAND THINGS HAVE NOT GONE WELL WITH THE MYSTERIOUS PASSENGER, NON?
HOW COULD YOU KNOW THAT ALREADY?
YOU'LL WANT TO GO TOWARD MONTENEGRO NEXT, DEAR FRIEND. I'D FLY YOU THERE BUT MY HELICOPTER, YOU KNOW...WAXING.
WHAT'S IN MONTENEGRO?
GAMBLING, NATASHA. BUT IT'S ALL HIGH DOLLAR, NOT YOUR THING.
NEVERTHELESS, I DIDN'T SAY IN MONTENEGRO. YOU'LL WANT TO GO NEAR IT. THE COAST.
YOU RECOGNIZE YOUR MYSTERIOUS STEALTH HELO, OUI? WELL. VOILA.
WHO IS BEHIND ALL OF THIS?
I'M NOT THE WONDERFUL WIZARD, NATASHA. JUST A MERCHANT, TRADING IN INFORMATION.
NOW YOU HAVE THE KEY, SO YOU GO UNLOCK THE DOOR.
CIAO.

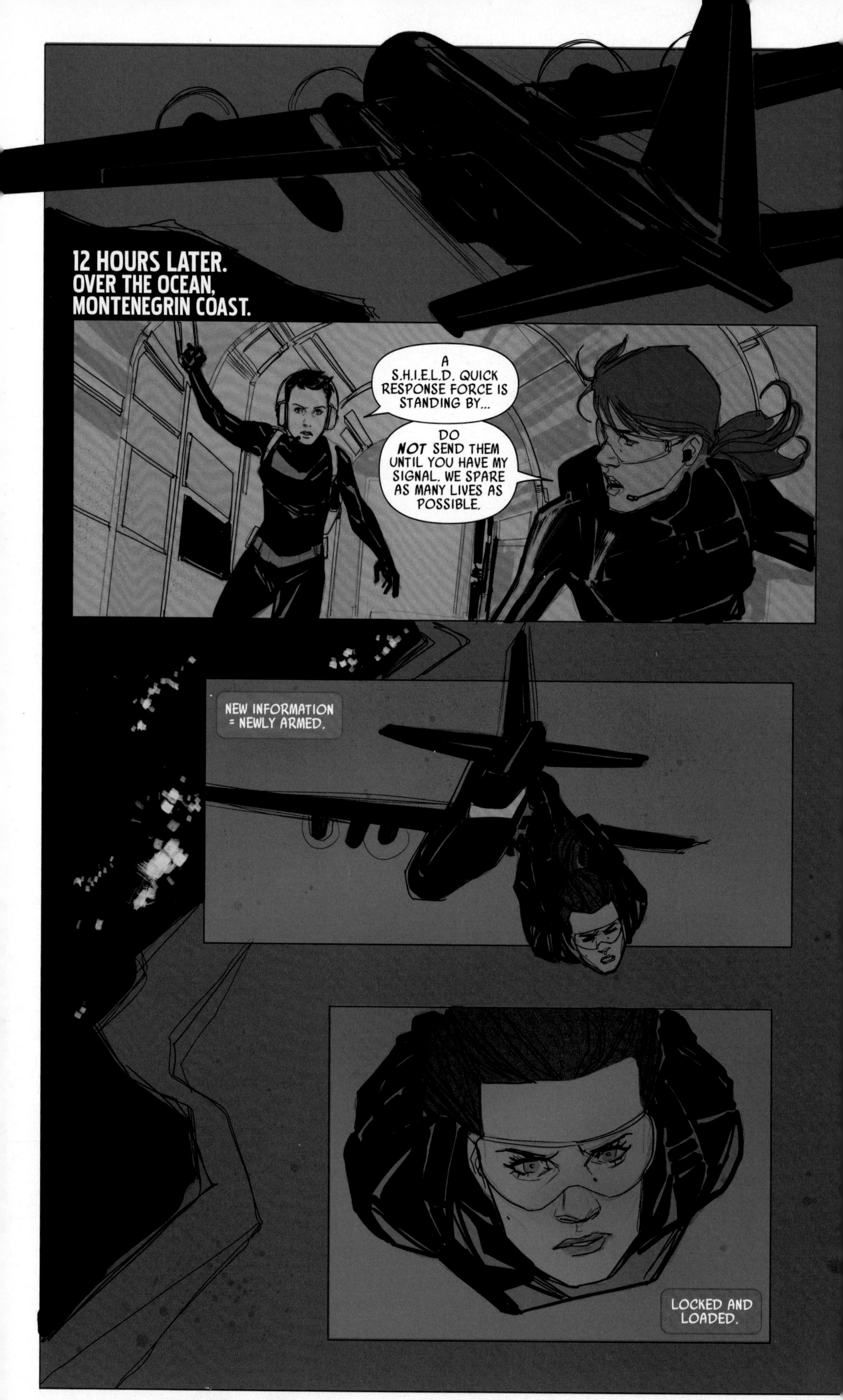
12 HOURS LATER. OVER THE OCEAN, MONTENEGRIN COAST.
A S.H.I.E.L.D. QUICK RESPONSE FORCE IS STANDING BY...
DO NOT SEND THEM UNTIL YOU HAVE MY SIGNAL. WE SPARE AS MANY LIVES AS POSSIBLE.
NEW INFORMATION = NEWLY ARMED.
LOCKED AND LOADED.

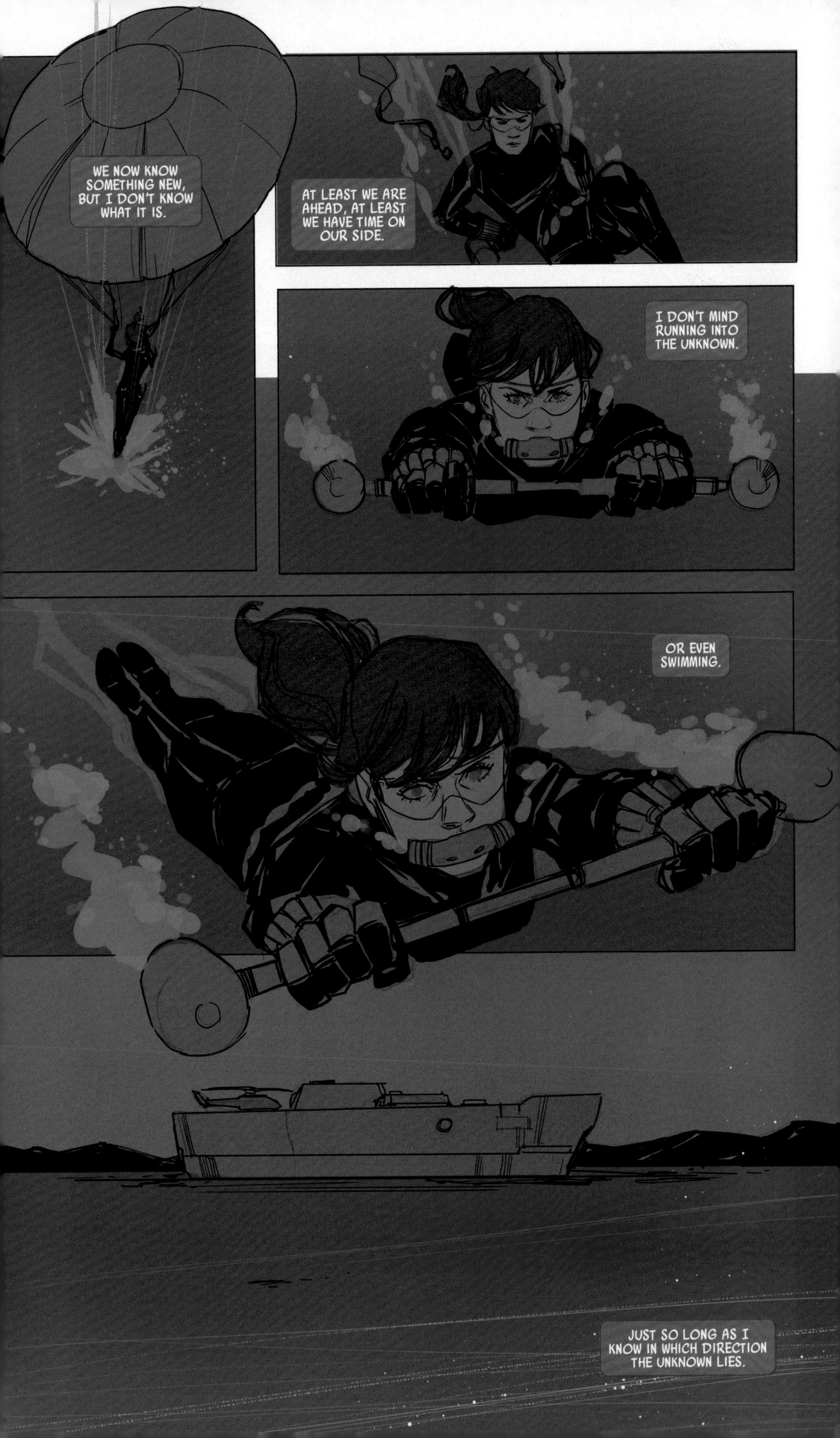
WE NOW KNOW SOMETHING NEW, BUT I DON'T KNOW WHAT IT IS.
AT LEAST WE ARE AHEAD, AT LEAST WE HAVE TIME ON OUR SIDE.
I DON'T MIND RUNNING INTO THE UNKNOWN.
OR EVEN SWIMMING.
JUST SO LONG AS I KNOW IN WHICH DIRECTION THE UNKNOWN LIES.

I SUDDENLY HAVE THAT SINKING FEELING AGAIN.

YEAH...

BLIND INTELLIGENCE IS LIKE AN UNPROVEN WEAPON.

IT SOMETIMES LEAVES YOU S.O.L.

IF YOU TRY TO MOVE, YOU WILL DIE.

THESE LASERS CAN HIT SOMETHING FIFTY FEET BELOW THE SURFACE.

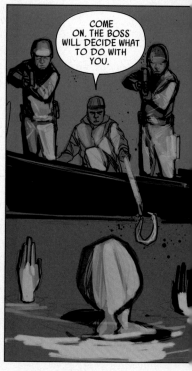

COME ON. THE BOSS WILL DECIDE WHAT TO DO WITH YOU.

NATALIA ROMANOVA, IS IT?

NOW SOMETHING BECOMES CLEAR...

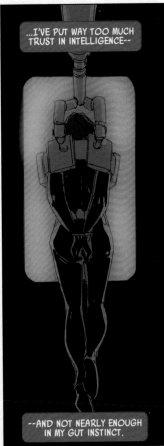

...I'VE PUT WAY TOO MUCH TRUST IN INTELLIGENCE--

--AND NOT NEARLY ENOUGH IN MY GUT INSTINCT.

I'M IN OVER MY HEAD, AND I HAVE NO ONE TO BLAME BUT MYSELF.

MISS NATASHA, YOU COME HERE, I HOPE, WITH SOME NEWS FOR ME.

DAMON DRAN?

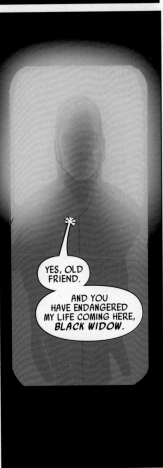

YES, OLD FRIEND.

AND YOU HAVE ENDANGERED MY LIFE COMING HERE, BLACK WIDOW.

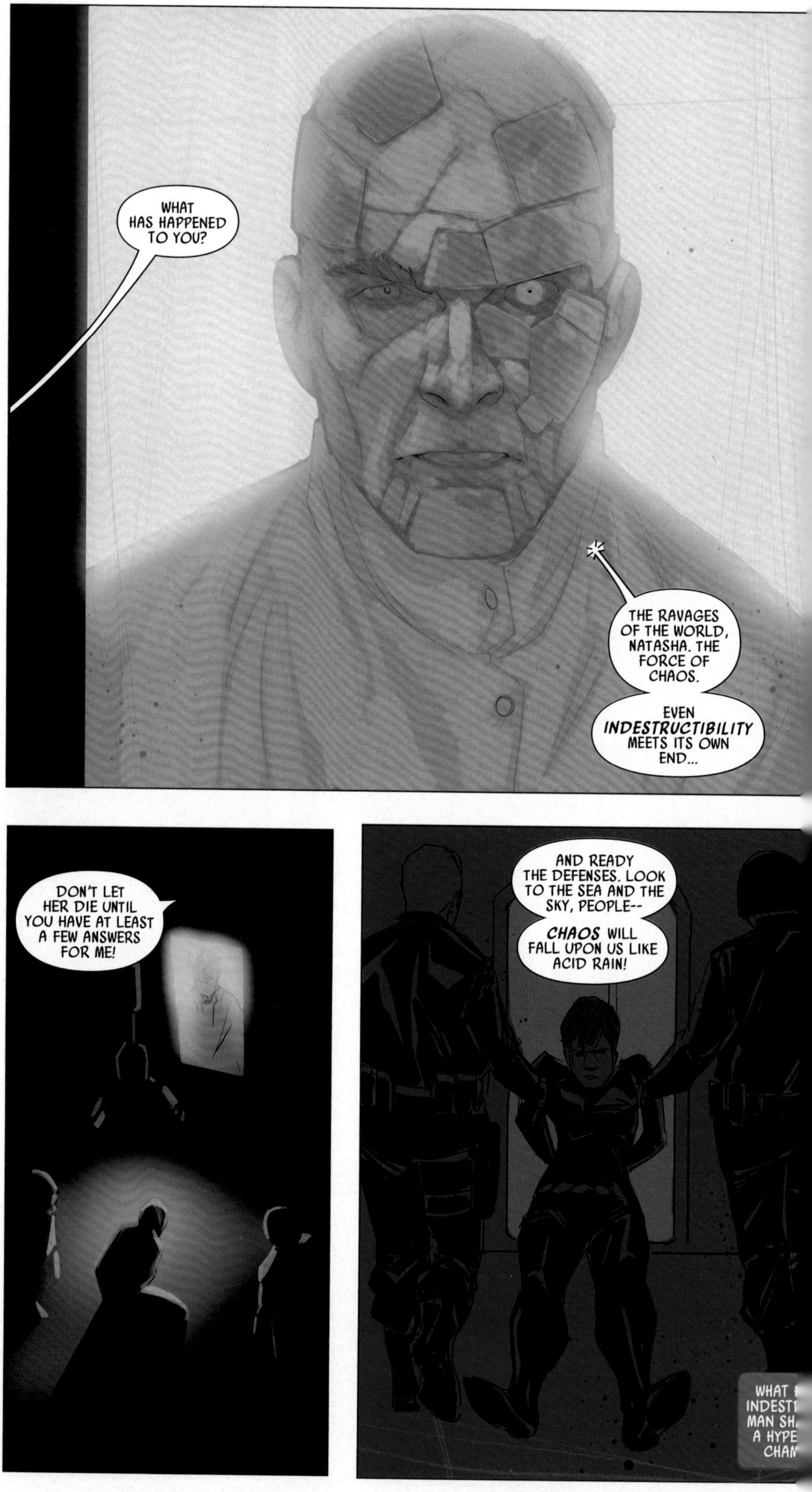
WHAT HAS HAPPENED TO YOU?
THE RAVAGES OF THE WORLD, NATASHA. THE FORCE OF CHAOS.
EVEN *INDESTRUCTIBILITY* MEETS ITS OWN END...
DON'T LET HER DIE UNTIL YOU HAVE AT LEAST A FEW ANSWERS FOR ME!
AND READY THE DEFENSES. LOOK TO THE SEA AND THE SKY, PEOPLE--
CHAOS WILL FALL UPON US LIKE ACID RAIN!

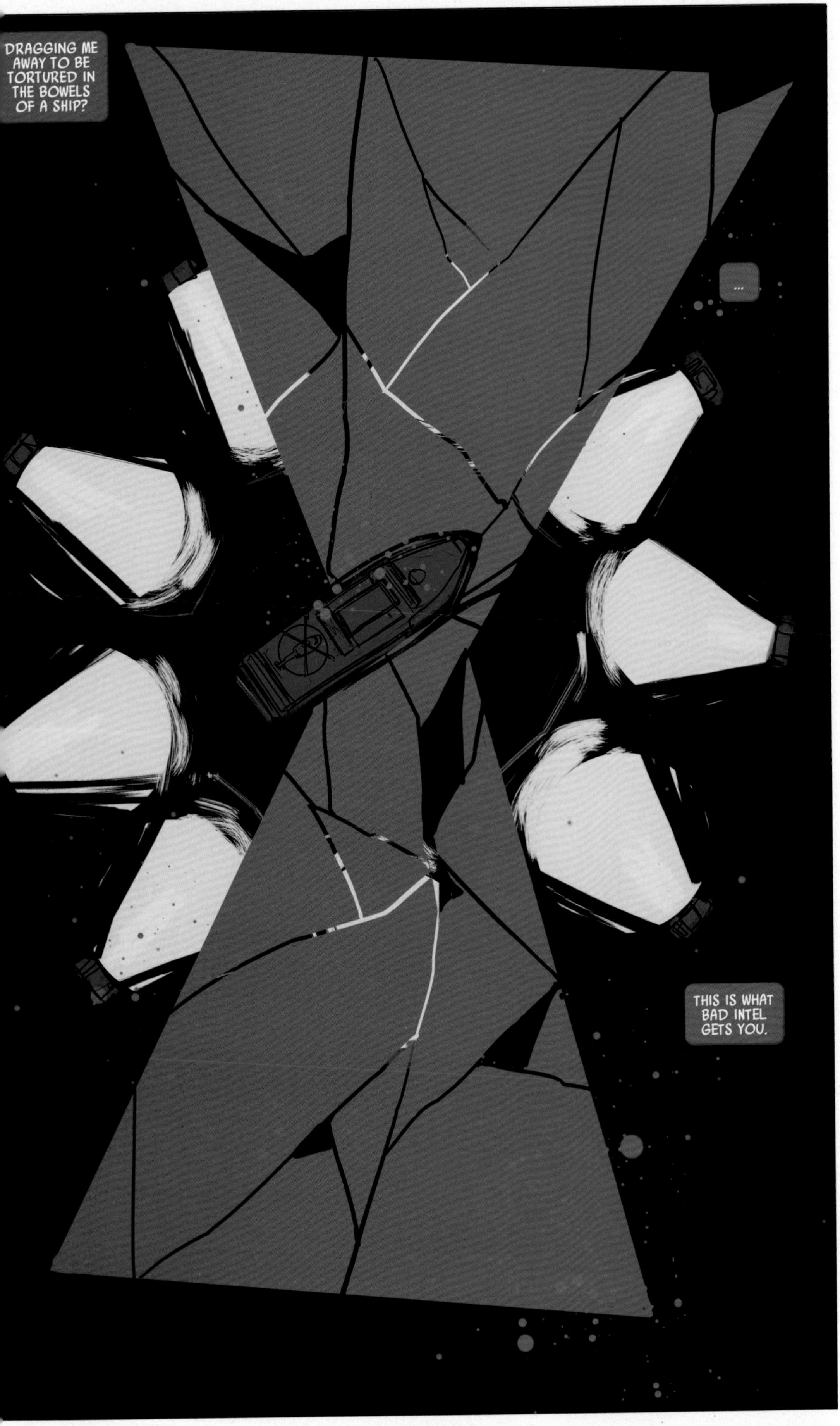
DRAGGING ME AWAY TO BE TORTURED IN THE BOWELS OF A SHIP?
...
THIS IS WHAT BAD INTEL GETS YOU.

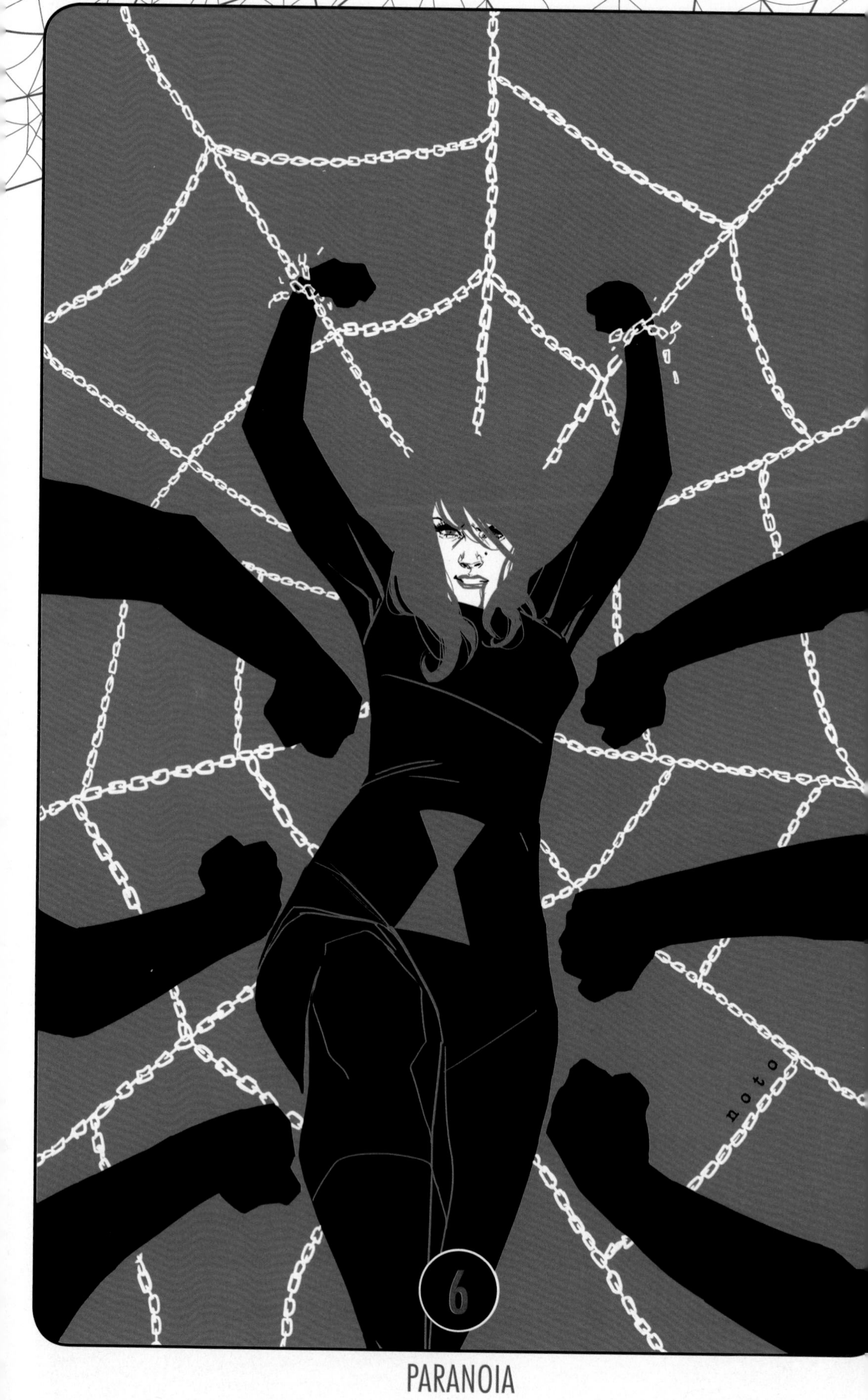
6

PARANOIA

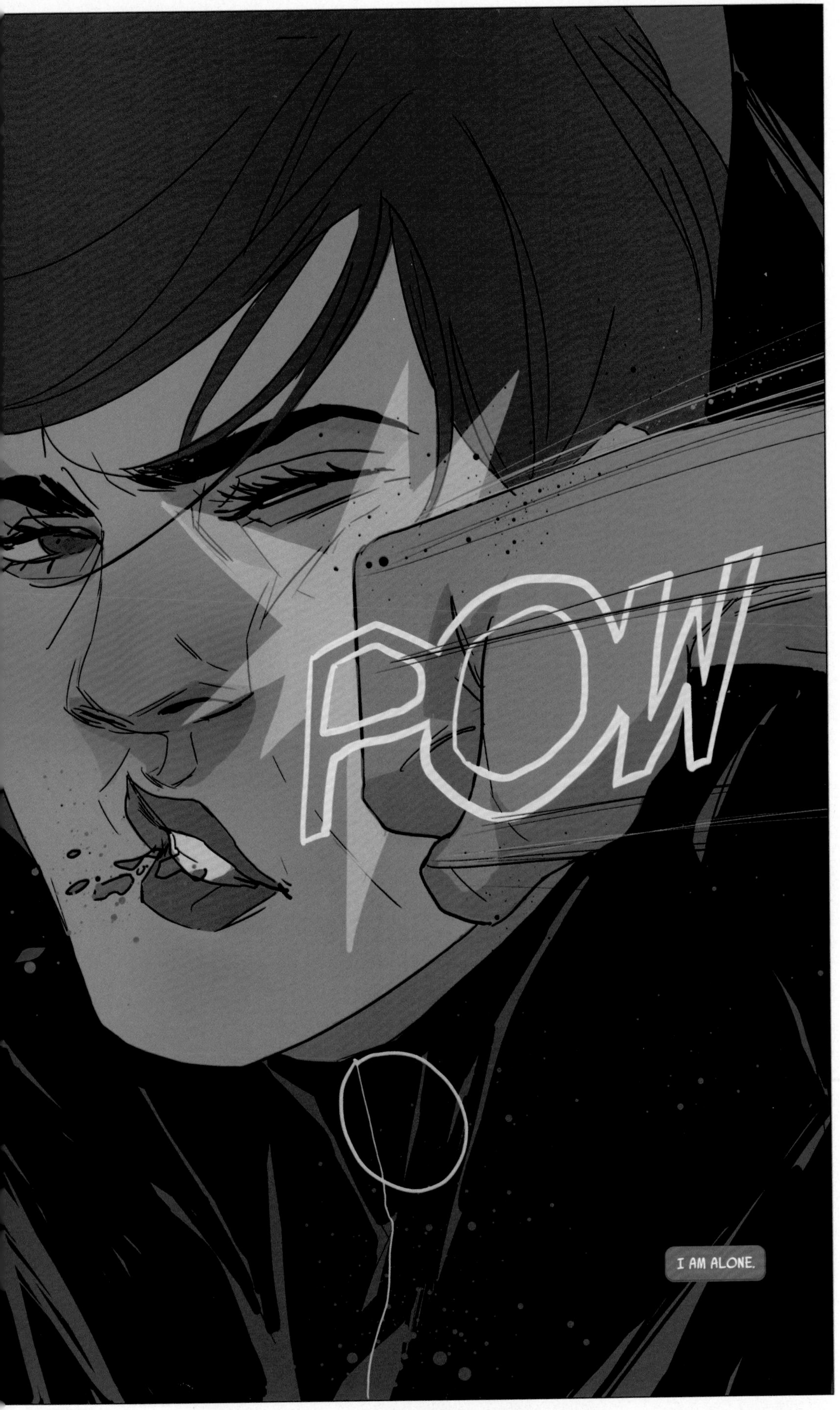
POW
I AM ALONE.

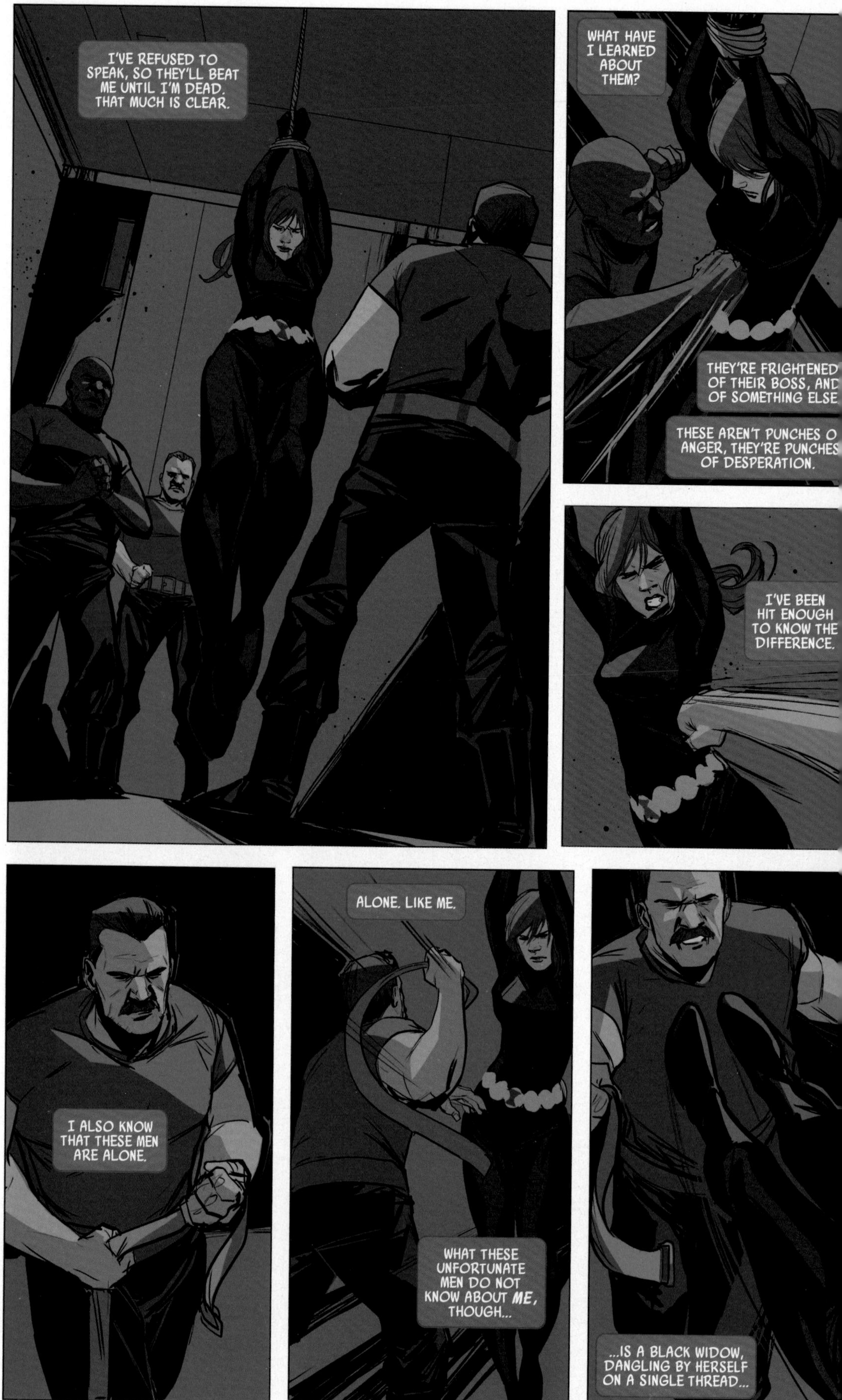
I'VE REFUSED TO SPEAK, SO THEY'LL BEAT ME UNTIL I'M DEAD. THAT MUCH IS CLEAR.
WHAT HAVE I LEARNED ABOUT THEM?
THEY'RE FRIGHTENED OF THEIR BOSS, AND OF SOMETHING ELSE
THESE AREN'T PUNCHES O ANGER, THEY'RE PUNCHES OF DESPERATION.
I'VE BEEN HIT ENOUGH TO KNOW THE DIFFERENCE.
I ALSO KNOW THAT THESE MEN ARE ALONE.
ALONE. LIKE ME.
WHAT THESE UNFORTUNATE MEN DO NOT KNOW ABOUT *ME*, THOUGH...
...IS A BLACK WIDOW, DANGLING BY HERSELF ON A SINGLE THREAD...

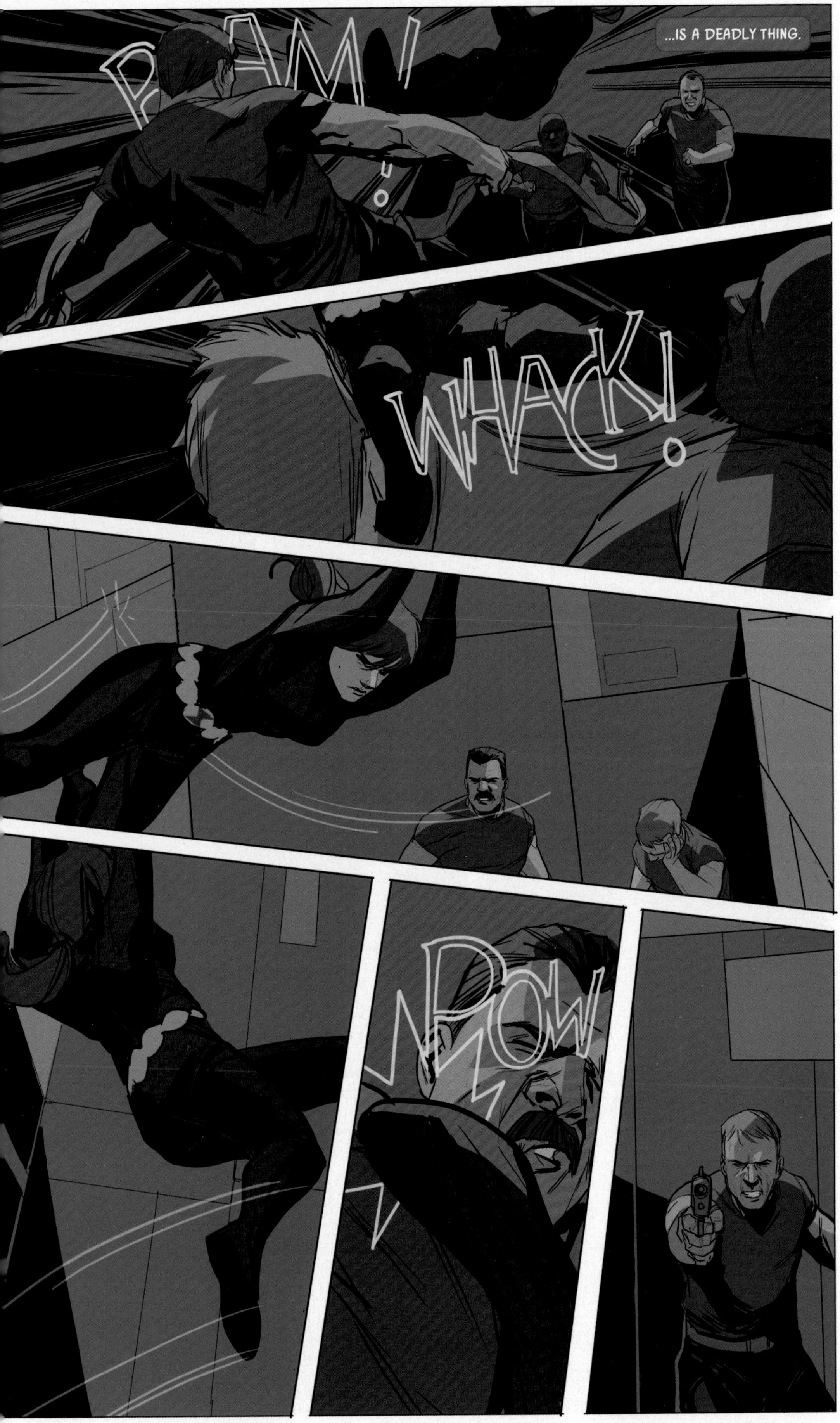
...IS A DEADLY THING.
BAM!
WHACK!
POW

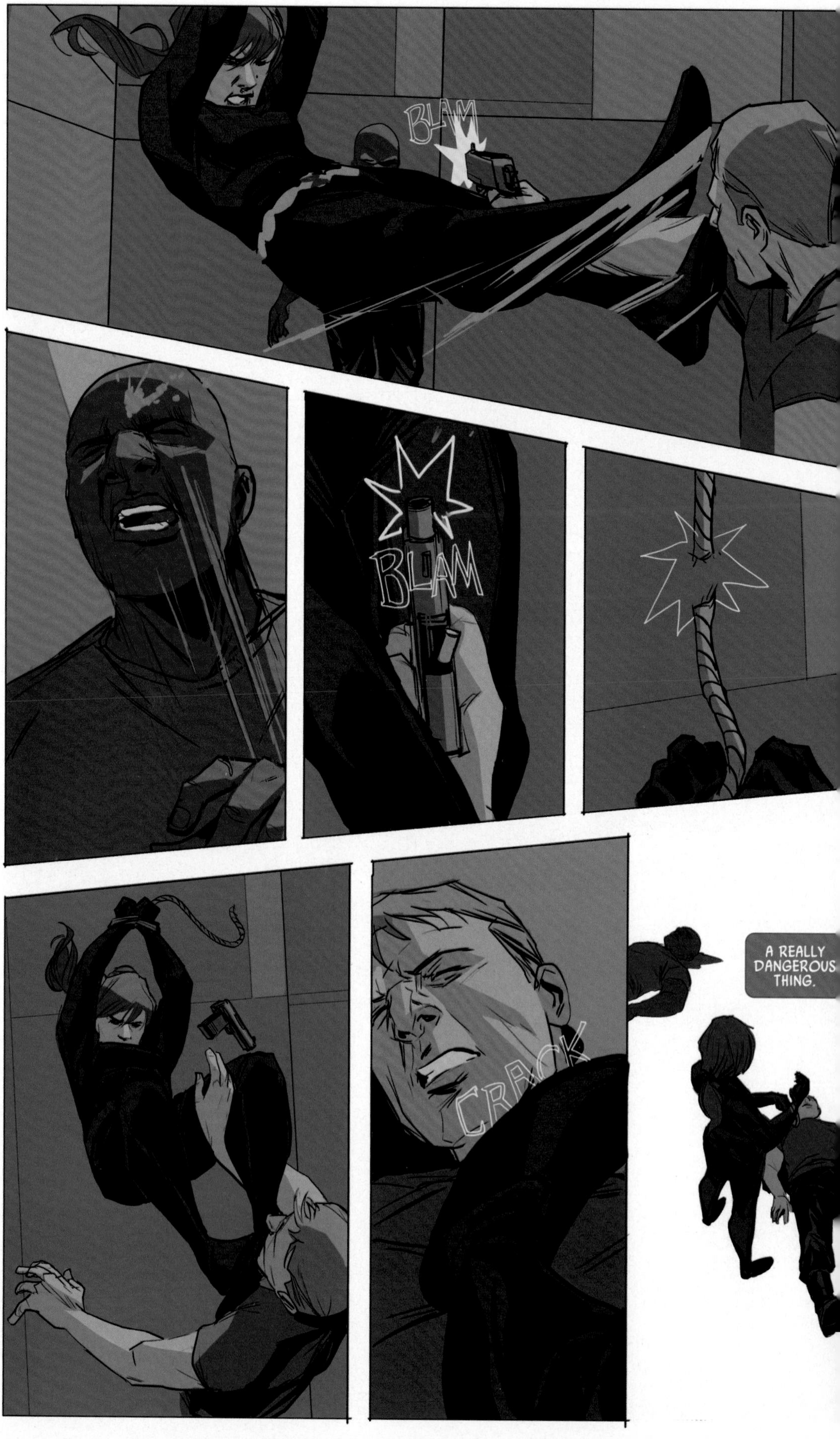
BLAM
BLAM
CRACK
A REALLY DANGEROUS THING.

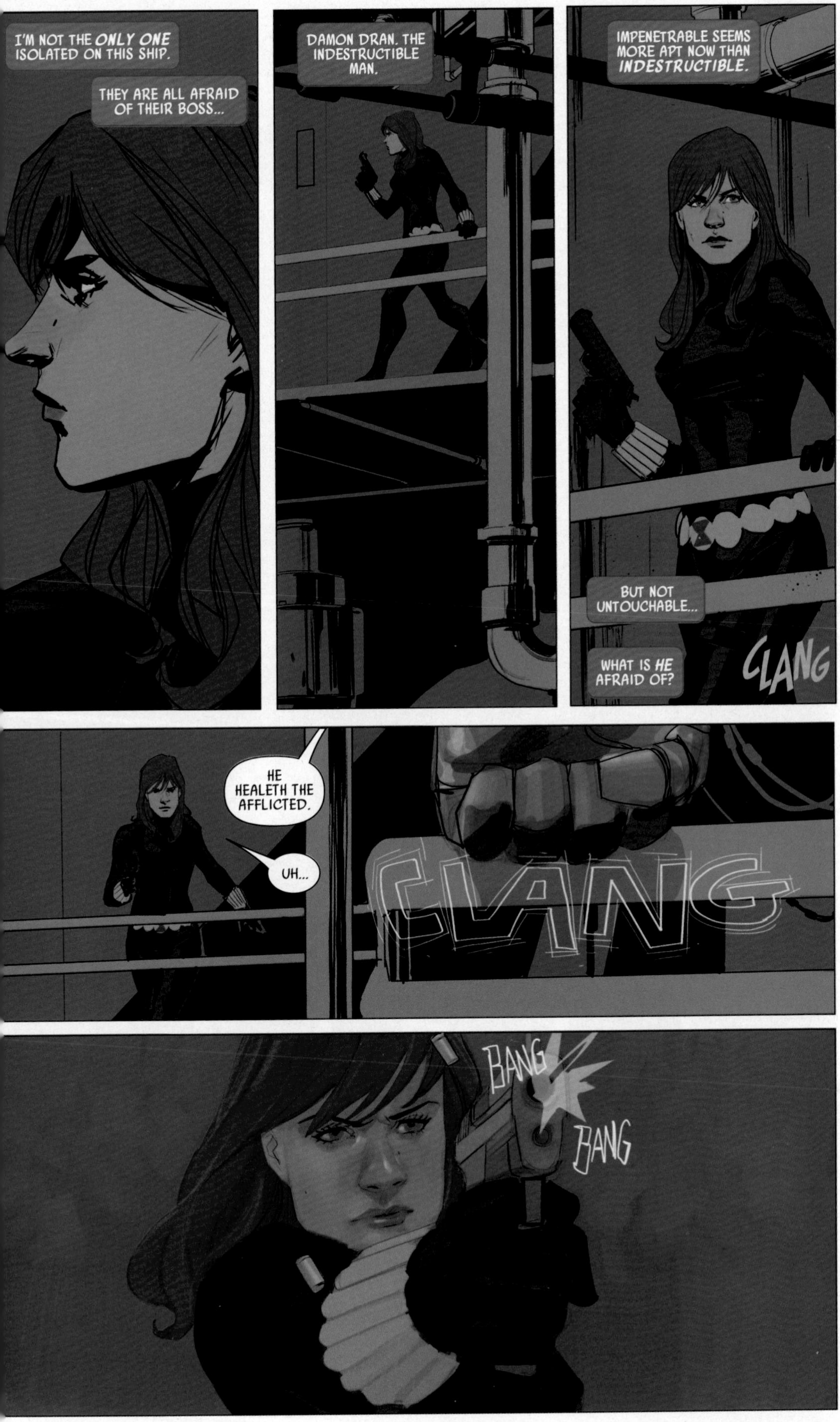
I'M NOT THE ONLY ONE ISOLATED ON THIS SHIP.
THEY ARE ALL AFRAID OF THEIR BOSS...
DAMON DRAN. THE INDESTRUCTIBLE MAN.
IMPENETRABLE SEEMS MORE APT NOW THAN INDESTRUCTIBLE.
BUT NOT UNTOUCHABLE...
WHAT IS HE AFRAID OF?
CLANG
HE HEALETH THE AFFLICTED.
UH...
CLANG
BANG
BANG

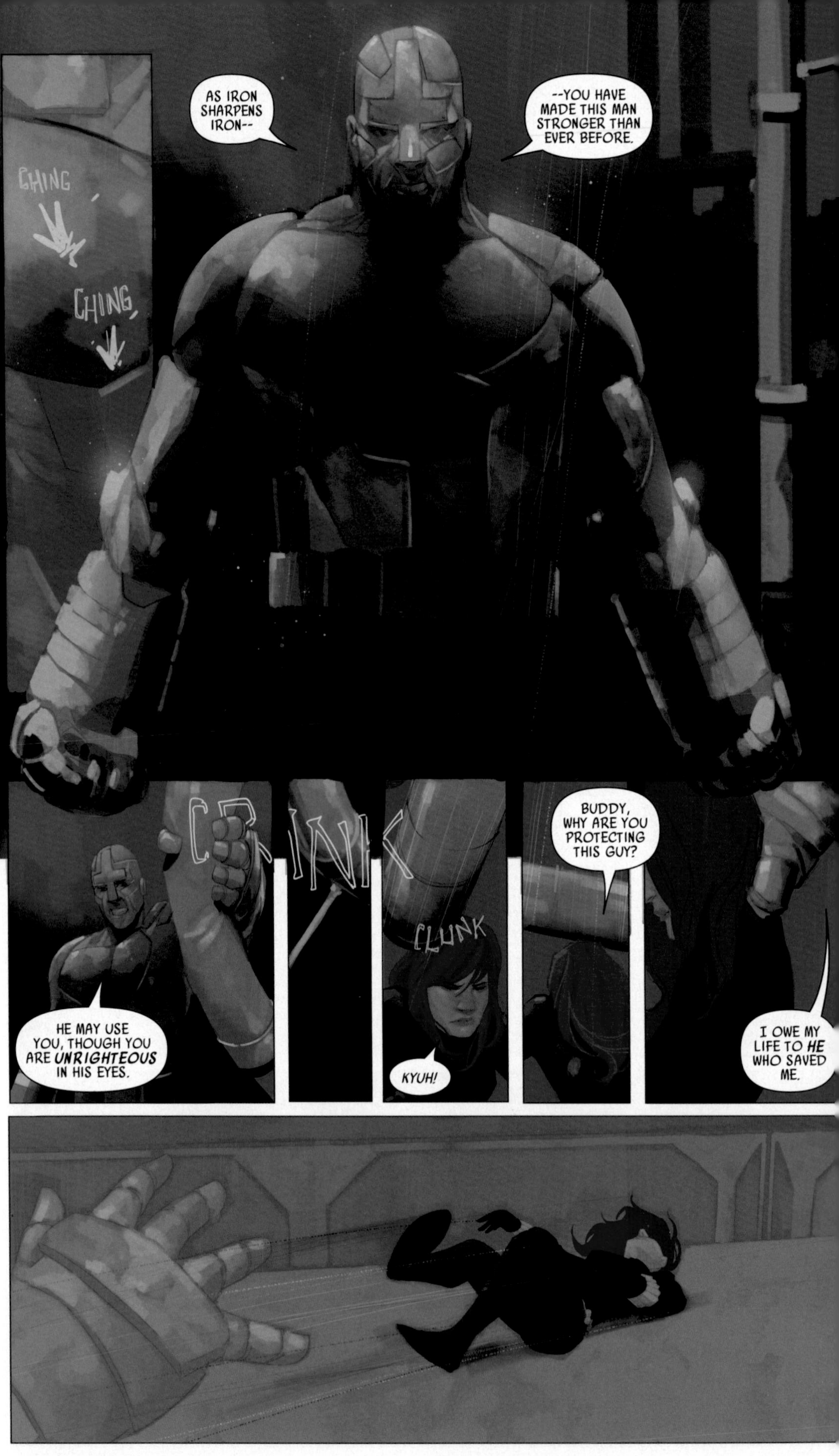
AS IRON SHARPENS IRON--
--YOU HAVE MADE THIS MAN STRONGER THAN EVER BEFORE.
CHING
CHING
CRINK
HE MAY USE YOU, THOUGH YOU ARE UNRIGHTEOUS IN HIS EYES.
CLUNK
KYUH!
BUDDY, WHY ARE YOU PROTECTING THIS GUY?
I OWE MY LIFE TO HE WHO SAVED ME.

IT'S BEEN FIVE HOURS.

WE HAVE TO TRUST BLACK WIDOW NOW.

WE WAIT FOR HER SIGNAL. SHE WAS CAUGHT JUST LIKE SHE ANTICIPATED.

DIRECTOR HILL, THEY'RE MOVING WESTWARD.

IF THEY HAVE MILITARY SUPPORT--

WE TRUST IN OUR AGENT.

AND IF SHE DOESN'T--

LIKE ALL OF YOU, SHE'S A DENIABLE ASSET, AGENT.

THIS ISN'T THE RED CROSS.

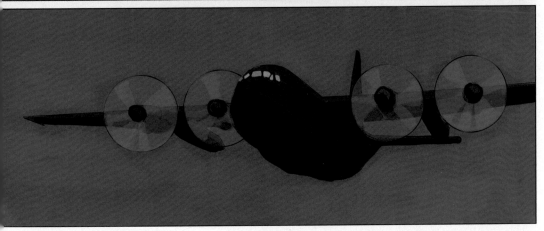

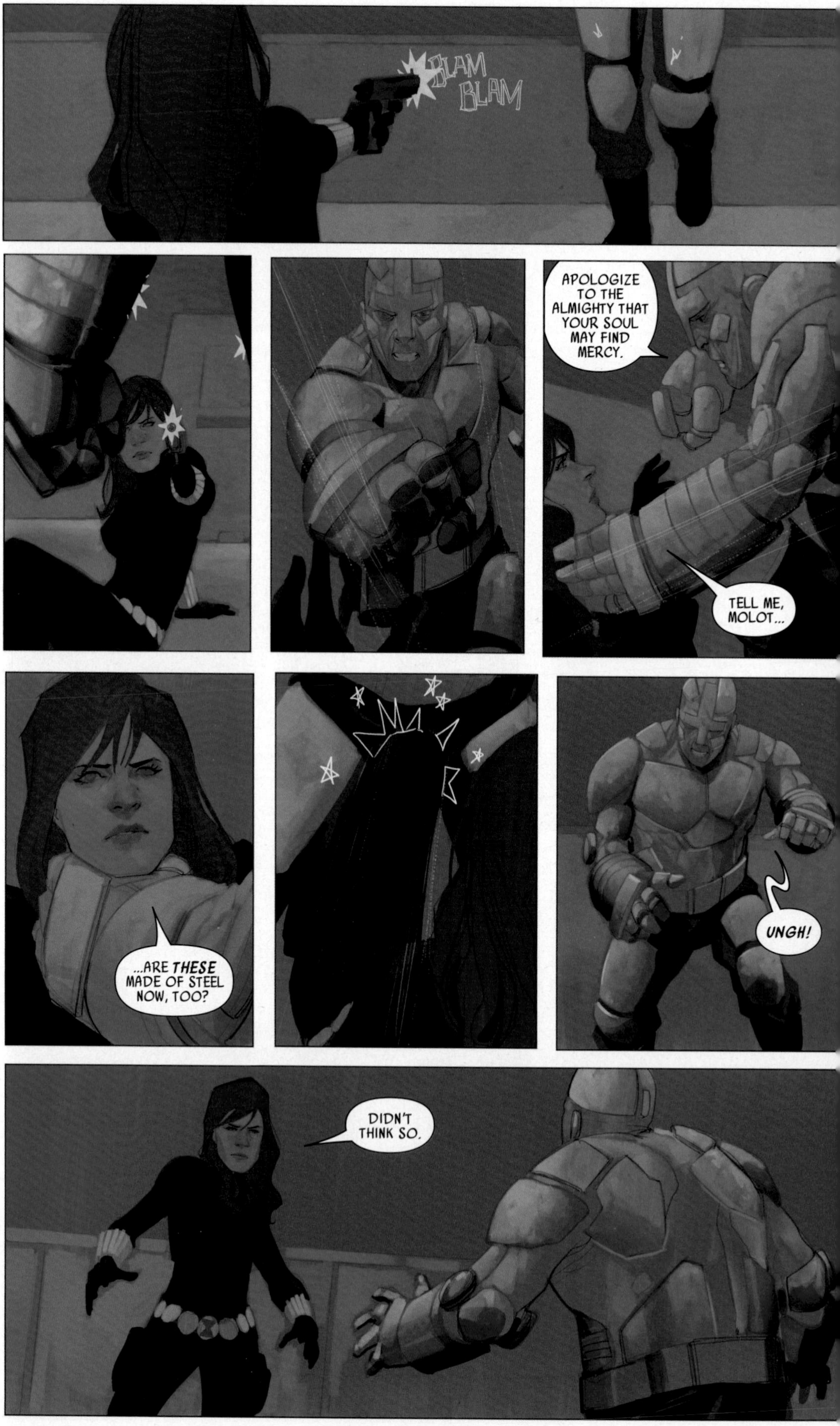
BLAM
BLAM
APOLOGIZE TO THE ALMIGHTY THAT YOUR SOUL MAY FIND MERCY.
TELL ME, MOLOT...
...ARE THESE MADE OF STEEL NOW, TOO?
UNGH!
DIDN'T THINK SO.

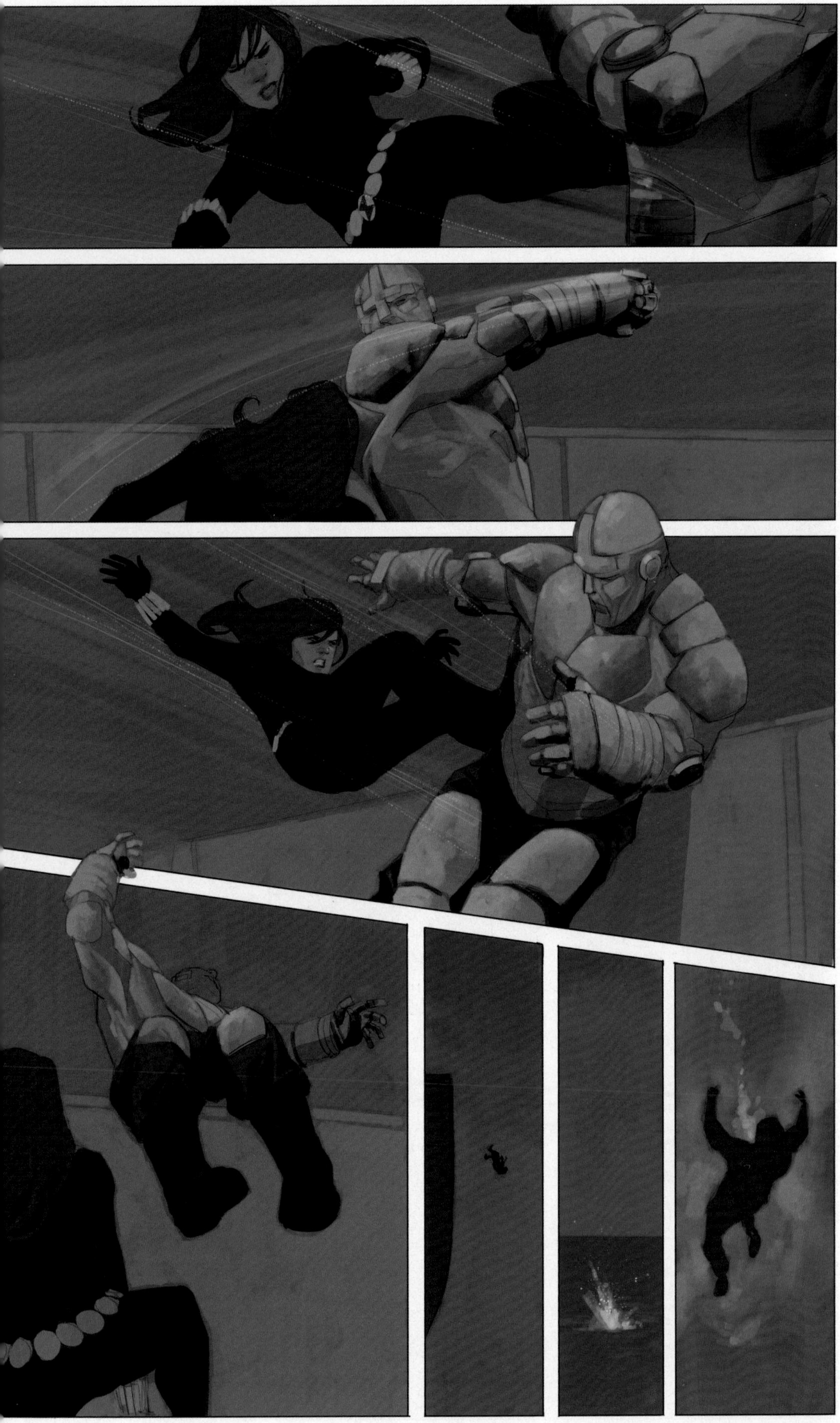

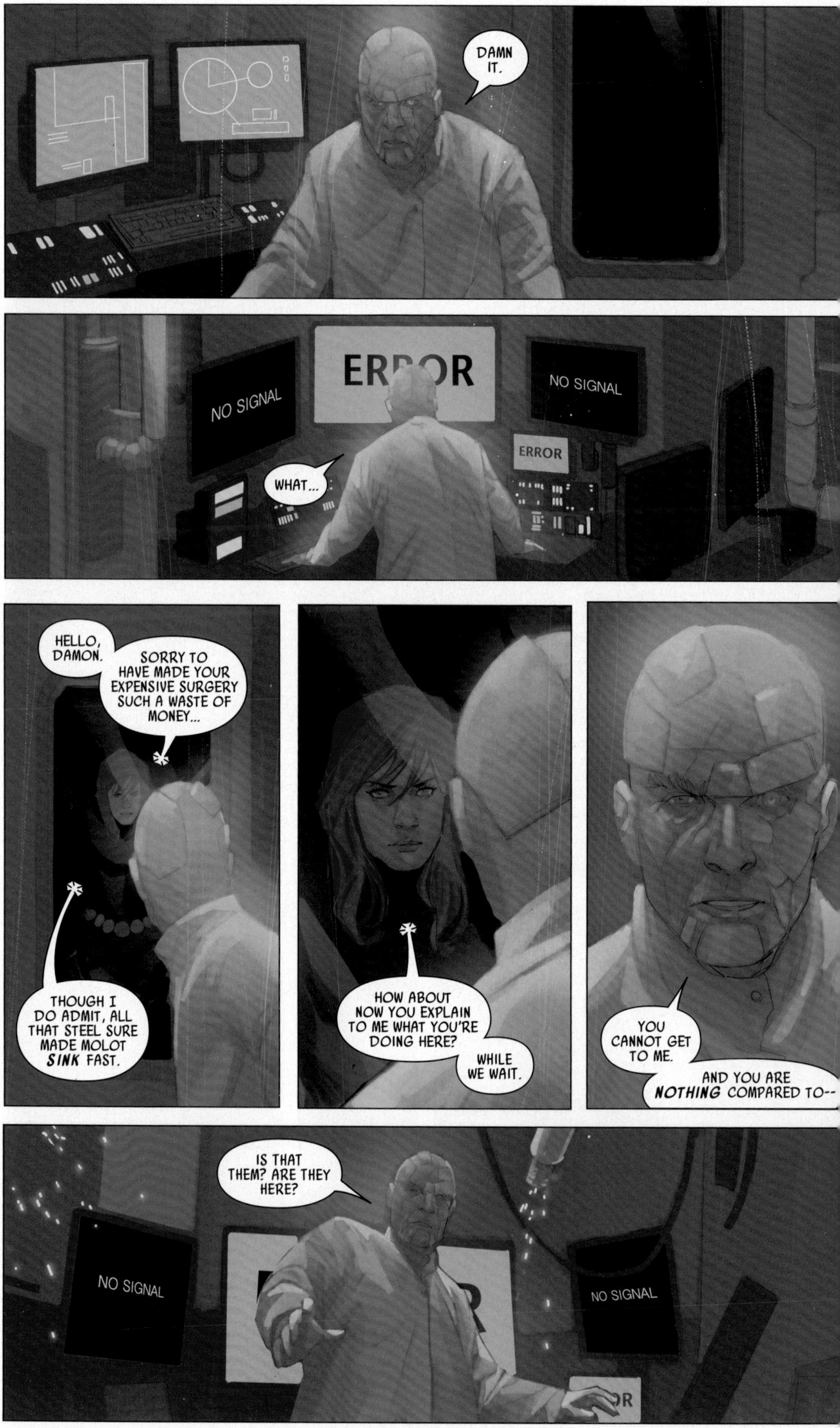
DAMN IT.
ERROR
NO SIGNAL
NO SIGNAL
ERROR
WHAT...
HELLO, DAMON.
SORRY TO HAVE MADE YOUR EXPENSIVE SURGERY SUCH A WASTE OF MONEY...
THOUGH I DO ADMIT, ALL THAT STEEL SURE MADE MOLOT SINK FAST.
HOW ABOUT NOW YOU EXPLAIN TO ME WHAT YOU'RE DOING HERE?
WHILE WE WAIT.
YOU CANNOT GET TO ME.
AND YOU ARE NOTHING COMPARED TO--
IS THAT THEM? ARE THEY HERE?
NO SIGNAL
NO SIGNAL

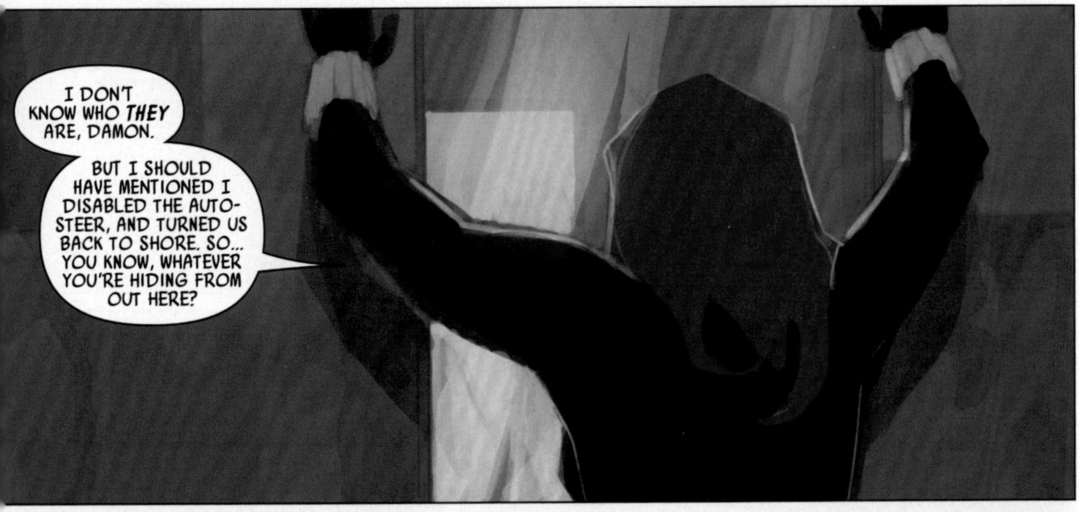
I DON'T KNOW WHO *THEY* ARE, DAMON.
BUT I SHOULD HAVE MENTIONED I DISABLED THE AUTO-STEER, AND TURNED US BACK TO SHORE. SO... YOU KNOW, WHATEVER YOU'RE HIDING FROM OUT HERE?

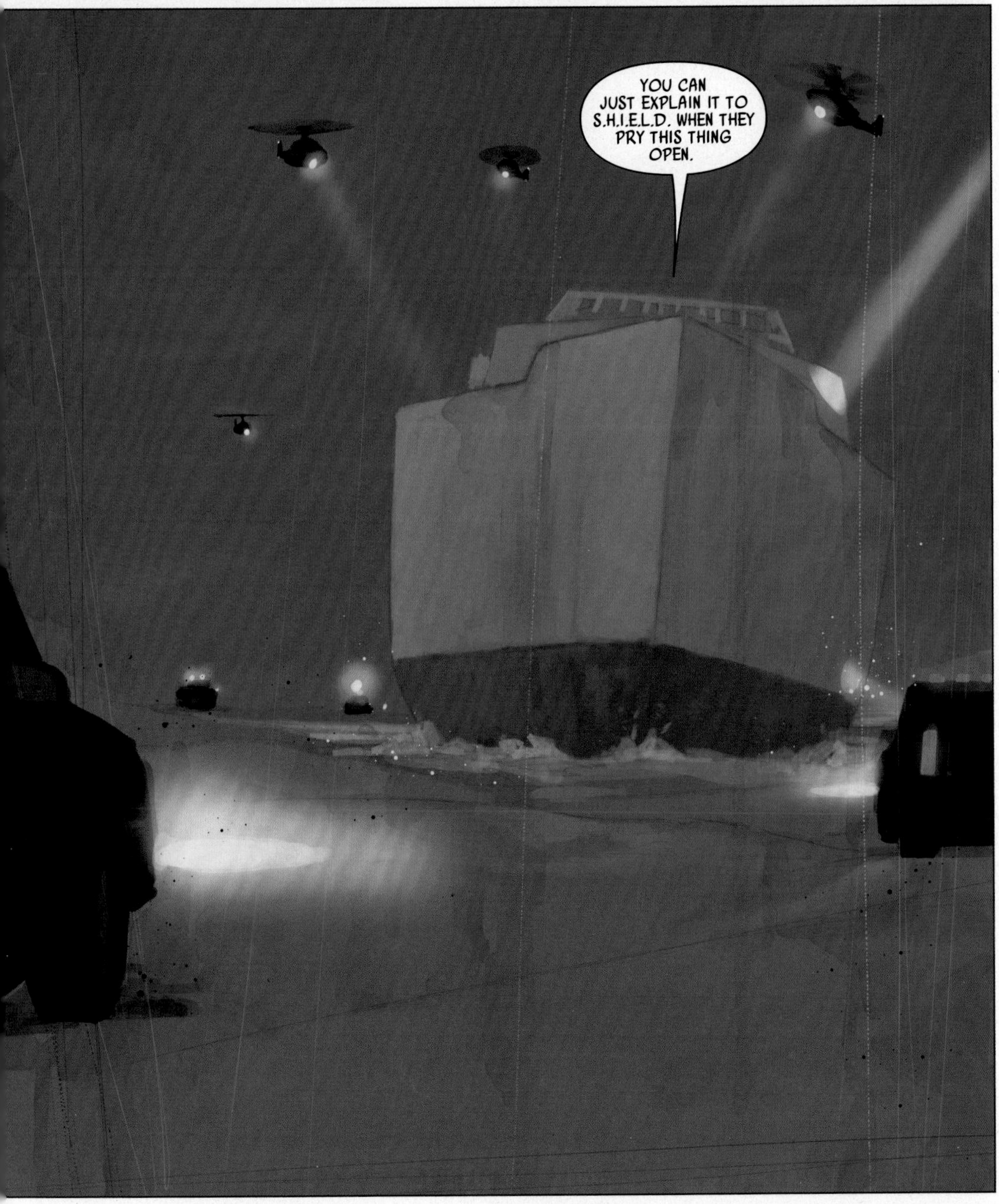
YOU CAN JUST EXPLAIN IT TO S.H.I.E.L.D. WHEN THEY PRY THIS THING OPEN.

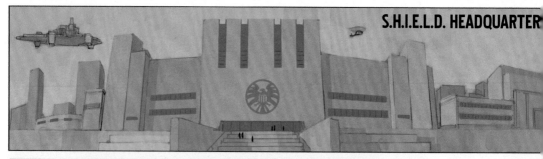

WE LOST TRACK OF DRAN EIGHT YEARS AGO.

APPARENTLY, THE SCIENCE BEHIND HIS INDESTRUCTIBILITY HAD AN EXPIRATION DATE...

HE TRIED TO BUILD THIS ARMOR INTO HIS BODY. HE USED U.V. LIGHT AND PILLS TO KEEP HIMSELF, WELL, IMMORTAL...

ALL THE WHILE GROWING MORE AND MORE PARANOID.

THAT'S WHEN HE BEGAN KILLING OFF HIS ENEMIES...

KILL ANYONE WHO MIGHT GET TO HIM.

THAT'S A SPY'S PARANOIA.

THAT'S WHAT BEING ALONE DOES TO YOU.

WELL, HE HAS COMPANY NOW.

INDEED. AND WE HAVE ALL THE TIME TO FIGURE OUT WHAT HE KNOWS.

CLICK

NO, NO.
NO, NO NO.
NO.

LUNCHTIME,
MR. DRAN.

A HAMBURGER
HOT OFF THE S.H.I.E.L.D.
CAFETERIA LUNCHLINE.

BURGER
TIME
B

CHAOS
RAINS, MR.
DRAN.

BURGER
TIME

ZZZZZTTTT

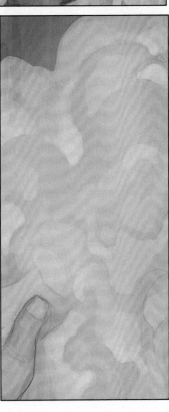

BANG
OH, NO.
NO! DON'T OPEN IT!
CAN'T-- ESCAPE-- CHAOS!
TRIED--TO-- ESCAPE--GACK--NO ONE ESCAPES!
CHAOS-- FALLS--LIKE ACID-- RAIN!
GET HAZMAT! QUARANTINE THE AREA!

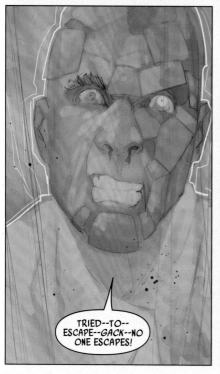

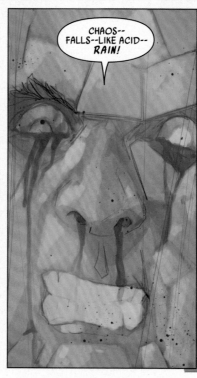

SEAL THE BUILDING!

"WE HAVE NO INTEL ABOUT WHAT HAPPENED, NATASHA.

"HOW THEY TURNED A SEASONED S.H.I.E.L.D. AGENT...

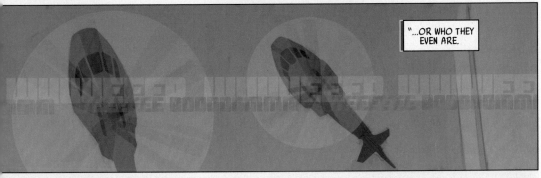

"...OR WHO THEY EVEN ARE.

"OUR JOB NOW IS TO FIND THEM. TO UNDERSTAND THEM."

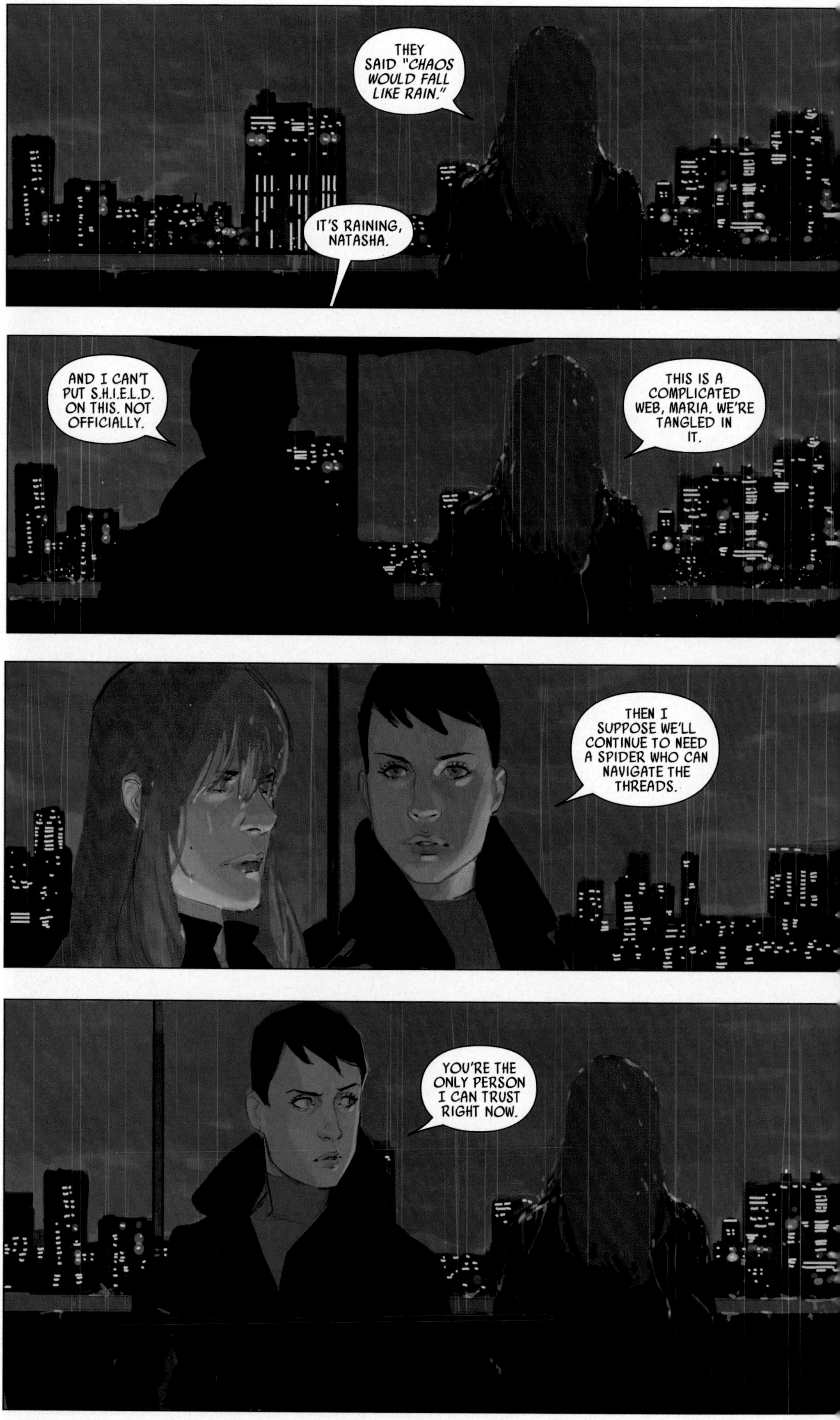
THEY SAID "CHAOS WOULD FALL LIKE RAIN."
IT'S RAINING, NATASHA.
AND I CAN'T PUT S.H.I.E.L.D. ON THIS. NOT OFFICIALLY.
THIS IS A COMPLICATED WEB, MARIA. WE'RE TANGLED IN IT.
THEN I SUPPOSE WE'LL CONTINUE TO NEED A SPIDER WHO CAN NAVIGATE THE THREADS.
YOU'RE THE ONLY PERSON I CAN TRUST RIGHT NOW.

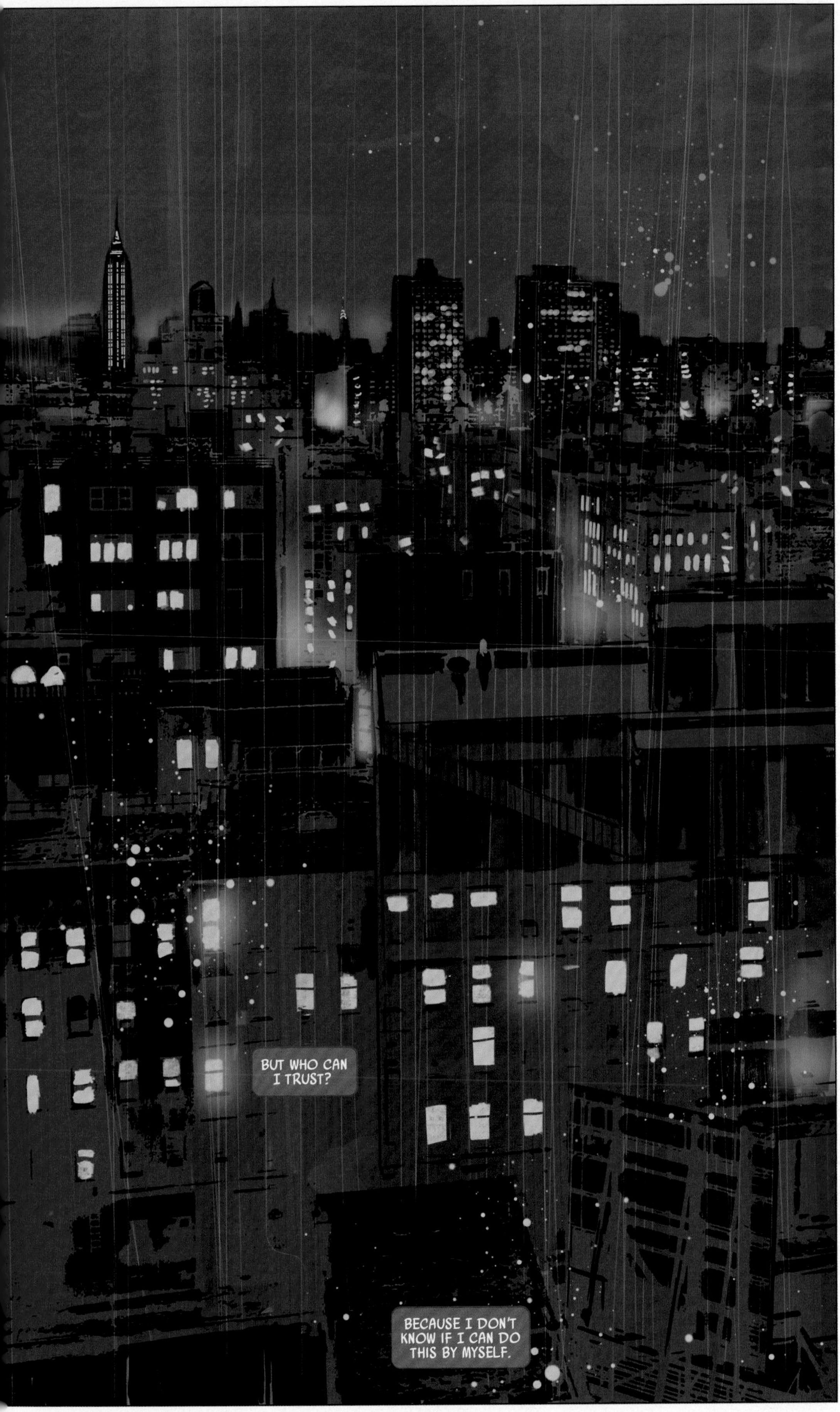
BUT WHO CAN I TRUST?
BECAUSE I DON'T KNOW IF I CAN DO THIS BY MYSELF.

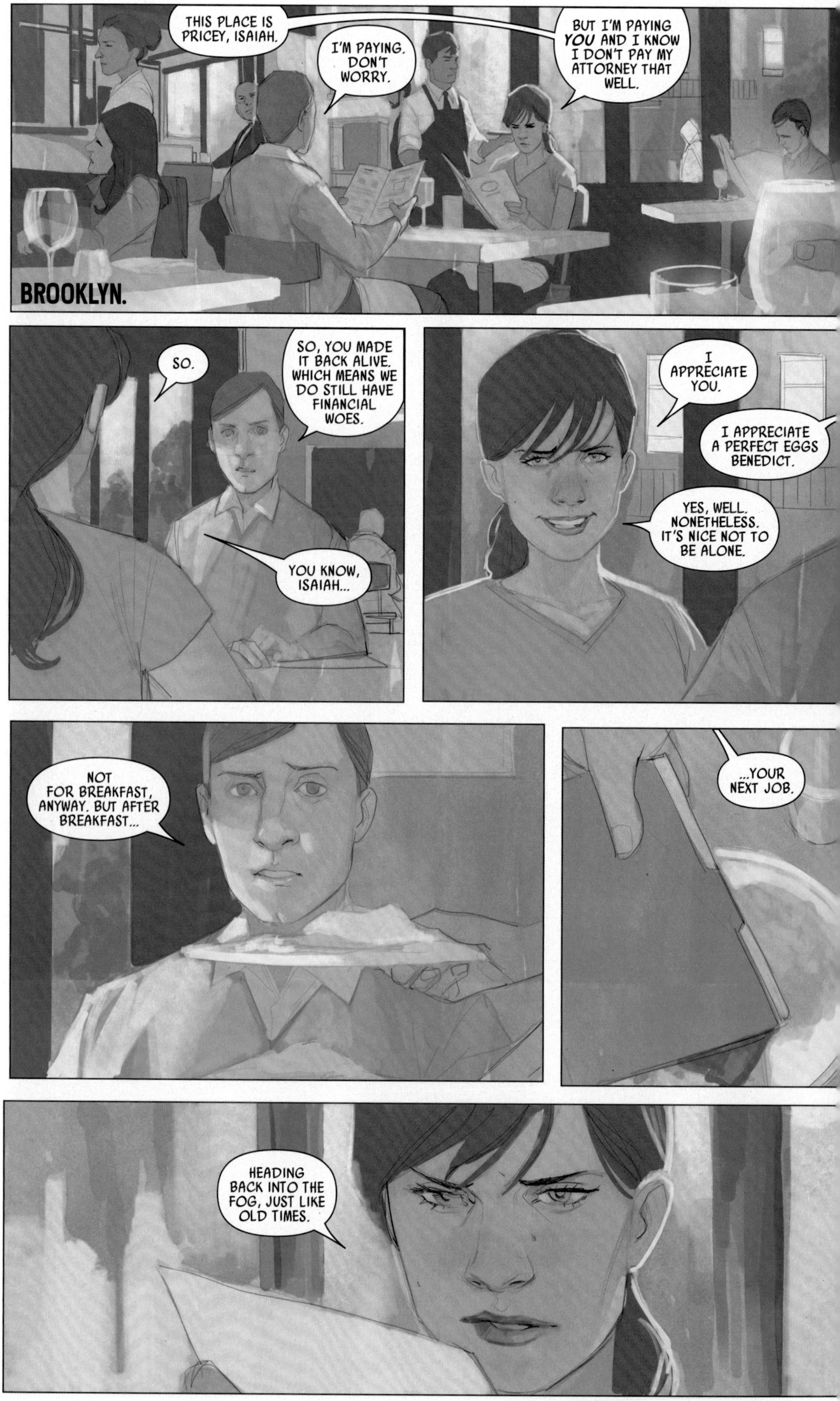
THIS PLACE IS PRICEY, ISAIAH.
I'M PAYING. DON'T WORRY.
BUT I'M PAYING YOU AND I KNOW I DON'T PAY MY ATTORNEY THAT WELL.
BROOKLYN.
SO.
SO, YOU MADE IT BACK ALIVE. WHICH MEANS WE DO STILL HAVE FINANCIAL WOES.
YOU KNOW, ISAIAH...
I APPRECIATE YOU.
I APPRECIATE A PERFECT EGGS BENEDICT.
YES, WELL. NONETHELESS. IT'S NICE NOT TO BE ALONE.
NOT FOR BREAKFAST, ANYWAY. BUT AFTER BREAKFAST...
...YOUR NEXT JOB.
HEADING BACK INTO THE FOG, JUST LIKE OLD TIMES.

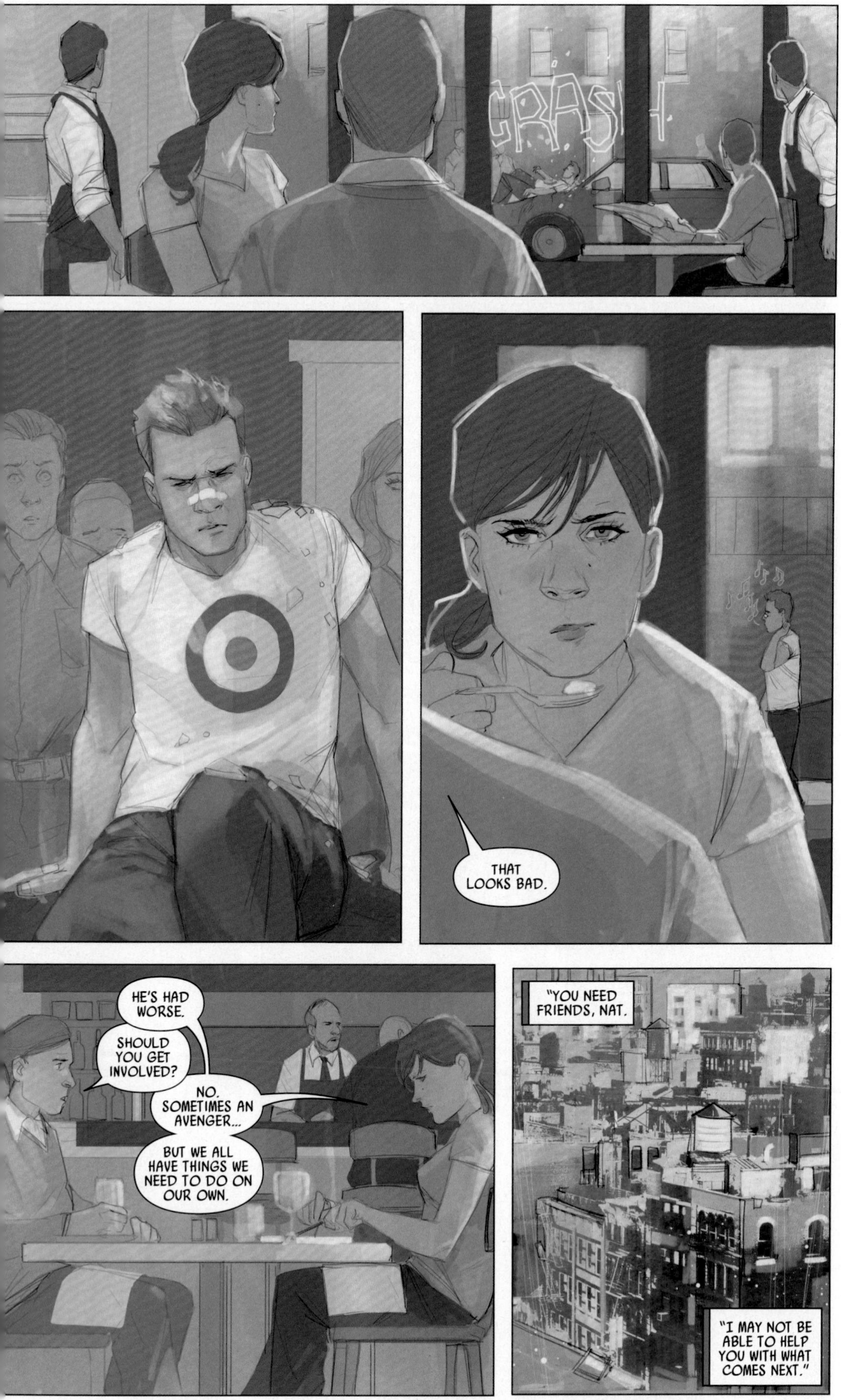
CRASH
THAT LOOKS BAD.
HE'S HAD WORSE.
SHOULD YOU GET INVOLVED?
NO. SOMETIMES AN AVENGER...
BUT WE ALL HAVE THINGS WE NEED TO DO ON OUR OWN.
"YOU NEED FRIENDS, NAT.
"I MAY NOT BE ABLE TO HELP YOU WITH WHAT COMES NEXT."

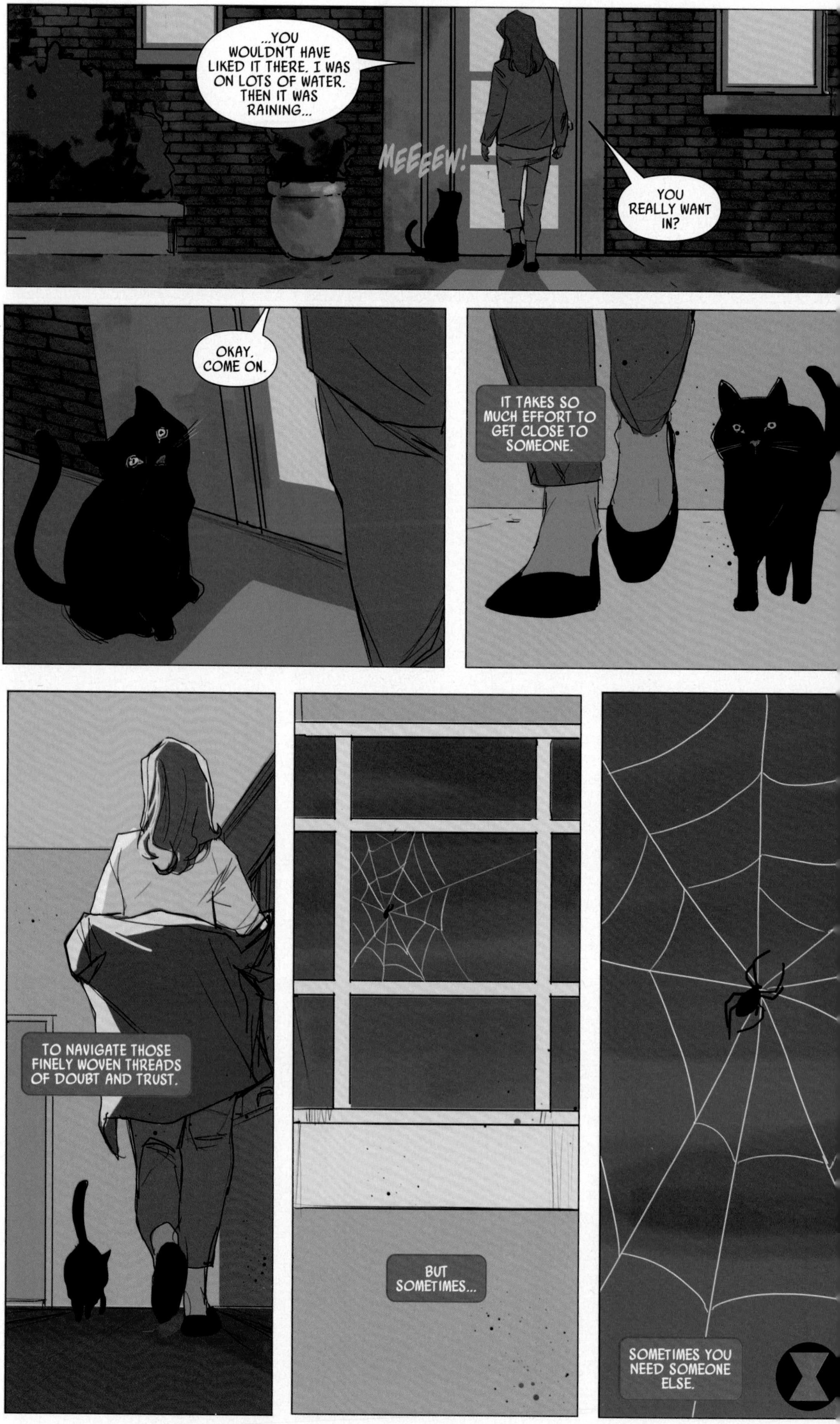
...YOU WOULDN'T HAVE LIKED IT THERE. I WAS ON LOTS OF WATER. THEN IT WAS RAINING...
MEEEEEW!
YOU REALLY WANT IN?
OKAY. COME ON.
IT TAKES SO MUCH EFFORT TO GET CLOSE TO SOMEONE.
TO NAVIGATE THOSE FINELY WOVEN THREADS OF DOUBT AND TRUST.
BUT SOMETIMES...
SOMETIMES YOU NEED SOMEONE ELSE.

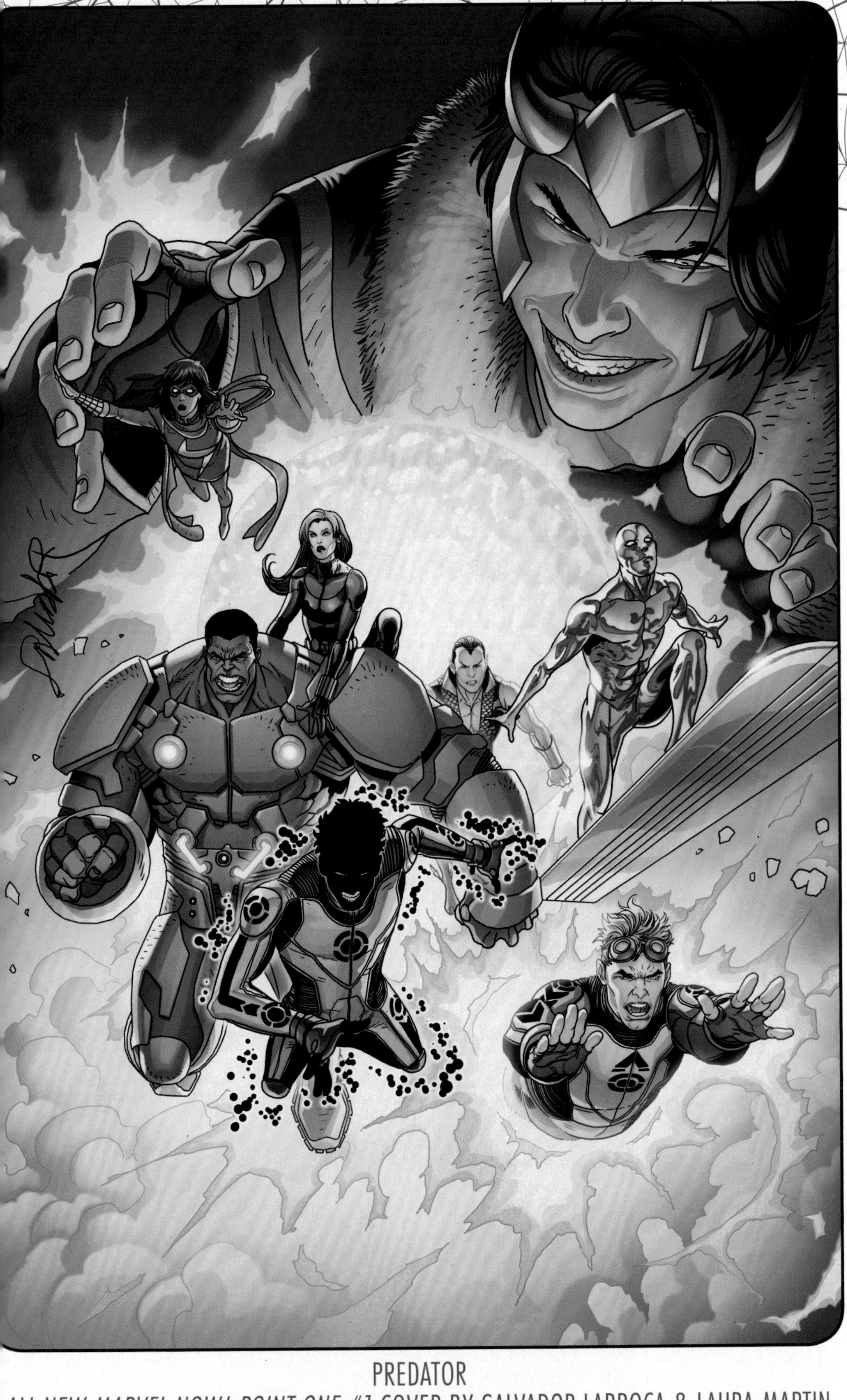

PREDATOR
ALL-NEW MARVEL NOW! POINT ONE #1 COVER BY SALVADOR LARROCA & LAURA MARTIN

WHAT KIND OF A PREDATOR AM I?

GOODBYE, BLACK WIDOW.

AND IS A PREDATOR A PREDATOR--

--WHEN IT HAS BECOME PREY?

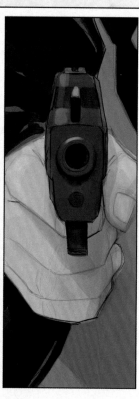

LET ME EXPLAIN WHAT HAPPENED THREE HOURS AGO...

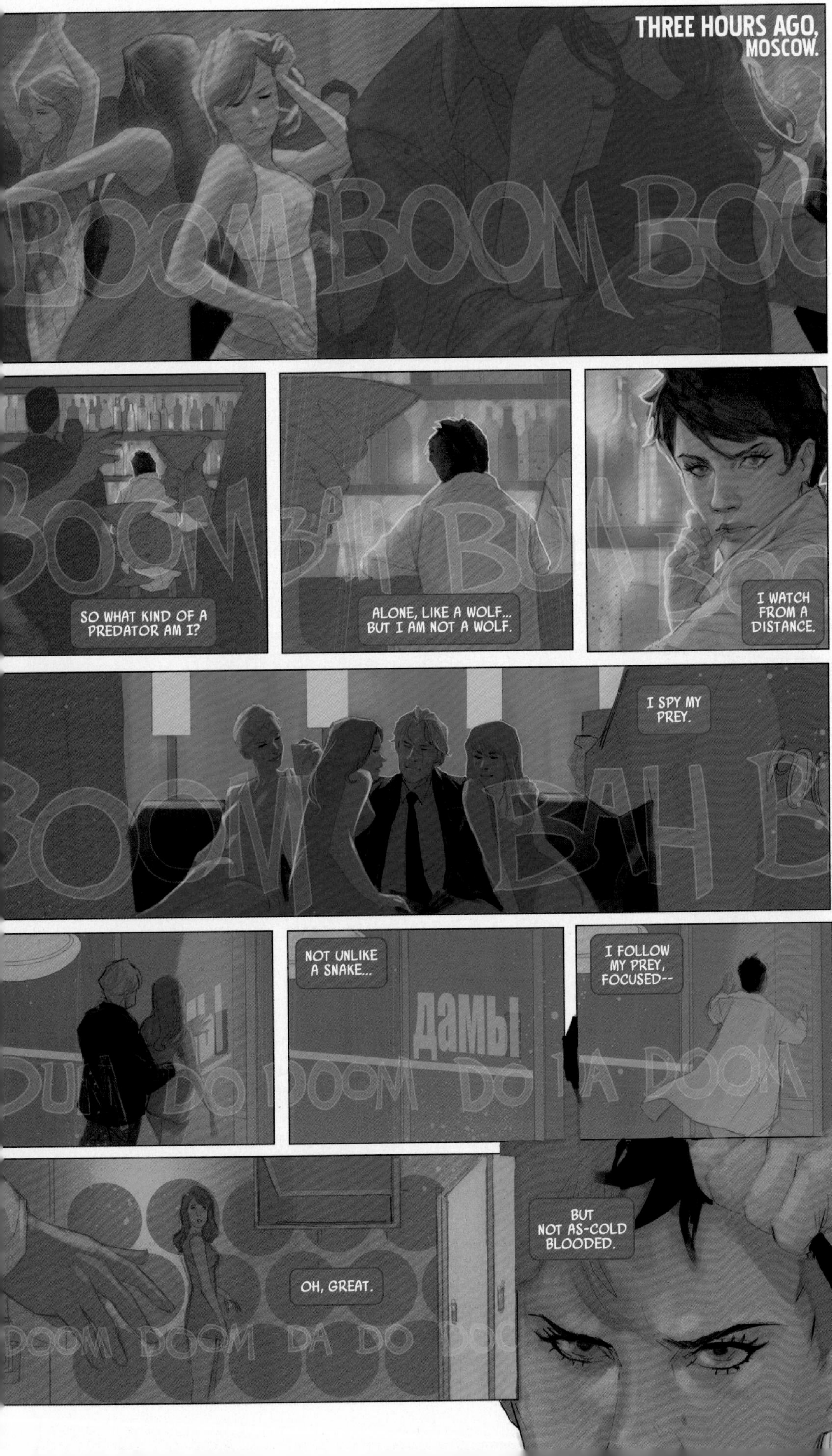
THREE HOURS AGO, MOSCOW.
BOOM BOOM BOO
BOOM
SO WHAT KIND OF A PREDATOR AM I?
BAH BUM
ALONE, LIKE A WOLF... BUT I AM NOT A WOLF.
I WATCH FROM A DISTANCE.
I SPY MY PREY.
BOOM BAH B
DUM DO
NOT UNLIKE A SNAKE...
дамы
DOOM
I FOLLOW MY PREY, FOCUSED--
DO DA DOOM
BUT NOT AS-COLD BLOODED.
OH, GREAT.
DOOM DOOM DA DO

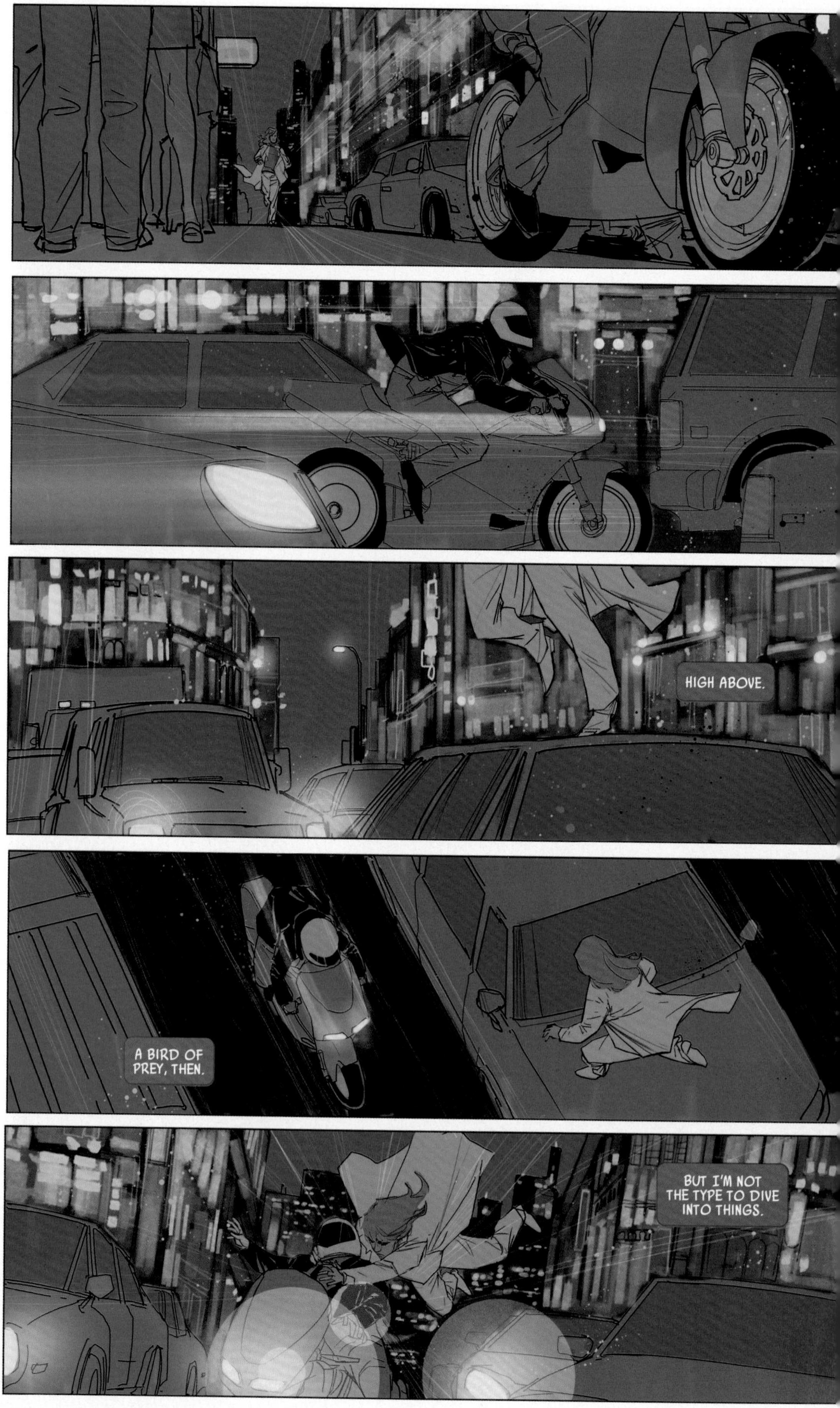
HIGH ABOVE.
A BIRD OF PREY, THEN.
BUT I'M NOT THE TYPE TO DIVE INTO THINGS.

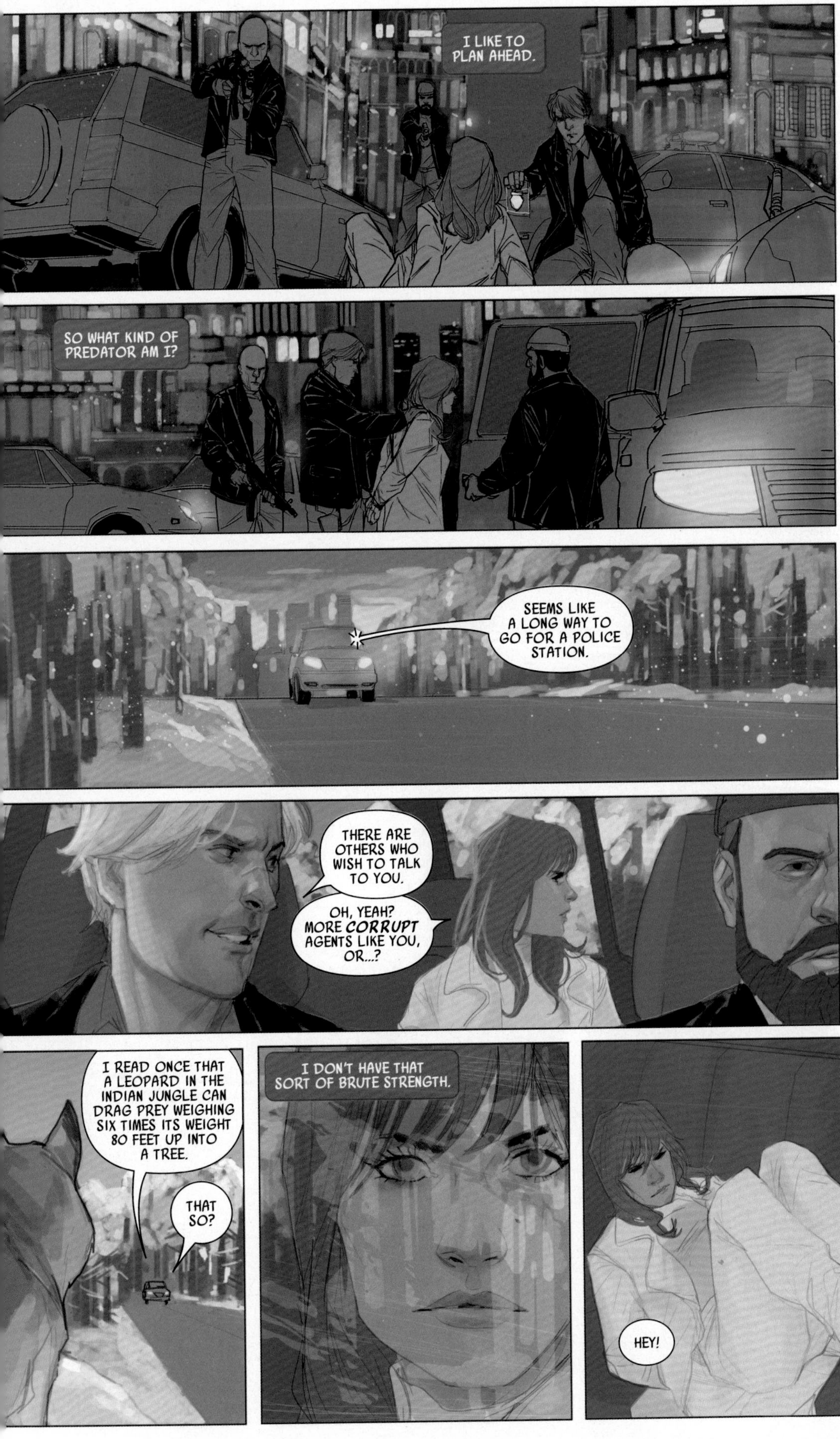

I LIKE TO PLAN AHEAD.
SO WHAT KIND OF PREDATOR AM I?
SEEMS LIKE A LONG WAY TO GO FOR A POLICE STATION.
THERE ARE OTHERS WHO WISH TO TALK TO YOU.
OH, YEAH? MORE CORRUPT AGENTS LIKE YOU, OR...?
I READ ONCE THAT A LEOPARD IN THE INDIAN JUNGLE CAN DRAG PREY WEIGHING SIX TIMES ITS WEIGHT 80 FEET UP INTO A TREE.
THAT SO?
I DON'T HAVE THAT SORT OF BRUTE STRENGTH.
HEY!

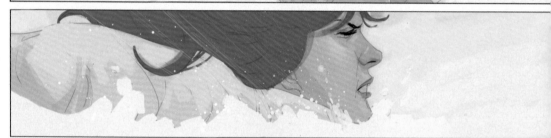

I'VE BECOME THE PREY...

CAUGHT...

GOODBYE, BLACK WIDOW.

EXCEPT, YOU KNOW, ONE THING...

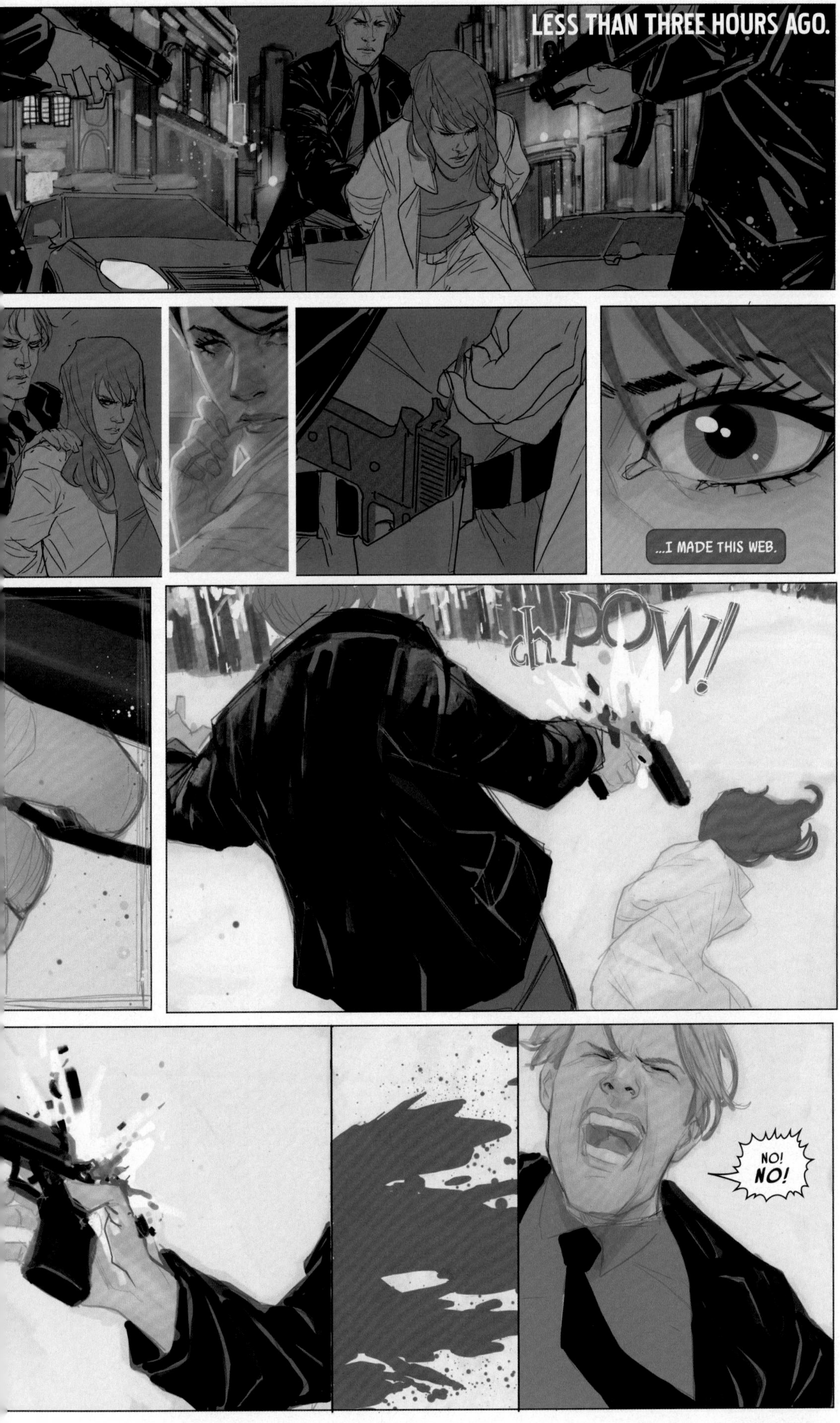
LESS THAN THREE HOURS AGO.
...I MADE THIS WEB.
chPOW!
NO! NO!

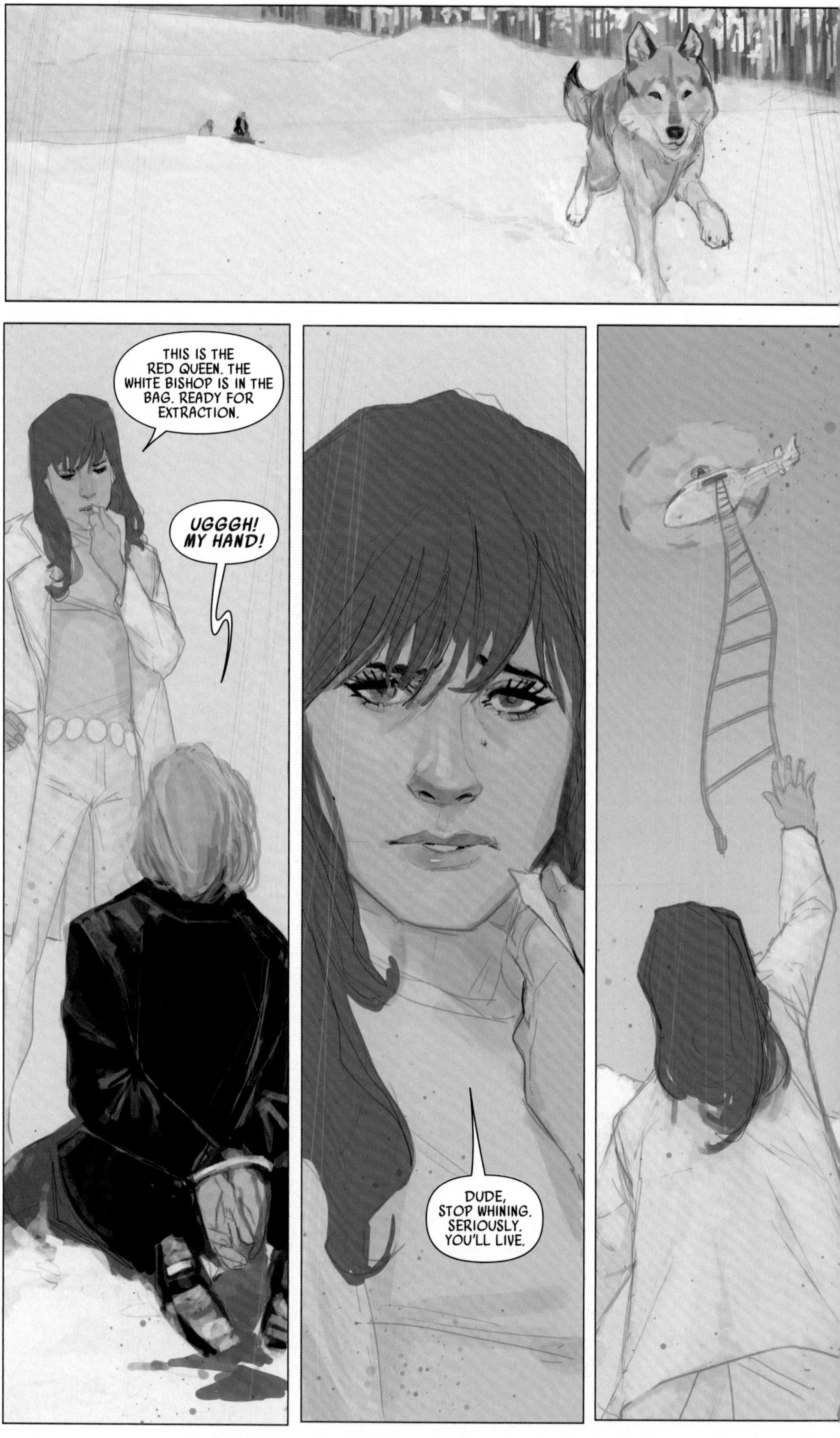
THIS IS THE RED QUEEN. THE WHITE BISHOP IS IN THE BAG. READY FOR EXTRACTION.
UGGGH! MY HAND!
DUDE, STOP WHINING. SERIOUSLY. YOU'LL LIVE.

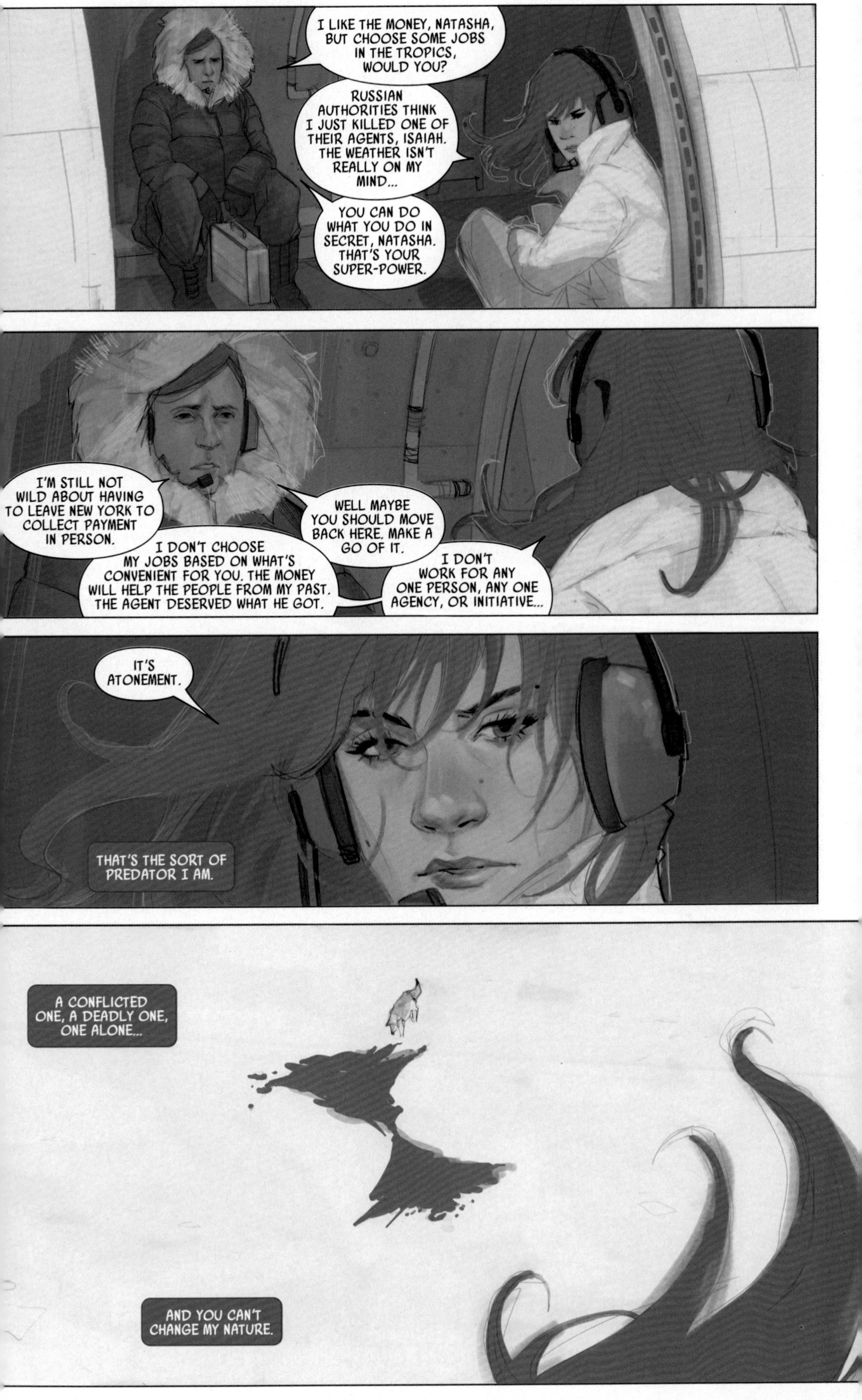
I LIKE THE MONEY, NATASHA, BUT CHOOSE SOME JOBS IN THE TROPICS, WOULD YOU?
RUSSIAN AUTHORITIES THINK I JUST KILLED ONE OF THEIR AGENTS, ISAIAH. THE WEATHER ISN'T REALLY ON MY MIND...
YOU CAN DO WHAT YOU DO IN SECRET, NATASHA. THAT'S YOUR SUPER-POWER.
I'M STILL NOT WILD ABOUT HAVING TO LEAVE NEW YORK TO COLLECT PAYMENT IN PERSON.
I DON'T CHOOSE MY JOBS BASED ON WHAT'S CONVENIENT FOR YOU. THE MONEY WILL HELP THE PEOPLE FROM MY PAST. THE AGENT DESERVED WHAT HE GOT.
WELL MAYBE YOU SHOULD MOVE BACK HERE. MAKE A GO OF IT.
I DON'T WORK FOR ANY ONE PERSON, ANY ONE AGENCY, OR INITIATIVE...
IT'S ATONEMENT.
THAT'S THE SORT OF PREDATOR I AM.
A CONFLICTED ONE, A DEADLY ONE, ONE ALONE...
AND YOU CAN'T CHANGE MY NATURE.

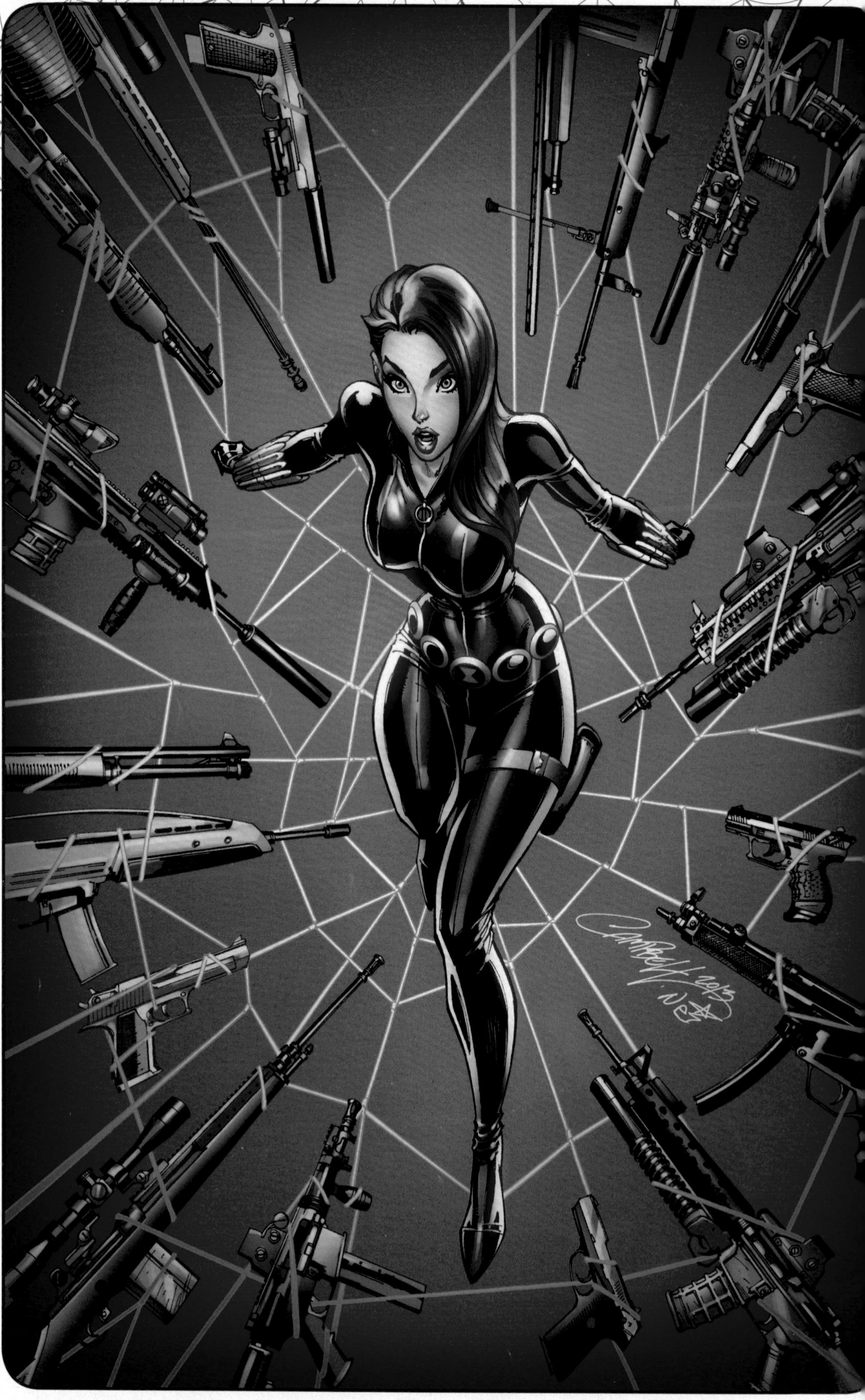

#1 VARIANT BY J. SCOTT CAMPBELL & NEI RUFFINO

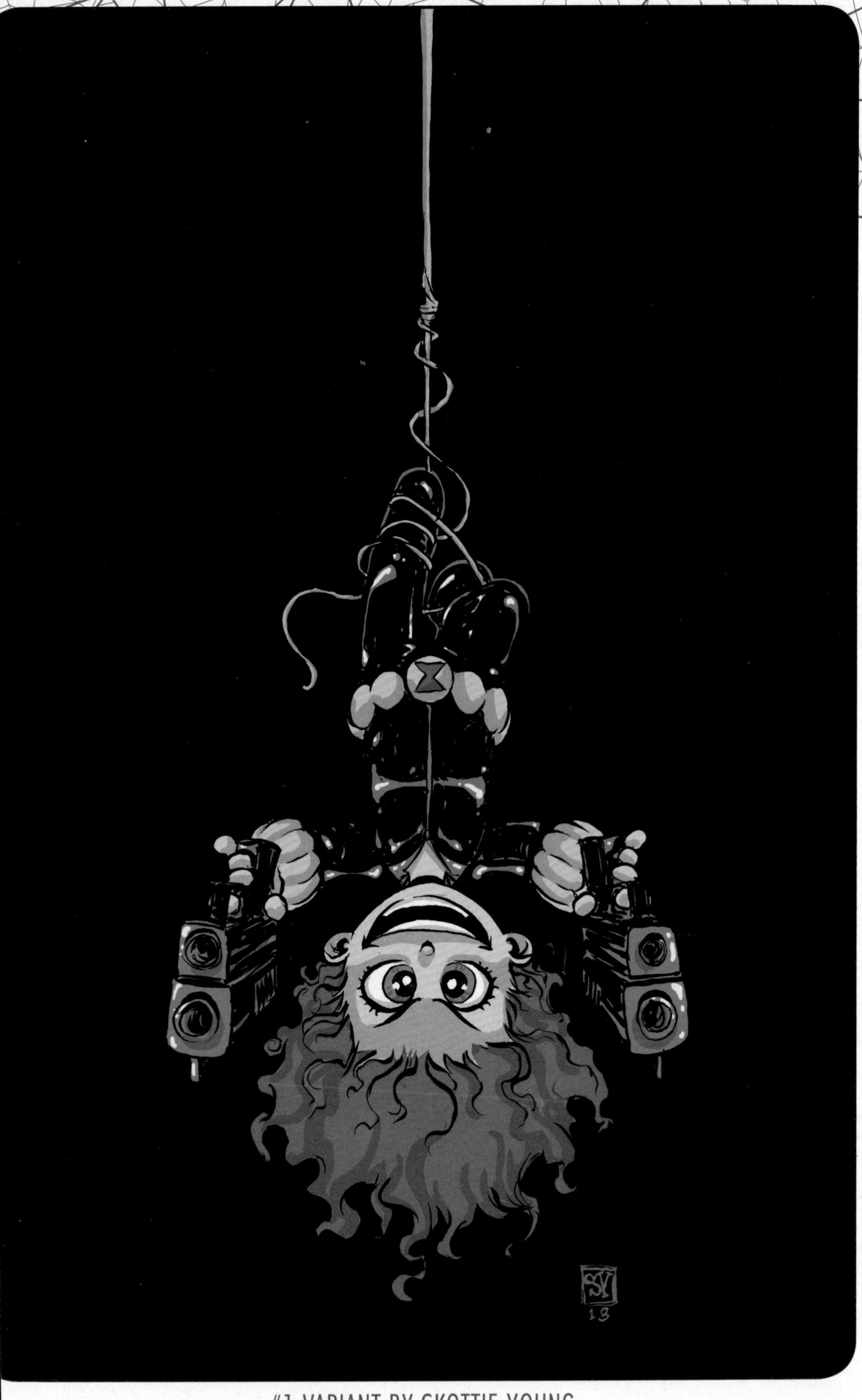

#1 VARIANT BY SKOTTIE YOUNG

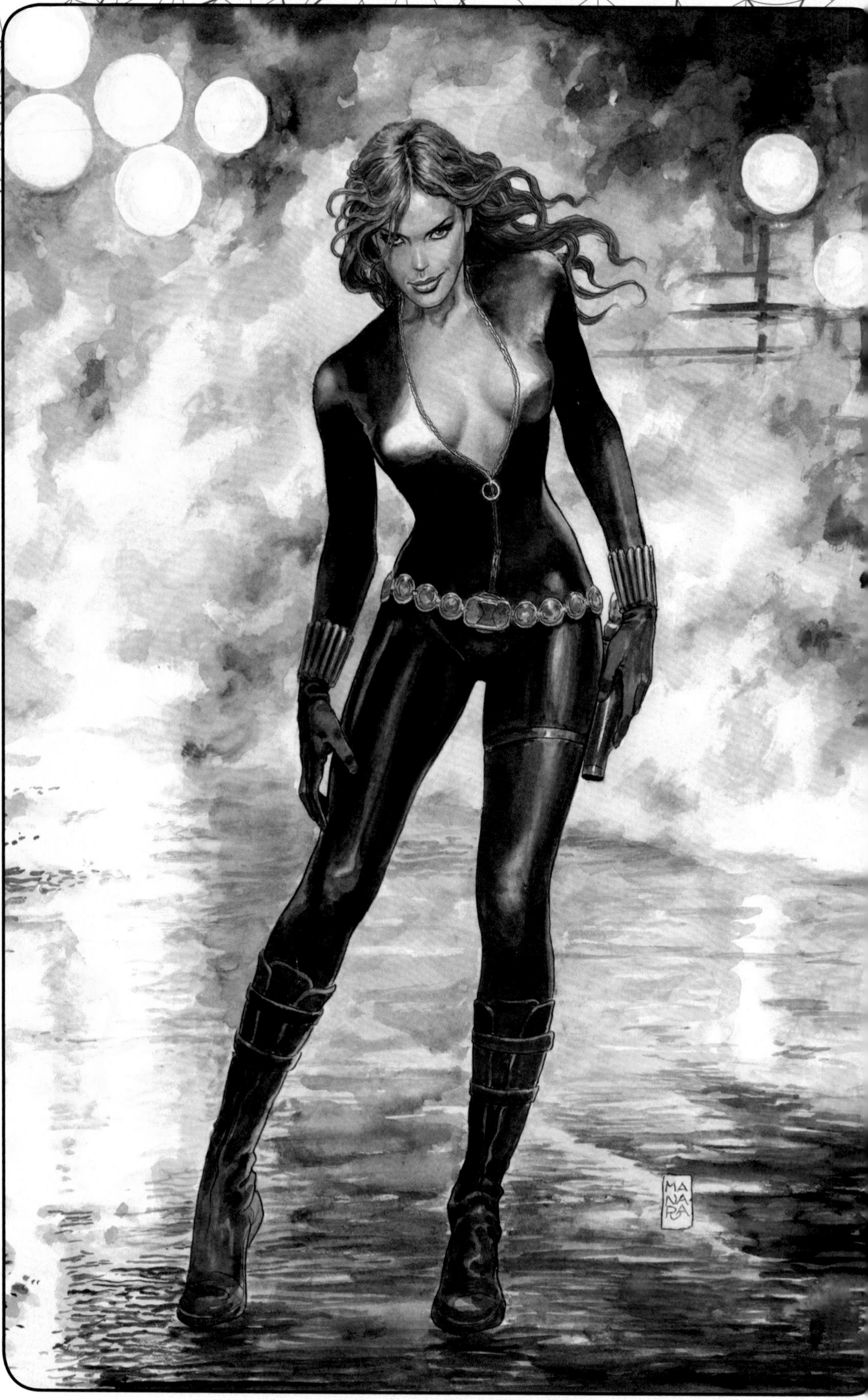
MANARA

#1 VARIANT BY MILO MANARA

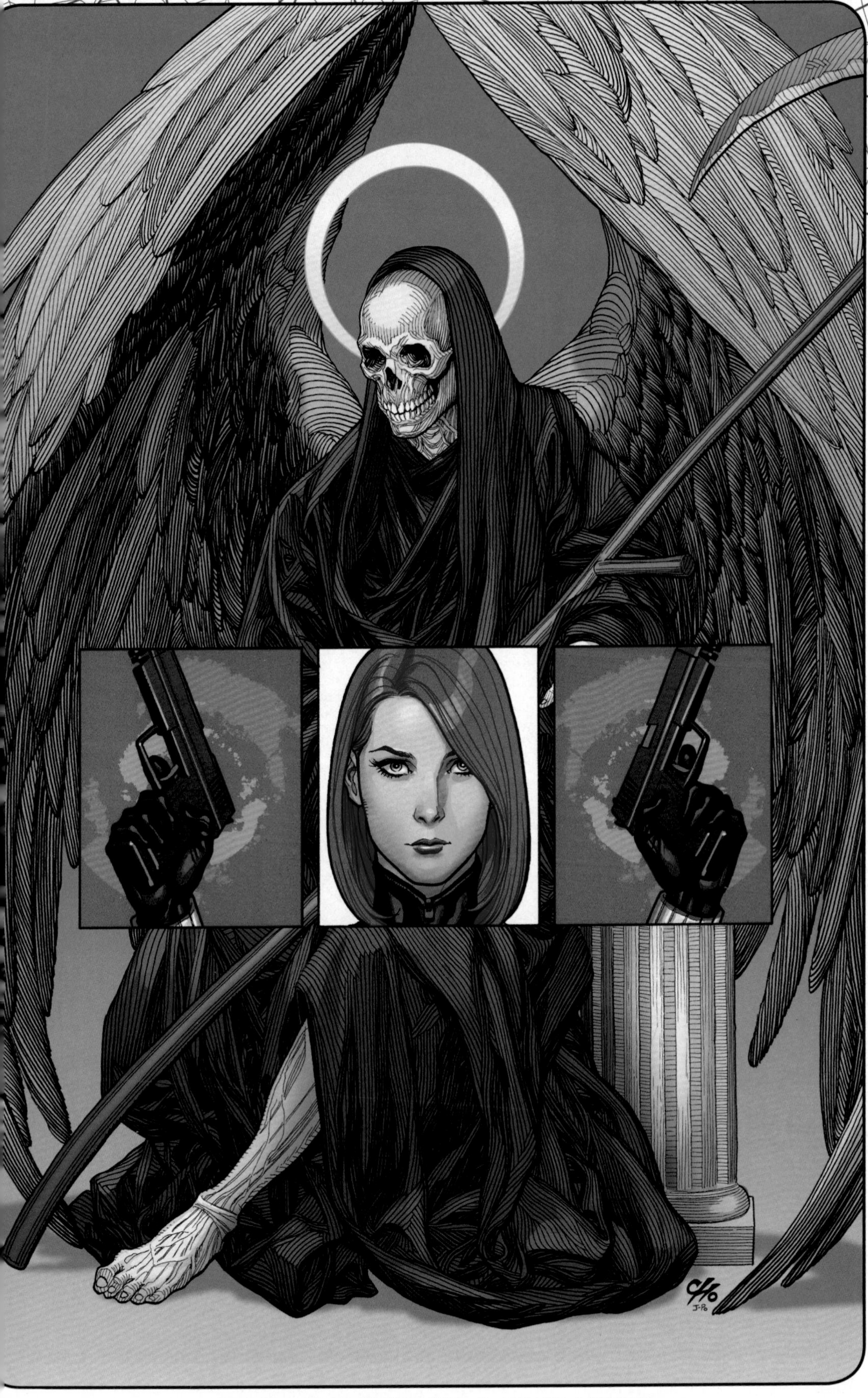
CHO
J-Po

#2 VARIANT BY FRANK CHO & JUSTIN PONSOR

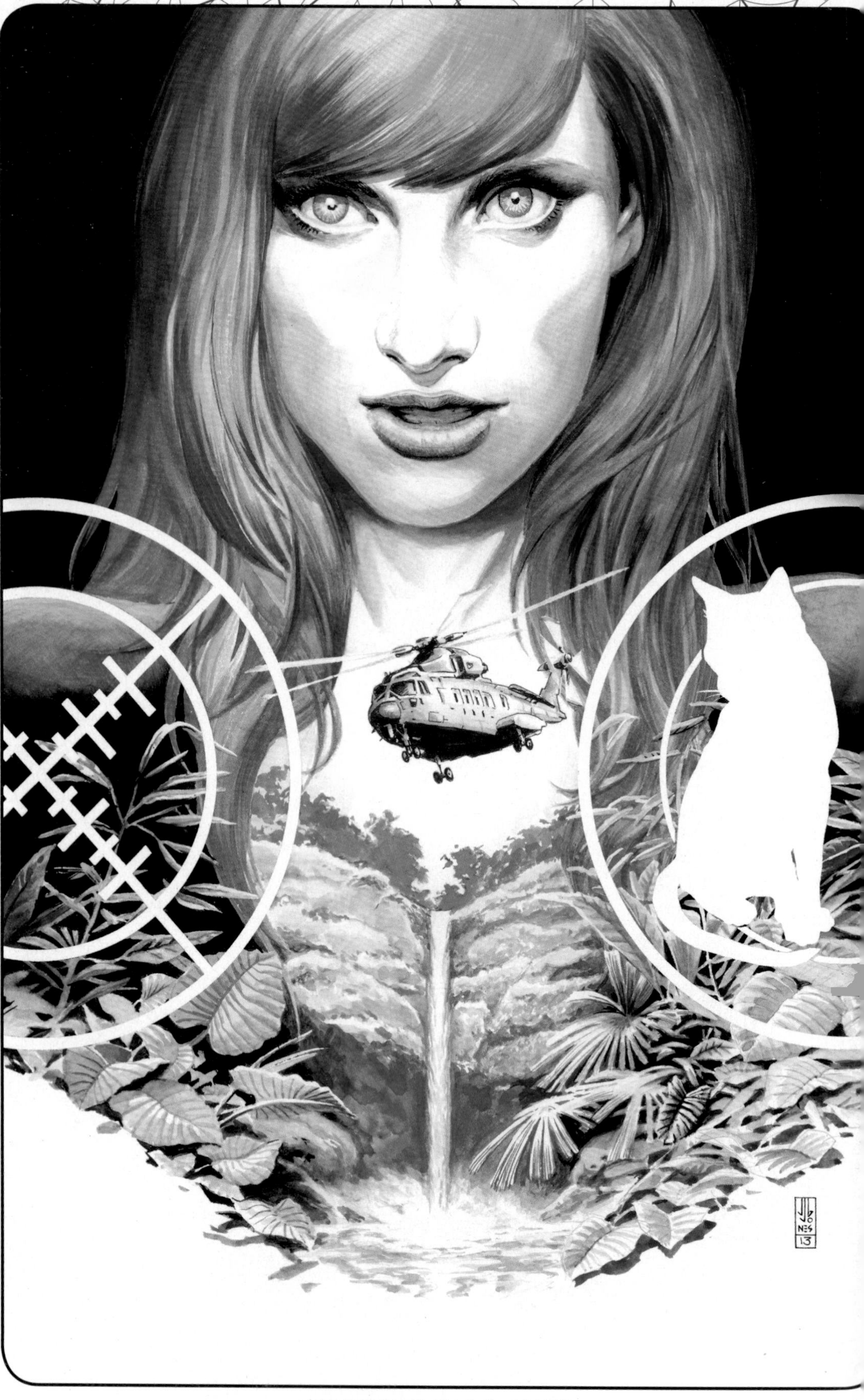

#3 VARIANT BY J.G. JONES